BEAUTY
AND TRUTH

A Study of Hegel's Aesthetics

STEPHEN BUNGAY

OXFORD UNIVERSITY PRESS
1984

Oxford University Press, Walton Street, Oxford OX2 6DP

London New York Toronto
Delhi Bombay Calcutta Madras Karachi
Kuala Lumpur Singapore Hong Kong Tokyo
Nairobi Dar es Salaam Cape Town
Melbourne Auckland

and associated companies in
Beirut Berlin Ibadan Mexico City Nicosia

Oxford is a trade mark of Oxford University Press

Published in the United States
by Oxford University Press, New York

British Library Cataloguing in Publication Data

Bungay, Stephen
Beauty and truth. –(Oxford modern languages
and literature monographs)
1. Hegel, Georg Wilhelm Friedrich.
Vorlesungen über die Aesthetik
2. Aesthetics
I. Title
700'.1   N64.H43
ISBN 0-19-815540-9

Set by Hope Services, Abingdon, Oxon
Printed in Great Britain by
Alden Press, Oxford

PREFACE

Nobody really knows for sure what Hegel wanted to do, let alone whether he actually managed to do it or not. But whatever it was, if the results are anything to go by, it was not easy. His work is abstract, subtle, and complex, and the genuine difficulties these features impose on the reader are compounded by the fact, mentioned by Rosenkranz in the first book of his biography, that Hegel was not very good at explaining himself. The result is that whilst any intelligent, educated person can pick up a work by Kant and get an idea of what his concerns are, it is possible to read page after page of Hegel without having any idea at all what it is all about, or why such matters as 'the pure relationship of Concept to itself', whatever that may be, should be of any consequence to anyone. In the English-speaking world the problems are compounded by the near impossibility of translating him, the deep-seated Anglo-Saxon preference for the immediately comprehensible, though incoherent, epistemological pictures proffered by the likes of Locke or Hume, and the xenophobia of the Anglo-American philosophical establishment. Small wonder that the *Lectures on Aesthetics*, though vaguely felt to be a work of the stature of Aristostle's *Poetics*, has been in practice ignored in universities. It is very long, very obscure, in a foreign language, and written by a man rumoured to have been a foolish old windbag, and probably a Nazi or a communist or both.

The first aim of this book is to provide a framework for understanding Hegel in order to remove some of that sense of disorientation which comes from the unfamiliarity of his idiom. The second aim is to expound and analyse Hegel's aesthetic theory, criticizing it in terms which I think he would have to have acknowledged as valid. And the third aim is to follow the theory through to the empirical level, drawing together a selection of Hegel's more important observations about works of art. I hope it may prove useful to have a book in English about the *Aesthetics* which condenses the main features of Hegel's lectures and to some extent explains them. I would hope too that the reader will find some of the rewards I found in my attempt to understand them. Hegel is a good example of one of those Germans who

dives deeper into murkier waters than the rest of us, and who not surprisingly comes up muddier. Perhaps a suitable role for an English
sceptic is washing off the mud and polishing some of the nuggets he
finds underneath. It is for the reader to judge whether or not the
glitter is that of gold.

I have also tried to cater for the needs of different sorts of reader.
Those whose main interest is theoretical will, I hope, find the argument
of the book continuous, moving from the general to the particular.
However, if someone wishes, for example, to find out about Hegel's
theory of ancient and modern drama, he should be able to turn directly
to that section and find it comprehensible with the help of the glossary
and a few earlier passages. My main regret is that there is no full exposition of the reading of Hegel's *Logic* which informs the whole account.
Such an exposition, justifying the view I have taken, formed the first
chapter of the doctoral thesis on which this book is based, but it has
had to be omitted here for reasons of length. I hope I have been able
to add what was necessary so that the present book makes sense, and
apologize now for any obscurity or dogmatism which may remain, and
which could only have been removed by making the book twice as long
as it is.

That this book exists at all is due to the generosity of my examiners,
Patrick Gardiner and Barry Nisbet, whose suggestions I have gratefully
taken up, and the Modern Languages Monographs Committee of Oxford
University, who put the thesis forward to the Press. The text is sub-
stantially that of the thesis, and I have not attempted to consider here
any literature published since the work was completed in 1981. However, I have had to spend some weeks working on translations, pre-
paring the glossary, and playing my part in producing the finished
article, and I would like to record my thanks to the London office of
The Boston Consulting Group, and in particular to the office admin-
istrator Anthony Habgood, who encouraged the project and allowed me
all the time off I required.

The original thesis would not have existed had it not been for
help from many quarters. I owe a considerable debt of thanks to the
Alexander von Humboldt-Stiftung, which is responsible for the Theodor
Heuß Research Fellowship through which I was able to spend two vital
years from 1978 to 1980 at the University of Tübingen. Without this
period of study at a German university work on the book could never
have been completed, but without the understanding of the Department
of Education and Science, which allowed me a third year of a Major

Award on my return to Oxford, it could never have been written down.

Intellectual debts, so many of which are oblique, are harder to acknowledge, but some of the more direct ones should be mentioned. In Oxford, Charles Taylor first aroused my interest in Hegel, Siegbert Prawer provided early encouragement as attention focused on the *Aesthetics*, while Patrick Gardiner and my supervisor, Raymond Lucas, helped to draw some coherence out of my first attempts to understand what it is about. In Germany, I have benefited from conversations with Rüdiger Bubner, Günter Wohlfart, and L. Bruno Puntel, but my greatest debt is to my supervisor in Tübingen, Klaus Hartmann, who provided unfailing moral, intellectual, and practical support and who has exerted a deep influence over the substance of this study. In addition, mention should be made of those who joined me in reading the *Logic* for several hours a week over a period of months, and who provided the conversations without which the final product would be immeasurably more inadequate than it is. I would particularly like to mention Ulrich Saßmann and Bernhard Milz, and Frank Kirkland and Robert Berman.

Finally, I would like to thank Peter Ganz for guidance in the final stages, and also Richard Parish and Deirdre Edwards for reading and correcting the typescript.

London,
January 1984

ACKNOWLEDGEMENTS

The author and the publisher would like to thank the Museum der Bildenden Künste, Leipzig, the Kunstmuseum, Düsseldorf, and The Trustees of the British Museum for permission to use the reproductions they supplied.

CONTENTS

LIST OF PLATES   xi

INTRODUCTION   1

Part One: PRINCIPLES   11

1 THE DETERMINATION OF ART   13

   The Object of Hegel's Aesthetics   13
   What Could a Philosophy of Art Be?   19
   Art as Absolute Spirit   26
   The Ideal   34
   Problems and Solutions   45

2 THE SYSTEMATICS OF ART   51

   The Moments of Concept   51
   Form and Content   62
   The End of Art   71
   The System of the Arts   89

Part Two: INSTANCES   97

3 FROM ARCHITECTURE TO MUSIC:
   OPENING UP THE INTERIOR   99

   Architecture   99
   Sculpture   109
   Painting   121
   Music   133

4 LITERATURE: THE REALM OF GOLD   142

   The Determination of Literature   142
   The Theory of Genres   146
   The Epic   153
   The Drama   165
   The Lyric   178

CONCLUSION   188
NOTES   193

CONTENTS

GLOSSARY 214
SELECT BIBLIOGRAPHY 220
INDEX 228

LIST OF PLATES

Plates are inserted between pages 132 and 133.

I. The Horse of Selene, Parthenon, 439–432 BC
   British Museum, London

II. Carl Ferdinand Sohn, *Rinaldo und Armida*
   Kunstmuseum, Düsseldorf

III. Wilhelm von Schadow, *Mignon*
   Museum der Bildenden Künste, Leipzig.

INTRODUCTION

It may not be completely wrong to say that there is just one issue which is specifically and uniquely philosophical. It may even be possible to argue that philosophy is simply the body of discourse concerned with that issue. Unfortunately, it is not possible to say what the issue is.

This embarrassing state of affairs has the one happy consequence of keeping the issue, and philosophy, alive. It had been stated and described many times, and called many things. It has been called the problem of forms and appearances, of ideas and instances, of categories and cases, universals and particulars, identity and difference, mind and body, substance and accidence, concept and intuition, theory and practice, being and existence. It manifests itself in theological traditions as the question of the Divine and the human, of God and man. The embarrassment is obvious—to say what the issue is, would simply be to give it another name, and then to say: '*That* is what everybody has *really* been talking about', without being able to prove it. To name the issue is already to have understood it in a certain way, and it does not exist apart from the way in which is it understood. To name it is to constitute it, and to say what philosophy is; which means that philosophy is its own problem, which it has solved when it completely understands itself. The issue cannot be described apart from the thinking of it, because it is a relation, and relations can only be thought. Any putative solutions cannot be correct or incorrect, because they cannot be checked; they can only make sense or fail to make sense.

The most revolutionary statement of the issue immediately before Hegel was Kant's. He understood it as the relation of concept and intuition. After Hegel, the most novel ways of understanding it have been as theory and practice and as ontological difference ('Sein' and 'Seiendes'). The novelty of Hegel's approach is that he tries to draw various answers together, and relate them in terms of the issue itself. The result is an account of thought thinking itself, as the thinking of determinacy. Hegel does not stop there, but goes on to investigate the issue of philosophy as it manifests itself in more concrete forms, and his lectures on aesthetics are his investigation of the issue as it shows itself in art. The present study names the issue in this case as that of principles and instances, that is, the relationship between the concept of art (the Ideal) and works of art. It is accordingly divided into two parts, but as the issue is a relation, they both deal with the same thing from a different point of view.

The first part will attempt to show that Hegel has claims to make about the systematicity and the historicity of art, and the second part will exemplify those claims. The relation between systematics and history is another example of the issue of philosophy, so in talking about art, philosophy is once more talking about itself. One of the first people to be irritated by Hegelian philosophy's liking for the sound of its own voice was Karl Marx, and he duly polemicized against it.[1] Marx had an important point, but his protests were misplaced, for philosophy can only legitimately talk about art, if art raises philosophical issues. If it does not, philosophy has nothing to say, and should keep quiet. If it does, the only way to talk about them is philosophically. The problem is, how do we know what philosophy can talk about, and why should we be interested in what this arcane Narcissus has to say?

Obviously, if Hegel's theory of art is to justify even its own existence, it must at least show that philosophy can talk about art in terms of itself, and that the exercise is not trivial. The point on which his argument turns is that both art and philosophy are systematic, and he expresses this by claiming that both are forms of a category he calls 'Idea'. The philosophical form of the category is the Idea of Truth, and the artistic form is the Ideal of Beauty. If his claim is justified, he has both shown that philosophy can say something about art, and said it. It is this relation between Beauty and Truth which itself explains the relation between the principle of art and its instances. Beauty and Truth are themselves instances of the principle of systematicity called 'Idea', and they are open to historical instantiation. The relationship between systematics and history is another example of the issue of philosophy. When this relationship is examined, it shows that the relation between Beauty and Truth encompasses the relation between art and social morality. One problem leads to another, and all are interconnected, in sometimes subtle ways.

The reason why these obscure and dubious assertions have been unloaded on the first pages of an introduction, is that it must be made clear that to get to grips with Hegel's *Aesthetics* means getting to grips with Hegel's philosophy as a whole. His philosophy of art has a context, and, as he himself said in his inaugural lecture in Berlin in 1818, it is only when the whole has been understood that the parts become comprehensible.[2] If we are not to rotate dizzily around the circle of circles which his philosophy constitutes,[3] we need some understanding of the system as a whole. The problem raised by the young Marx is really the general problem of the status of 'Realphilosophie', of which the *Aesthetics* is a part. We cannot expect to open the text at page one and have all our questions answered, for if we do, we will not even know what we are reading. What sort of a theory is it? What is its object? What terms does it use? Why, and what do they mean?

In the past, Hegel has succeeded in inspiring virulent passions, and Hegel reception, in sorry contrast to the impressive history of Kant scholarship, has been a history of vituperation and adulation. However, since about 1960 scholars in Germany have produced some of the badly needed commentaries on central texts, primarily the *Logic*, and a period of cool analysis has brought us back up to the level of Rosenkranz, Rötscher, Weisse, and others among Hegel's contemporaries who have seemed to be alone in their sober and insightful discussion of Hegel's achievements and failings. Lack of space unfortunately precludes the sort of exposition of the system which is really required before tackling the *Aesthetics*, but in order to make what follows comprehensible, I shall dogmatically lay down what I take to be certain key aspects of his thought as a whole without any attempt to justify them. Some issues are dealt with more fully in the main text, and I have added a glossary to act as an aide-mémoire. This reading of Hegel is no doubt not the only possible one, but it reflects recent research, makes sense of the text, and takes his thought seriously. Further support for this view will be found in works in the bibliography.

The object of Hegel's philosophy is not the world, but thought; it is not out to tell us how the world has to be, but how we have to think about it. It starts out with the ordinary notions and images embodied in language, and draws certain of them together into a system, in a process which will be referred to as 'reconstruction'. Reconstruction consists in the translation of the vague picture we have of something, which Hegel calls a 'Vorstellung', into pure thought, a Concept ('Begriff') from which the picturing element is eliminated. Clearly some concepts, such as cow, do not admit of reconstruction, because they are empirical. Others, such as identity, do, because nobody can check whether there is such a thing as identity by going out and pointing to it (as one might with a cow); one can only argue over whether or not it makes sense to talk about things in terms of identity. If it does, it will be reconstructed, and its meaning determined by the system. The rationale for the system is that the relations set up by concepts already reconstructed imply further ones, and the process continues until the system closes in on itself like a circle. Each concept is the concept it is, that is, it is determined, by virtue of its relation to other concepts, and claims to explain the thought it reconstructs. The validity of the relations set up is guaranteed by the fact that they constitute a method, which Hegel calls the 'speculative method', and which is reflected upon at the end of the first part of the system, the *Logic*, under the title 'the Absolute Idea'. The general pattern followed by speculative method is that one concept is found to imply another with which it stands in contrast, in other words, it is what it is only by virtue of what it is not. (To put it crudely, identity is only identity because it is not difference; to talk about identity makes no sense without talking about difference.) Such concepts, which negatively imply each other, are called 'dialectical'. They in turn imply a concept in terms of which their relationship can be understood, and it is this positive implication of a negative relation which is the speculative moment of method—hence its name.

There are a number of distinctions within the system which will concern us in what is to come. There are three main areas of the system: Logic, Nature, and Spirit. The place of aesthetics is at the end of Spirit. Whilst Logic gives a basic account of method by reconstructing the most fundamental categories of thought, Nature and Spirit give an account of what might be called regions which are determinate with respect to space and time (the first categories of Nature). Together, they constitute 'Realphilosophie' or regional philosophy, and call upon the conceptual framework of Logic. Recurrent reference will be made to the three main sections of Logic, the *Logic of Being*, the *Logic of Essence*, and the *Logic of Concept*. They differ in the types of relations obtaining between their concepts. In Being, progression from one concept to the next is by *transition* (Übergehen), whereby each of a pair of dialectical concepts stands in immediate contrast to the other; for example, the concepts 'Something' and 'Other' stand in immediate contrast, meaning that Something is not-Other and Other is not-Something. But the relationship between the two is indeterminate: they are relatively indifferent to one another. In Essence, the pairs of categories stand in a determinate relation, and determine each other in a relationship called *reflection* ('Reflexion' or 'Scheinen in Anderes'). An example would be the categories of 'Thing' and 'Property', whereby a thing is what it is by virtue of its properties, and the properties are what they are by virtue of being properties of that thing. Essence considers each concept as a moment of a relation through which they are held together as distinct. The final section of Logic, called Concept, considers that relation as itself a moment of what therefore becomes a triadic structure, which does not alter, but only *develops*. The three moments of this structure (called 'Concept-structure') are *universality*, *particularity*, and *individuality*. Hegel's claim is that Concept gives a framework for understanding products of the human mind (as well as thought and subjectivity themselves) which have universal formal properties, are particular with respect to space and time, and are irreducibly individual because they embody a universal property in a particular context. Accordingly, Concept-structure is used to build up the theories of regional philosophy, including the theory of art.

Before opening a page of the text known as the *Aesthetics*, we can therefore say quite a lot about what we will find there. We should find a theory which translates historical and current thoughts about art into concepts which determine art satisfactorily, distinguishing it from its neighbours in the system, neighbours such as religion, philosophy, decoration, entertainment, and the like. It will not tell us whether x is a work of art, but give us criteria for making such empirical, judgemental assessments ourselves—it will not tell us about things, but about how we think about things. It should show art to be universal, that is it must develop a Concept of art which will play the role of a general theory, and then proceed to show that art is necessarily particular and individual, giving an account of both. We must expect the general theory to encompass a justification of the whole undertaking, some reason for believing that art is open to speculative reconstruction. We must understand that it is in principle possible for the Concept of art to correspond to reality, that is, to be true.

Hegel's theory of truth, which he places at the end of the *Logic of Concept* under the title 'Idea', has complex ramifications, but must be briefly considered as it plays such a crucial role in this study. In a nutshell, his theory combines two traditional strands of thought: of truth as coherence, and of truth as correspondence. The Idea is the unity of Concept and reality, which is to say that a systematically coherent theory actually corresponds to the way things are. One could understand a truth claim as combining the claims: 'This is a possible way for things to be, because this is how we can think about them' (Concept/coherence), *and*: 'This is the way things are' (reality/correspondence). Therefore, within 'Realphilosophie' we will be able to judge the adequacy of empirical instances (in our case works of art) by the degree to which they correspond to the Concept which has been developed. This, one could say, is Hegel's systematic notion of truth.

Within Spirit, however, there is another notion of truth to be found, which is fundamentally a historical one. Hegel talks freely about 'the truth of the Greeks', 'the truth of Oriental consciousness', 'our truth', and the like. He means the seriously held beliefs of societies, the way people understand themselves and their God or gods. This seems to be something quite different from the theoretical Idea, and so indeed it should be. Hegel, alas, believes he can translate the existential and religious beliefs held throughout history into the conceptual terms of his system, and that they will culminate in a fully adequate reconstruction of the God of Christianity as the categories of the *Logic*. In other words, he thinks that historical and systematic developments parallel each other, and this belief of his, which is never adequately defended, is one which plagues all 'Realphilosophie', not least the Aesthetics. It will occupy us all too often, but should be distinguished from the perfectly legitimate use of historical material to provide examples, and from the theory of history contained in his systematic consideration of it. Briefly, he distinguishes historical from natural events by arguing that historical events are such as to alter the context of their own possibility, with the consequence that history is ruled by the principle of non-repetition: it is that particular context, all of whose results are individual. This Concept of history will be of some importance for us, and is rather more interesting than the Hegel of legend, who had the World Spirit and its mystical minions pushing Napoleon across the Alps.

Texts

The text known as Hegel's *Aesthetics* was put together from lecture notes by Gustav Heinrich Hotho, and published in 1835. The material dates from between 1818, when Hegel was still in Heidelberg, and the 'Wintersemester' of 1828–9 in Berlin, and includes Hegel's own notes as well as Hotho's and those made by various students. Hotho's work has in general been highly praised, but in 1931, Georg Lasson's revised edition appeared in the Meiner Verlag, containing serious criticism of Hotho, and attempting to provide a text which more accurately reflected Hegel's own ideas. However, Lasson had none of Hegel's own notes, and only five of the ten student scripts available to Hotho, and his edition has not replaced Hotho's. At the time of writing, Frau Dr. Annemarie

Gethmann-Siefert is working on a scholarly edition of the lectures at the Hegel Archiv in Bochum. All the existent manuscripts are in Bochum, including some late ones Lasson did not have, but no edition will be appearing in the foreseeable future. Until one does, Hotho's work must remain the basis of any study. This is not too serious, for it seems unlikely that modern editorial methods will produce radical changes in the text, and in any case, Hotho's edition has been accepted for a century and a half, and exerted strong influence over many people, so it is an important historical document in its own right.[4]

The textual situation means that we are not dealing with a book, a text signed by an author, but with a mixture of the author's notes and reports on what he said in lectures spread over a decade. Hegel often improvised freely in his lectures, so he undoubtedly said different things, and used different examples, at different times. This makes it all the more important that as much reliance as possible be placed on the texts of the *Encyclopedia* and *Logic* which Hegel did publish. I have chosen to work from the Suhrkamp *Theorie-Werkausgabe* in twenty volumes of Hegel's works (and lectures), and it is volumes 13, 14, and 15 of this edition, edited by Eva Moldenhauer and Karl Markus Michel, which will be the text of the *Aesthetics* quoted throughout. The edition is reliable, contains all the valuable additions to the *Encyclopedia* and *Philosophy of Right*, and is easily available. The three volumes of the *Aesthetics* also have minor claims to superiority over others (see chapter 2). They will be referred to as $\ddot{A}$ I, $\ddot{A}$ II, and $\ddot{A}$ III, corresponding to volumes 13, 14, and 15 of the *Werke*. Only in the case of the *Phänomenologie des Geistes* and the *Wissenschaft der Logik* did I feel that better, and more generally used editions were available, and they have been quoted in the Meiner Verlag editions, edited by Hoffmeister and Lasson respectively, referred to as *PhG* and *WL* I or *WL* II. In order to reduce the number of notes, page references to Hegel's works will be put in the main text as far as possible. References to the *Encyclopedia* will follow standard practice by giving the paragraph number, followed by 'Zus.' (Zusatz) in the case of an addition. The lengthier quotations have English translations appended to them. In the case of shorter passages in the body of the text, I have often used English alone unless the meaning of the German is clear. All quotations, whether English or German, refer to a German text, and all translations are my own. Translators face a conflict between the requirements of accuracy and those of readability, and as some of Hegel's language is technical I have in general inclined towards the former, on occasion coining phrases of my own (no-one would normally render 'Scheinen' by 'reflection').

The main object of this study remains some one-thousand-six-hundred pages without an author, and the aim is to make them more transparent. In doing so, their lack of sanctity can be turned to advantage, for it makes the reader more ready to accept the text's weaknesses as well as its strengths. The purely hermeneutic approach, which has dominated German literature on Hegel for a long time, concentrates on finding coherence and harmony in his texts, as if they were novels. This approach fails to take him seriously, for he is concerned with issues and is making claims which can only be understood if they are questioned. The text must be understood, but then interrogated. The tendency in other quarters, particularly in England, has been to attack apparent weaknesses, and make him sound ridiculous. The issues once more disappear, and the attacks are directed against positions which Hegel never held. Hegel had a more sophisticated understanding of the nature of criticism:

> Die wahrhafte Widerlegung muß in die Kraft des Gegners eingehen und sich in den Umkreis seiner Stärke stellen; ihn außerhalb seiner selbst angreifen und da recht zu behalten, wo er nicht ist, fördert die Sache nicht (*WL* II. 218).

A genuine refutation must acknowledge the strength of the adversary, and take him on at his strongest points; the issue will not benefit if one attacks a position he does not hold, and is correct about a point he has never challenged.

If we are really interested in the issues, 'die Sache', then we must discover Hegel's strengths, and that can only be done through close reading. Argument and hermeneutics are not alternatives. Only if the reader is prepared to help the text to make the best case possible, can he then ask the right questions, and, perhaps, discover genuine incoherence. And then, perhaps, one could see how some of the incoherence might be avoided. The text can become a discussion partner, and in order to illuminate the issues, others can be invited to contribute. This is why other positions have been considered when they throw light on some matter. I have made no attempt to cover all the major writers on aesthetics, which would be self-defeating anyway, but have simply tried to get some outside perspectives on Hegel, in order to make clear what he is saying, and what he is not saying. Pure textual immanence has limits, and a proper understanding of a text thinks on both sides of them.

Of course, one might wonder whether it is at all worth while to take Hegel seriously. The relationship between Beauty and Truth may have been an issue once, but nobody is interested in these pretentious Platonic nouns any more—they belong on the scrap-heap of history. This may be true. I shall argue that it is not, and that when Hegel's alien language is penetrated, subtle solutions to modern problems emerge. At the end of it all, one may decide that it was not worth the effort, but that is not a foregone conclusion. After all, if we in the late twentieth century are above the level of Germany's early-nineteenth-century idealism, we should have no trouble in showing that we can attain it. We may be in for a humbling, but instructive surprise.

Part One:
PRINCIPLES

Wir kannten nicht sein unerhörtes Haupt,
darin die Augenäpfel reiften. Aber
sein Torso glüht noch wie ein Kandelaber,
in dem sein Schauen, nur zurückgeschraubt,

sich hält und glänzt. Sonst könnte nicht der Bug
der Brust dich blenden, und im leisen Drehen
der Lenden könnte nicht ein Lächeln gehen
zu jener Mitte, die die Zeugung trug.

Sonst stünde dieser Stein entstellt und kurz
unter der Schultern durchsichtigem Sturz
und flimmerte nicht so wie Raubtierfelle;

und bräche nicht aus allen seinen Rändern
aus wie ein Stern: denn da ist keine Stelle,
die dich nicht sieht. Du mußt dein Leben ändern.

Rainer Maria Rilke

1

THE DETERMINATION OF ART

'Wer nicht weiß was er sieht oder hört, genießt nicht das Privileg unmittelbaren Verhaltens zu den Werken, sondern ist unfähig, sie wahrzunehmen.'[1] ('Those who do not know what they are seeing or hearing do not enjoy the privilege of immediate access to the works concerned, but are incapable of perceiving them.') This uncompromising assertion is one of Adorno's justifications for philosophical aesthetics: if we do not know what we are looking at, we do not see; if we do not know what we are listening to, we do not hear.[2] It remains an assertion, and philosophical aesthetics remains a branch of philosophy in ill repute, recently described as 'a continuing intellectual disaster'.[3] The very enterprise of aesthetics is deeply problematic. Is anything to be gained from reflection on art? Could such reflection be distinctly philosophical? Can one say what art is, and should one even try to?

Hegel would clearly have given a positive answer to all these questions, and, like Adorno, would have denied that the purpose of art is to give us an immediate feeling of pleasure which could only be sullied by reflection.[4] Hegel has undertaken to say what art is, to give its determination. There are reasons in plenty to be critical of his execution of the project, but I shall try to gain a better understanding of him and his theory by considering what he could have said, as well as what he did say. The first step must therefore be to try to clarify what he was trying to do, and how he tried to do it.

The Object of Hegel's Aesthetics

Unfortunately, the apparently simple task of saying what the *Aesthetics* is about leads directly into controversy. Hotho's text opens as follows:

Diese Vorlesungen sind der *Ästhetik* gewidmet; ihr Gegenstand ist das weite *Reich des Schönen*, und näher ist die *Kunst*, und zwar die *schöne Kunst* ihr Gebiet (*Ä* I. 13).

These lectures are dedicated to *Aesthetics*; their object is the broad *realm of the Beautiful*, their concern being more specifically *art*, that is to say, *fine art*.

Hegel proceeds to criticize the term 'Ästhetik', because it suggests a science of the senses, of feeling (Empfinden), and also rejects the term 'Kallistik' on the grounds that 'die Wissenschaft, die gemeint ist, betrachtet nicht das Schöne überhaupt, sondern rein das Schöne der *Kunst*'— 'the science designated by this term does not consider the Beautiful as such, but simply the Beautiful in *art*' (*Ä* I. 13).[5] This suggests that his object is beauty as such, be it in art or not. However, he concludes his brief introduction by calling his science '*Philosophie der Kunst*', or more precisely '*Philosophie der schönen Kunst*', and then launches into the first topic for discussion by remarking: 'Durch diesen Ausdruck nun schließen wir sogleich das *Naturschöne* aus'—'In using this expression we immediately exclude *natural beauty*' (ibid.). So, is his object beauty, or is his object art? Is natural beauty included or excluded?

The answer to these questions is that natural beauty excludes itself from the enquiry, because to deal with beauty is to deal with art. Hegel explicitly states that he is not leaving out natural beauty for pragmatic reasons (*Ä* I. 14, 15), and he devotes some fifty pages to it, in which he attempts to justify his view. It is, as it were, only the exclusion of nature which is included in the *Aesthetics*, but this exclusion involves giving an account of natural beauty; Hegel can only avoid the subject by dealing with it.[6] Natural beauty is an inadequate realization of the Concept of Beauty, what might be called its *deficient mode*: it is not a product of a free intelligence, and is therefore abstract, restricted to things such as symmetry, regularity, and harmony.[7]

This is particularly interesting from a historical point of view because it is such a stark contrast to Kant, whose *Kritik der Urteilskraft* could be said to contain a twofold primacy of natural over artistic beauty: natural beauty is the paradigm of all beauty to the extent that art is only beautiful when we know it is art, but it looks like nature (§45); and nature rules art through the genius: 'Genie ist das Talent (Naturgabe), welches der Kunst die Regel gibt'—'Genius is the talent (gift of nature), which supplies art with its precept' (§46). Admittedly, Kant also says that there is a form of aesthetic interest in nature, which occurs when we discover its products appearing to be intentional like art, 'nach gesetzmäßiger Anordnung und als Zweckmäßigkeit ohne Zweck'— 'ordered as if according to rules, showing purposiveness without purpose' (§42), but in Hegelian terms this is only to regard art from the point of view of natural beauty—the point of view of 'ordering as if according to rules'. The artist's model is God's Newtonian design.

For Hegel, nature's model is art: natural beauty is 'ein Reflex des dem Geiste angehörigen Schönen'—'a reflex of the beauty which falls within the province of Spirit' (*Ä* I. 15). This represents a radical rejection of the ancient notion that art is 'mimesis', the imitation of nature,[8] and instead defines the source of art as human freedom (*Ä* I. 18).[9] Hegel's thesis is that we derive our notions of aesthetic value primarily from art, and regard nature as beautiful only in so far as it can be regarded from the point of view of art.[10] The point has been well put by Solger: 'Betrachten wir die Natur unter der Form des Schönen, so tragen wir den Begriff der Kunst auf die Natur über.'[11] ('When we consider nature from the point of view of the Beautiful, we are transferring the concept of art on to nature.') Formulated in stricter theoretical terms, Hegel is saying the following: nature and art can both be understood by means of *one* concept of beauty; natural beauty involves nothing which is not also involved in artistic beauty; artistic beauty does, on the contrary, involve factors which do not arise in nature; therefore, a concept of beauty must be a concept of art.[12] Whether or not this is valid will depend on the theory of art itself, which must be such as to allow us to understand symmetry, regularity, and so on, as its deficient instances.[13] These are the things which Hegel regards as constituting natural beauty—his treatment of natural scenes and landscapes is very perfunctory, but he is consistent in saying that they are regarded as beautiful if they appear to express something human, by exciting our interest or awakening some feeling (*Ä* I. 176, 177).

Three things should be clear from all this: first, that Hegel bans the concept of mimesis from aesthetics; second, that art is a product of human freedom, and stands in contrast with nature; and third, that nature can be beautiful only if it is treated as if it were a work of art, that is as if it were a human product. This means that things which are not art can have certain aesthetic effects when they are viewed as if they were.[14] But they do not thereby become art—it takes more than a few happy effects to produce a jump in ontological status.

We might now say that Hegel's *Aesthetics* is a *speculative theory of art as the locus of beauty*, which reconstructs in purely categorial terms the essential content of what, in the tradition of Western thought up to the beginning of the nineteenth century, has been taken to distinguish art from anything else. The input of the theory, the source of 'Vorstellungen', will be the distillation of two and a half millenniums of sophisticated and unsophisticated discourse about beauty and art. This body of discourse is the object of the theory, in the sense of 'material', and the determination of art is its object, in the sense of 'aim'. The most sensible and the most Hegelian thing to do now, is to make it clear what this means by making clear what it does *not* mean. I shall turn first to the question of the aim, and deal with the more difficult question of method presently.

It is not part of Hegel's aim to discuss the artist or artistic production, as there is nothing philosophical to be said about either. Once more, the subject is included with the express aim of saying that it is to be excluded from philosophical consideration ($\ddot{A}$ I. 362). Hegel devotes some space to general remarks about the artist, largely because the subject was so popular at the time (ibid.), and they are soberly realistic ($\ddot{A}$ I. 362-85). More importantly, the philosopher is not one of the 'doctors of art' ($\ddot{A}$ I. 31) who try to prescribe rules for the artist, in an attempt to determine what art ought to be. The philosopher wants to say what art is; he will be descriptive rather than prescriptive. Hegel seems here to abandon any claim to normativity, but it is apparent that the Concept of art is in some way evaluative, for it is supposed to tell us what true art is. Hegel's intention thus seems to be to leave everything as it is, and let artists do what they like, but then to give grounds for the evaluation of what they do. It remains to be seen how he does it.

The other thing which Hegel is most significantly failing to do, is to give a theory of aesthetic judgement, of the type exemplified by Kant's third critique.[15] Kant is concerned with the status of a type of judgement, and wishes to discern what is necessary in order to call an object beautiful.[16] The object of the judgement is merely the occasion of it, and could be anything at all; Kant's interest is in the subject doing the judging, and in what makes the judgement a judgement of taste, with the peculiar status of subjective universality. This theory is a quite different type from Hegel's and they are not in competition for that reason. However, Kant also has another theory in the *Critique of Judgement*, a theory of art which *is* in competition with Hegel's and its relationship to the theory of judgement is very unclear.[17] As a pure judgement of taste involves no intellectual interest (§16), and art is distinguished by 'aesthetic ideas' (§§42 ff.), aesthetic judgements appear to have nothing to do with art; indeed, artistic judgement must be intellectual as well as, or even rather than, aesthetic.

This raises an interesting problem about the relationship between the philosophy of art and the philosophy of aesthetic judgement, for although they appear to be doing quite different things, they are not in fact indifferent to one another. For Kant, it was irrelevant that art is the principal object of aesthetic judgements, but if this is found to be unacceptable, as it is by Roger Scruton, the question arises of how they link up.[18] Scruton sets out to give 'a systematic account of aesthetic experience in terms of an empiricist philosophy of mind'.[19] Having given a theory of the aesthetic attitude in those terms, he argues in the second part of his book that it would be odd if such an attitude were only contingently related to art, and undertakes to show that 'the thoughts and feelings involved in aesthetic interest can acquire a full elaboration only if the aesthetic object possesses just those features which are characteristic of art', an undertaking which he admits involves 'supplementing our theory in ways inimical to traditional empiricism'.[20] So having given a theory of the aesthetic subject, Scruton supplements it with a theory of the aesthetic object (i.e. a philosophy of art), and then tries to show that they fit together. However, given his un-Kantian notion of the aesthetic, his supplement renders the original theory superfluous.

The root of the trouble can be found in the theory of the aesthetic attitude, which in fact contains a lot of discussion about art. Having argued that an aesthetic attitude is normative, in that it 'seeks to found agreement in reason, and not in some chance convergence of opinion',[21] Scruton tries to ground this in the linguistic habits of an unspecified first-person plural, who has the philosophical function of serving as an ideal subject. It is the 'we' which, for unknown reasons, possesses normative aesthetic responses. If this 'we', for example, finds a film boring, he tries to convince other people that it was boring, and would actually be misusing the term 'boring' if he did not do so.[22] In the face of this, one grows curious about how this opinionated and intolerant creature knows that its feelings and value-judgements, and its eccentric views about correct English, are normative. The latter is not explained; the former lies in the fact that its response is 'appropriate'.[23] What is 'appropriate'? Clearly, if the answer is just that 'we' use words correctly and are not philistines,[24] the vicious circle of explanation has been closed. The alternative is to say that what is appropriate is that response which fully realizes the nature of the object, the work of art. But to say this is to make the account of the aesthetic attitude otiose, for aesthetic response is grounded in the nature of the work of art. If the aesthetic attitude is simply that response which is appropriate in the case of art, it is theoretically irrelevant, for it is a consequence of a theory of art; and furthermore, the only way of grounding what is an appropriate response is through a philosophy of art. Scruton has produced the wrong type of theory by beginning with an account of the aesthetic *subject*, when he needs a theory of the aesthetic object in order to ground it. If he can show that art is a rational object, he has grounded the *possibility* of a rational response, but he will never show that a rational response is *necessary*. The response as such is irrelevant, and varies even for one subject. If, for example, I am trying to sleep, I may be irritated by the sound of a piece of music I greatly admire; or I may feel great affection for a piece I regard as very bad, because, for example, it reminds me of childhood. Response *as such* is contingent.

Scruton's problems are interesting, for they show a very able aesthetician levering himself out of the impoverished tradition of empiricism and the later Wittgenstein, because the issues he is confronting burst the framework it offers, and indicate what advantages are offered by the Hegelian theory-type. But they also show that in producing a theory of art, Hegel has *ipso facto* produced a theory grounding a certain type of appropriate response to art, that type of response which is not concerned with passing a subjective judgement of taste on works of art, but with objectively judging what the qualities of works of art are at the empirical level. This would be a mode of discourse committed to giving reasons for what it says about art, and committed to giving an adequate empirical account of its object. As it is part of the object language of speculative philosophy, it too is the object of reconstruction, and it is determined along with art. It would be reasonable to call it *art-critical discourse*, and this would then be the rational core of the 'aesthetic attitude', as Scruton understands it. This has nothing to do with the aesthetic in Kant. Kant does not have Scruton's problems because he is not concerned with the aesthetic *attitude* at all, and, in accordance with eighteenth-century usage, does not see any necessary connection between what is meant by 'aesthetic' and art. He approaches the judgement that something is beautiful as a judgement of *taste*, and it is the judgement of taste which constitutes the object of his inquiry. That such a judgement is aesthetic is the first thing he has to prove, and by 'aesthetic' he means a judgement 'dessen Bestimmungsgrund *nicht anders* als *subjektiv* sein kann'—'the rationale for which *cannot be other than subjective*' (*Kritik der Urteilskraft*, § 1). 'Aesthetic' means 'subjective' for Kant, so the attempt to prove that the aesthetic attitude is objective would be a contradiction in terms, a simple misuse of language. To criticize Kant for not making art the principal object of aesthetic judgement is to criticize normal eighteenth-century German usage for not corresponding to normal twentieth-century English usage, a criticism which we would normally call 'odd'.

Hegel's *Aesthetics* therefore represents an attempt to give the determination of beauty and of art in speculative terms, and thereby say what the first-level discourse of art criticism could be. However, the text is far more heterogeneous than this suggests, for it contains a wealth of empirical discussion, both critical and historical, sections on the artist, other passages on the public and aesthetic judgement, and at least the outlines of a sociology of art.[25] Some of this material is there because Hegel liked to be comprehensive, but some has a theoretical function which will be investigated in due course. We can at least be confident that if we turn to the text expecting a theory of art, we will not be disappointed. But we do not yet know what to expect from the theory, in particular, we do not know that it will not be one of those disastrous disappointments for which aesthetics is renowned. Is a philosophy of art possible, even in principle?

What could a Philosophy of Art Be?

The world 'art' has been used to cover phenomena of such disparity that it seems prima facie quite implausible, and indeed arrogant, to presume to say what art is, and reduce it to some abstract philosophical formula. The only fair and honest attitude, it seems to some, is to resign in the face of positive facts, and not attempt to make distinctions where none are now possible. We should face up to the fact that anything could be art, or indeed, that everything is art; that, as the American artist Don Judd is reported as saying, 'If somebody calls it art, it's art.'[26]

   There are reasons to believe that we would be ill advised to resign so soon.[27] The problem with this sort of anarchic scepticism is that if everything is art, the concept becomes empty, because there is nothing it excludes. If a concept is to be meaningful, it must stand in contrast with something, which means that although the limits of a concept can be extended, there must still be limits. A new artistic product can challenge the tradition only if it has some relation to it. If it has nothing whatsoever to do with what has been taken to be art, the break is so radical that it no longer makes sense to refer to it as art at all. Judd's apparently passive tolerance masks the fact that he is making a very strong and difficult claim to the effect that there is no difference between art and anything else, which means that he must deny that there is anything distinctive about *Hamlet*, the Mass in B minor, the Sistine Chapel, or any of the other things which have commonly been thought to have peculiar qualities, and therefore been described as 'art'.

He must deny that there has been any reasoning behind the selection of certain objects as works of art.

Judd recommends a sort of positivism which demands that the curious would-be aesthetician be quiescent, and believe everything he is told. Indeed, there are those who would assert that a mere theoretician has no right to challenge what is said by practising artists about art.[28] The trouble with this is first, that anybody can then declare himself to be an artist and say that whatever he does is art, and second, that the question is not itself aesthetic but theoretical. Deciding what the limits of meaningful discourse are does not produce works of art but theories, and if artists do try to say what art is, they are encroaching on the province of the philosopher.

Philosophers may then decide that there is nothing to be said. Some have devoted considerable energies to explaining why they have nothing to say, and why it is important to say so, and they have criticized 'traditional' or 'idealist' aesthetics for erroneously assuming that art is a unity, pointing out that there are in fact neither universal merit-conferring properties shared by fine works of art, nor universal criteria by which to judge them.[29] What is a virtue in one work may not be one in another. This would mean that however a philosophy of art does contrive to talk about its object, it will not discuss shared properties, for the properties of individual works are indeed very different. They are also empirical, so they are unlikely to offer much promise if we are concerned with the a priori. The empiricist sceptic, for whom the only way to talk about art is to talk about the properties of works of art, is faced with some embarrassment when he considers criticism. He must either say that it has no criteria for its judgements, and is therefore irrational and arbitrary;[30] or he can admit that some criticism does seem to make sense, and be unable to explain why.[31] The empiricist usually reacts to this by pointing out that we do what we do and say what we say, and there is nothing to be gained from asking for reasons. There are authorities in these matters, and we should accept what they tell us.[32] The recommendation is once more to be quiescent, in this case not to anarchy but to authority. We should trust that the way we have always done things is right, and as empiricism is unable to explain why we do what we do, it dismisses the question.

The problem remains whether it is possible to give a unitary account of art, given the fluctuating limits of the concept and the disparity of its instances. It might be plausible, in the light of Wittgenstein's theory of 'family resemblances', to suggest that there is no common 'thread' running through all works of art. It might be the case that work A has features in common with work B, and work B with work C, but that A and C share no features at all. This is unlikely to be true in the case of art, because of the importance in art of historical precedents. If something is to be accepted as a work of art, it is compared with all previous works of art, not just a few immediate predecessors, because we refer to all the historical examples as 'art' at the same time. Raphael's Madonnas are still here, so we cannot lose sight of them in saying what art is. The concept may widen, but it can never be such as to exclude what it once included; we are always relating A and C. If there is nothing whatsoever relating a Beuys honey-pump and *Hamlet*, then one of them is not art. The example should make it clear that what links them is not an empirical feature–but it might be a function.[33] Art is an institution, and plays a role in human affairs, and it may be this which makes us relate the apparently unrelated. We relate them, not perhaps, because they have something in common, but because they each bear some relation to a centre, which might be a central body of 'classic' works, which we take to determine what art is. A theory of art might be content with some very abstract oppositions to determine the limits of art in a restricted way (such as the opposition between art and nature), and then try to locate the centre. It is clearly not the business of philosophy to judge what individual cases should be included or excluded, precisely because it is a matter of judgement, and judgement can only be empirical. Philosophy may, however, be able to provide some rational criteria for such judgements.

If philosophy does do this, could there be any reason to accept it? It seems, after all, that most aesthetic theories privilege certain works at the expense of others, and it has even been suggested that aesthetic theories are nothing more than rationalizations of prejudices.[34] In Hegel's case, it seems plausible to suggest that he has a bias towards the Ancient Greeks, so perhaps his own personal enthusiasm for Greek art led him to praise it over all the rest. If this were true, it would mean that Hegel was guilty of unsystematic empirical reasoning, of starting with a body of works and declaring them to be normative. But he is trying to determine principles, and principles are not empirical generalizations. Hegel must forget about any real examples, and reconstruct the discourse which is given purely systematically, or he will be guilty of bias. Any bias remaining will be one present in his object language.

If Hegel is not exactly guilty of rationalizing prejudice, then surely his theory is for all that tendentious, because the Concept of art is taken to legislate over reality, and it is a theory which privileges classical art.[35] Now indeed, we shall have to consider whether Hegel does have grounds for giving central importance to Greek art, and to other classicisms, but we may discover that his reasons are good ones. Philosophy ought to be neutral, and free from any evaluative preferences, and if it turns out not to be, we shall have grounds to criticize it. For example, Hegel wishes to argue that sculpture is the central art, with the same systematic importance that is attributed to classicism. Yet it is obvious that he personally is far more interested in literature. To claim that sculpture is the centre of art is to make a theoretical claim, and that means that we can assess it in view of the reasons given for it, its coherence, and its explanatory power. Of course, speculative theory cannot be verified empirically, because it is investigating our conceptual framework, so we cannot go and have a look at some sculpture to see if it really is the centre of art. We have to think about it.

Once we have thought about it, the conclusions reached will govern our judgement. If, for example, we were to be faced with an object which was excluded from art by the theory, we could dismiss it with a clear conscience, because we would be in a position to explain why. Anyone who disagreed would either have to convince us that we had misjudged the object, and that it did in fact fit the criteria which our theory stipulated, or he would have to attack the theory, and explain that he had a better one. The ultimate court of appeal would therefore be philosophical aesthetics, which is responsible for comparing the merits of competing theories. The success of a theory can only be decided through comparing it with other theories, by comparing one view of what art is with another. The sceptic will always pretend that he has not got a theory, but this strategy will not save him for long. He can either mean that he has no idea whatsoever what the word 'art' means, in which case he can be ignored, or that does have some idea, but not enough to constitute a theory. In this case, he can be invited to reflect upon his intuitions, and he will have begun to do philosophy. If he refuses, he has shown himself up as the real dogmatist, for dogmatism is not having clear and rational views on a subject, but refusing to discuss or think about the views one has. It is scepticism, not theory, in which prejudice can take refuge.

Whatever the results of a theory, they will be particular results, and that means that alternatives are possible. At a time when there is less consensus about the nature of art than ever before, it may seem self-defeating to face the challenge. It is interesting to note, therefore, that it is precisely the lack of consensus about art in his own day that Schelling gives as the major reason for lecturing on the philosophy of art. It is, he says, only when there are no recognized standards or criteria for assessment that philosophical reflection is necessary at all, but it is needed if the advocates of all the various opinions are to understand each other.[36] Hegel similarly sees aesthetics as a demand raised by contemporary art, and by the public of his day, the first-person plural whose views he is reconstructing:

Was durch Kunstwerke jetzt in uns erregt wird, ist außer dem unmittelbaren Genuß zugleich unser Urteil, indem wir den Inhalt, die Darstellungsmittel des Kunstwerks und die Angemessenheit und Unangemessenheit beider unserer denkenden Betrachtung unterwerfen. Die *Wissenschaft* der Kunst ist darum in unserer Zeit noch viel mehr Bedürfnis als zu den Zeiten, in welchen die Kunst für sich schon volle Befriedigung gewährte. Die Kunst lädt uns zur denkenden Betrachtung ein, und zwar nicht zu dem Zwecke, Kunst wieder hervorzurufen, sondern, was die Kunst sei, wissenschaftlich zu erkennen. (*Ä* I. 25–6.)

What works of art provoke in us these days is not just immediate pleasure, but a judgement, as we subject the work to a thoughtful consideration of the appropriateness or inappropriateness of the content and the means of expression. Thus it is that in our own day the *science* of art is a far more pressing need than it was in such times when art in itself provided complete fulfilment. Art invites us to reflect, not in order to produce more art, but in order to arrive at a scientific understanding of what art is.

It is because we no longer know what we are doing when we look at paintings, read poems, or listen to music, that we must think about it. This passage is a most interesting example of typically Hegelian self-reflection, for it tells us about the 'we' to which all reflective thought must have recourse for its raw material, and which Hegel specifies. 'We' means the sophisticated, intellectual public of early-nineteenth-century Germany which is not content with looking at something and finding it nice, but is concerned to judge and assess what it sees. 'We' make demands of art some may not care about, by, for example, comparing the content and the execution. From such passages, in which Hegel explains the position of his own theory, it becomes clear that he knew that his philosophy of art would ground a certain type of intellectual judgement on art.

To sum up, we might say that a possible philosophy of art would do at least four things:

it would begin with vague established notions about art, not a body of exemplary works;

it would consider art as a whole, and try to be comprehensive in order not to be tendentious;

it would consider the role of art as an institution, not just the features of works of art;

it would concentrate on locating a theoretical centre, and leave the drawing of limits to empirical judgement.

There are likewise four things we could hope to gain from such a theory, so that its success might be measured by the extent to which these hopes are satisfied:

clarity about what we mean by 'art';

precision in distinguishing it from similar phenomena (such as entertainment or decoration);

rationality, in being able to give reasons for our views;

criteria for our own critical judgements which will liberate us from received opinion, charlatans, and experts.

To conclude, it seems reasonable to say that the only type of theory with a chance of modest success would be a Hegelian one, attempting to reconstruct art in speculative terms, and this is so because of the nature of art itself. Having looked at some of the issues involved in the project of philosophical aesthetics, we can now better appreciate the significance of Hegel's own reflections on method in 'Realphilosophie'. The penultimate chapter of the *Logic*, called 'Die Idee des Erkennens', contains a general examination of analytic and synthetic procedures and their appropriate objects, and the section of the *Introduction* to the *Aesthetics* entitled 'Wissenschaftliche Behandlungsarten des Schönen und der Kunst' applies the general principles to the case of art. Hegel's conclusion is that art is an object which can only be adequately understood through the sort of procedure I am calling 'reconstruction'.

Analytic method is a purely a priori form of conceptual analysis, which treats its object in universal, non-empirical terms, and simply analyses what it contains (*WL* II. 442–5). It is limited because it is universal, and therefore cannot account for particular and individual differences. It is thus suitable in mathematics (*WL* II. 445-50), because mathematics is a universal science, a product of pure thought. However, a purely analytic approach to art would result in an abstract idea, with no clear relation to empirical reality, and such an approach Hegel believes to be exemplified by Plato (*Ä* I. 39). Plato treats the Concept of Beauty in the moment of universality, and ignores its further differences of particularity and individuality. Such a theory cannot account for the full determinacy of art.

The need then arises for a synthetic method to take up the empirically given. The first stage of the synthetic procedure common in natural science is to define the object. Definitions are in order in the case of objects which always are what they are supposed to be, as in the case of geometry (*WL* II. 451-4). A triangle, for example, is what it is defined to be, it is what it is because we make it that way. However, if we are to take up the given, and the given has many properties, it is by no means clear which properties are essential, and definitions lose their value because they make arbitrary stipulations. Hegel gives the example of a professor of anatomy called Blumenbach, who discovered that no animals have ear-lobes, and concluded that ear-lobes were defining characteristics of human beings (*WL* II. 455). Definitions always have a decisionistic element to them which is inappropriate in the case of complex objects which are given, and must be accounted for.[37] Thus, as we have seen, a purely empirical approach to art, relying on features, would be doomed to failure, because it would be arbitrary (see *Ä* I. 29-38).[38] To avoid this, a universal determination of the object must be followed by an account of its particular differences in the division of the subject-matter (*WL* II. 458-64), and proceed further to instantiate itself in real individual cases (*WL* II. 454-77). A determination is not a definition because a definition excludes possible examples by delimiting the object at the outset. A determination is a theory, a framework of universal explanation, which then must demonstrate its own explanatory power through its differences and its instantiation.

Hegel is not then seeking to define art, because all that may legitimately be defined in philosophy are terms; a theory is always a theory *of* something, it has a commitment to the given, the explanandum. Speculative reconstruction is a combination of analytic and synthetic methods.[39] It is analytic and a priori in as much as its rationale is systemic, and its procedure is one of conceptual analysis. It is synthetic and a posteriori in as much as the concept it takes up is a result of distinctions which have been made historically in the course of previous discussion of the nature of art, and it is committed to explanation of actual works of art, in all their variety. Whatever cannot be interpreted as an instance of the resulting Concept, no matter how deficient an instance it might be, is not art. If Hegel's theory makes more and better sense than our intuitions about art, it would be irrational of us not to accept it. It is to that theory that we now turn.

Art as Absolute Spirit

The first two sections of this chapter run roughly parallel to the first two sections of Hegel's *Introduction* (*Ä* I. 13-40), and attempt to entertain his ideas by discussing the issues in more modern terms. The next section of the *Introduction* is by far the longest, consisting of some sixty pages, and is called 'Begriff des Kunstschönen' (*Ä* I. 40-99). It is divided into a section on usual common sense ideas about art, and a 'historical deduction of the true Concept of art' (which is in fact where the discussion of Hirt, Meyer, and Goethe in section two, pp. 33-8, really belongs). However, the opening of this third main section informs us that the Concept of Beauty does not need to be deduced, but can be taken up as given from the *Encyclopedia*, which provides a systematic deduction of art (*Ä* I. 40-3). I wish to argue that Hegel needs both a systematic and a historical 'deduction', and will now follow up Hegel's allusion to the former. Art is given its systematic location in the third part of the *Encyclopedia*, the *Philosophy of Spirit*, where it is situated in the third and final category called 'Absolute Spirit'.

Absolute Spirit (Absoluter Geist) is one of those heady terms which seem to be an invitation to free-associate, but which had a strict technical sense for Hegel. The *Philosophy of Spirit* deals with individuality, considering the possible avatars of subjectivity (individuality and subjectivity are usually equated, as in, for example, *Enzyklopädie* §391). It divides into the three regions of Subjective, Objective, and Absolute Spirit, which relate to each other as Being, Essence, and Concept relate to each other in Logic. Their common concern is concrete subjectivity, 'Geist', which I am translating as 'Spirit' (although in normal German it means 'mind') because it is a technical term, designating what has reasonably been regarded as the central object of Hegel's thought.[40]

What the term means in its minimal, and therefore fundamental, form, can be seen from its first occurrence at the end of the introduction to chapter four of the *Phenomenology*. We read:

Es ist ein *Selbstbewußtsein für ein Selbstbewußtsein*. Erst hiedurch ist es in der Tat; denn erst hierin wird für es die Einheit seiner selbst in seinem Anderssein . . . Indem ein Selbstbewußtsein der Gegenstand ist, ist er ebensowohl Ich wie Gegenstand.–Hiemit ist schon der Begriff *des Geistes* für uns vorhanden (*PhG* 140).

Here we have a *self-consciousness for a self-consciousness*. Indeed, it is only now that we can properly speak of self-consciousness at all, for only now does its own unity in its Other become apparent to itself . . . In as much as it has self-consciousness as its object, the object is both Ego and object–With this, we have before us the Concept of Spirit.

We have an instance of Spirit when one self-consciousness meets another, and knows it, so that their meeting is mutual recognition. The *Phenomenology* continues to discuss deficient instances of Spirit, where one self-consciousness treats another as if it were a thing with properties, and the full realization of Spirit is not achieved until chapter six, which is entitled 'Der Geist'. The relationship between self-consciousness and its object is further explored until self-knowledge is complete. The completion of self-knowledge is only possible through self-consciousness being confronted with different objects, for Hegel wishes to argue (in ways which cannot be gone into here) that self-knowledge is only gained as a result of mediation through an object. Thus self-consciousness is fully self-conscious when it recognizes, and is recognized by, another fully self-conscious subject. At the end of the process of gaining self-awareness, it is possible to see that the first stages of consciousness were not something completely different, but led to the realization of Spirit. They were in fact deficient instances of Spirit, though this was not clear at the time when they were considered. Because a consideration of the forms of consciousness leads to the full self-awareness of consciousness, the science of appearing knowledge is properly called 'Phenomenology of Spirit, not 'Phenomenology of Consciousness'.

'Spirit' does not therefore designate some entity, but, as is usual in Hegel, it is a category designating a relation. It is one form in which Concept manifests itself in 'Realphilosophie', and is not itself anthropological or psychological; it is rather a concept in terms of which anthropological and psychological phenomena can be understood. We must not be tempted to read Hegel's principles through their instances, and equate Spirit with real, thinking human subjects. For example, reading a text can be understood as an instance of Spirit, despite the fact that a text is not a self-conscious subject in a psychological sense. In a categorial sense, the sense which matters to Hegel, a text is a subject to the extent that it embodies thought, and the thought it embodies could very well be self-conscious. Reading is an activity of Spirit to the extent that it involves self-reflection, and a text is a relatum of that relation if it mediates the self-awareness of the reader. Self-consciousness can be mediated through anything, but if it is mediated through a natural object, the knowledge gained will be very abstract. Hegel tends to restrict his use of 'Spirit' to less deficient instances when self-consciousness is mediated through human products, which could be political and social institutions (the realm of Objective Spirit), or the even purer form of self-reflection provided by religion, philosophy— and art.

Art is covered by the category of Absolute Spirit. The word 'absolute', when used as an adjective, indicates a relation of identity, such that all otherness is eliminated and the subject is not dependent upon anything outside itself: an absolute relation is a pure self-relation. So Absolute Spirit will be the category of Spirit's awareness of itself, which means that the relationship between the two logical subjects[41] involved will be such that the relationship itself forms part of the reflection: the subject reflects upon himself, and knows it. As an illustration of what this implies, one can contrast voting at a general election (an example of Objective Spirit), with going to the theatre (an example of Absolute Spirit). A general election is the self-reflection of the state, which comes about because its citizens reflect upon it by voting. They reflect upon the state, not upon themselves, except in their role as citizens. Therefore, their self-reflection is not absolute. However, when the same subjects go to the theatre, they are engaged in absolute self-reflection. The reflection involved in voting is particular—it is specifically political. But the sort of reflection involved in the theatre will not be restricted to a specific subject, it will be self-reflection of a universal nature, which at the same time will be reflection upon themselves as individuals, and will be determined by the individual play watched. So in indulging in the sort of reflection invited by art, one indulges in a universal activity in a particular context, and the reflection is therefore individual, as well as absolute.

It follows from the general structure of Hegelian systematics that the range of art is unrestricted because it presupposes all the previous categories of the *Philosophy of Spirit*, by virtue of its position at the end. It will mediate reflection upon what is universal and abstract, and upon what is particular and specific, just as Spirit begins with the abstract natural determinations of subjectivity, through to the highly mediated ones of politics or religion.[42] Thus the most universal themes of art will be ones which concern natural determinacies of subjectivity, such as ageing, sex, the change of seasons, and so on, and what it can say about them will be relatively abstract, because such things are universal and do not change. But art will also be a product of a particular form of ethical life, and in this respect, its socio-historical determinacy, art will be far more specific, for the socio-historical is the realm of difference. A consequence of this is that if one does look for universal themes in art, the results will be banal: people fall in love, summer follows spring, and the like. The specific content of these themes will be constituted by the specific way in which they are treated, and this specificity arises from the fact that the work of art will have been produced in a particular society at a particular time. It has typically been left to Marxists to draw due attention to this level of the socio-historical,[43] with the difference that Marx regarded Objective Spirit, which he understood as the realm of the socio-economic, as in some way primary in the constitution of subjectivity, the base on which a superstructure arose.[44] In Hegel's system, it would be arbitrary to make Objective Spirit the essence of Spirit in this way—it is just more specific than Subjective Spirit.

If art is to have a place in the *Philosophy of Spirit*, it must in some sense be necessary.[45] Clearly, if art is necessary in some sense, it is not in the existential sense. Art is not a necessity of life like warmth, food, and shelter.[46] It has been claimed that art is the product of a fundamental human drive, but it is not clear how this can be proven.[47] It is a course not open to Hegel, for it would not prove art's necessity, but simply root its existence in a contingent anthropological fact. What Hegel has to show is that art is a 'need of Spirit' ($\ddot{A}$ I. 24), which means that an account of Spirit would be incomplete without it. If then, art is systematically necessary, it must provide an irreducible form of self-reflection, mediating knowledge of Spirit in a way that only it can. To consider it from this point of view is to consider it as an end in itself, and as free. It is this view which Hegel adopts:

In dieser ihrer Freiheit nun ist die schöne Kunst erst wahrhaft Kunst und löst dann erst ihre *höchste* Aufgabe, wenn sie sich in den gemeinschaftlichen Kreis mit der Religion und/Philosophie gestellt hat und nur eine Art und Weise ist, das *Göttliche*, die tiefsten Interessen des Menschen, die umfassendsten Wahrheiten des Geistes zum Bewußtsein zu bringen und auszusprechen. ($\ddot{A}$ I. 20–1.)

It is only in this freedom that fine art is truly art, and it only fulfils its *highest* function when it takes its place alongside religion and philosophy as a way of becoming aware of and expressing the *Divine*, the deepest interests of mankind, the most all-embracing truths of Spirit.

This has two implications:

art must be regarded as autonomous and irreducible;

art which does not fulfil its highest function is in some sense deficient.

Both these implications are of central importance, and both raise problems. Only if Hegel can account for art as a unique and irreducible category is a philosophy of art possible. If the content of art can be reduced to religion or philosophy, it ought not to be dealt with at all. Thus Hegel insists that it is not the servant of morality or religion, for if it is nothing more than an attractive wrapping for edifying truths, it has been turned into 'a pointless accessory, a covering' (*Ä* I. 77). Art cannot be considered as a didactic conveyor of moral principles; it must be shown that in fulfilling its own function, and considered purely as it is in itself, art is 'the first *teacher* of peoples' (*Ä* I. 76). Nor can art be viewed as the purveyor of religious ideas, for it is placed alongside religion as its equal, and with the common object of Truth. It is true, Hegel notes, that art has at times been in the service of religion, but adds:

Wo die Kunst jedoch in ihrer höchsten Vollendung vorhanden ist, da enthält *sie* gerade in ihrer bildlichen Weise die dem Gehalt der Wahrheit entsprechendste und wesentlichste Art der Exposition (*Ä* I. 140).

But where art is present in its highest perfection, it is *art* which, with its use of images, provides the form of exposition which gives the most adequate account of the content of Truth.

Hegel is insistent and unambiguous on this point, marking as it does a significant rupture with a tradition which sought to justify art with reference to its moral effect.

   Unfortunately, however, art is also supposed to have the same content as religion and philosophy, and there is no doubt that although the three should be equal, one comes out on top, in such a way that the ungenerous might question the regal impartiality of Hegelian science:

die Philosophie hat mit Kunst und Religion denselben Inhalt und denselben Zweck; aber sie ist die höchste Weise, die absolute Idee zu erfassen, weil ihre Weise die höchste, der Begriff, ist (*WL* II. 484).

philosophy shares both its content and its purpose with art and religion; but the highest way of understanding the Absolute Idea is through philosophy, because the means it provides is the highest—conceptual thought.

This has led to the widespread view that Hegel regards art as a sort of inferior philosophy,[48] a view which has some immediate plausibility to it, but which collapses in the face of the textual evidence and theoretical requirements expounded above. The problem is both hermeneutic and theoretical, and has two aspects: the relationship between art, religion, and philosophy as the three modes of Absolute Spirit; and the meaning of 'content', which they are supposed to share.

The relationship between art, religion, and philosophy, both in the supposedly strict account in the *Philosophy of Spirit* (*Enz.* §§ 553-77) and in the looser discussion in the lectures (*Ä* I. 127-44), is very obscure. This was first pointed out in the review of the *Aesthetics* by Christian Hermann Weisse, largely because many of Hegel's followers assumed that the relationship was clear, and that art was a transitory phase in mankind's progression to complete illumination in philosophy, a view which Weisse believes could hardly have been held by Hegel himself.[49] Weisse's analysis of the confusion which reigns under the title of 'Absolute Spirit' is very acute: he suggests that Hegel has illegitimately conflated the methods of 'Realphilosophie' and Phenomenology, by reinterpreting the three moments of Absolute Spirit as three forms of consciousness which are passed through and left behind.[50] This indeed seems to be the case. Hegel's distinguished pupil Karl Rosenkranz states in his review what ought to be there instead. Absolute Spirit parallels Concept in Logic, so it ought to consist of three equally essential moments. However, because this ought to be the case, Rosenkranz assumes that it is.[51] He is wrong, for Hegel clearly intends a linear progression from art to religion to philosophy: art is said to have 'its future' in 'true religion' (*Enz.* §563). This suggests, as Weisse observes,[52] that Hegel is replacing a theoretical rationale with a historical one, and the suspicion is confirmed in the *Aesthetics*, where we learn that art is earlier because consciousness forms sensuous representations before concepts with no sensuous content (*Ä* I. 144). This is one of the cases in which dubious history and questionable psychological premises masquerade as systematic theory, and Weisse was well advised to raise an eyebrow.

In this case, as in many others, it is hard to say where our problems as interpreters end, and Hegel's problems begin, in other words, whether we are failing to understand him or whether his theory is incoherent. At such points, we need to recall first principles. Absolute Spirit ought to have the structure of Concept. We would expect to find a logic of development through three moments, distinguishing universal, particular, and individual modes of self-reflection.[53] The content should indeed be the same for each moment of Concept, but by 'content' one should understand nothing more than 'self-reflection'. In the same way, the *Logic of Concept* deals throughout with the same content: subjectivity or pure Thought. There should be development from one moment to another, showing an increase in determinateness in the way in which self-reflection is articulated. This would be quite plausible: the meaning of a work of art would be relatively indeterminate; religion could contain areas of indeterminacy (mysteries, irrationalities); and philosophy would be committed to full clarity and complete explanation.

Hegel probably intends something like this, but it is not what we find. Instead of the moments of Concept, we have a progression from art as immediate, through religion to philosophy as fully mediated, and as somehow a synthesis of the first two (*Enz.* §§556, 572), with the comment that religion is the sphere of the particular (*Enz.* §566), the only residue of the *Logic of Concept*. The distinction between the three forms of Absolute Spirit is made instead by simply using the three forms of theoretical knowledge distinguished in the *Psychology*, the third part of *Subjective Spirit* (*Enz.* §§445–68). This gives art as 'intuition' ('Anschauung'), religion as 'representation' ('Vorstellung'), and philosophy as 'pure Thought' ('Denken') (*Enz.* §§556–8, 565, 572). This procedure of mapping an earlier section on to a later one is unprecedented, and it is also unfortunate, for two reasons. First, it fails in its purpose of differentiating art and religion, because literature is determined as 'Vorstellung' (*Enz.* §556; *Ä* I. 123), which would make it indistinguishable from religion; and secondly, the three modes of knowledge in the *Psychology* are not, despite the misleading title, psychological modes of access to a common object, but different forms of Spirit, that is of the subject–object relation. This means that if we take Hegel at his word, the content of art, religion, and philosophy must be different, for the object of intuition, representation, and conceptual thought is different in each case.

Such are the problems of the text: on the one hand, the mutually dependent moments of Concept, on the other a linear progression through inadequately distinguished differences which is reinterpreted as historical; on the one hand identity of content, on the other hand difference. The text is confusing, but the framework of the theory allows some coherence to be established. Hegel discusses how forms of the same content differ at various points, for the issue is important in justifying the translating procedure of reconstruction—the content remains the same, only the form alters. However, we are told at one point that the alteration in the form of access which the mind has to a content does alter, or appears to alter, the content itself:

In irgendeiner dieser Formen oder in der Vermischung mehrerer ist der Inhalt *Gegenstand* des Bewußtseins. In dieser Gegenständlichkeit *schlagen sich* aber auch *die Bestimmtheiten dieser Formen zum Inhalte*; so daß nach jeder dieser Formen ein besonderer Gegenstand zu entstehen scheint und, was an sich dasselbe ist, als ein verschiedener Inhalt aussehen kann' (*Enz.* §3; cf. §19, Zus., and §22).

In any one of these forms, or in a mixture of several, the content is the *object* of consciousness. But in this objectivity, *the determinacies of these forms* also *penetrate* the content; so that in the case of each of these forms a specific content seems to arise, and, which really amounts to the same thing, it can look like a different content.

In view of this passage, we could take the common content of art, religion, and philosophy as the activity of self-reflection, their common position as Absolute Spirit. Differences would arise within this identity, assuming that the object of the self-reflection is different in each case, because the form of reflection has an effect on the content, as the above passage suggests. One might wish to elaborate this by saying that the content of art is universal, the content of religion different according to socio-historical context, and therefore particular, and philosophy is individual because universal themes are understood in a particular way. It is when fulfilling the role of Absolute Spirit, and expressing awareness of man's highest interests, that art is truly art, and fulfils its highest function.

Simply by virtue of giving it the systemic position it has, Hegel has committed himself to considering art from the point of view of its highest function, and art which does less than that is deficient. Art is an expression of self-awareness, and a means of expanding it. It may sound arbitrary to approach the subject like this, for surely most art is just entertaining or enjoyable.[54] However, there are compelling theoretical reasons for adopting Hegel's approach. If one were to say that the function of art is entertainment, because that is what most art seems to be (which may or may not be true), one would be unable to explain how it was that some art has religious significance. There would thus be important facts about art which would remain unexplained, and inexplicable. Only if the theory aims to cover the totality of possible significance for any work of art, can it cover all cases. Being entertained or amused can be understood as a deficient mode of self-reflection, but the reverse is not the case. If any work of art has had, or could have religious significance, it shows what art's full potential is, and it is then a fact about all other art that it does not reach the full potential. This is not to be unfair, or to legislate over the quality of non-religious work, but to make an observation about the value which is ascribed to art which does reflect man's highest interests. If no art did, we might be happy with amusement as a normative function. All that is meant by using the term 'deficient' is that the instance concerned fails to fulfil all the possible determinacy of art, so the word has a neutral theoretical function, indicating that the value attributed to the work is not as great as the value attributed to other works.

To fulfil its highest function, art must mediate the self-knowledge of the subject so that the knowledge is complete and essential, in other words, so that it constitutes the subject's identity. It would be knowledge of the absolute principles governing human life, and in human culture such principles are normally embodied in what men call the Divine. Hegel believed that art fulfilled this role in ancient Greece, and Greek art provided in consequence the supreme example of what art could be, so that one could say that it was normative. However, this must be immediately qualified, for the norm is not real, but theoretical, a vital distinction which can be clarified by contrasting Winckelmann. For Winckelmann, classical Greek art was a real norm, because it was a norm for imitation by practising artists.[55] For Hegel, it is a theoretical norm because it realizes a totality of determinations. We will later see that Hegel actively rejected the imitation of classical models. The theoretical norm is no more than the centre of art, the apex on which the aesthetician stands in order to view and understand the world of art. Hegel calls this centre the 'Ideal'.

The Ideal

It is only because art is placed under Absolute Spirit as a mode of articulating man's self-understanding and highest interests that philosophy is able to say anything about it. For if it has this role the content of art will not be arbitrary, and neither will the forms in which that content manifests itself ($Ä$ I. 28–9). Philosophy is obliged to prove the necessity of its objects, and the history of art contains much that is contingent, and about which philosophy can accordingly say nothing. The one aspect of art which according to Hegel does show some necessity is the relationship between form and content, and so we may conclude that the *Aesthetics* will be largely, if not exclusively, concerned with that subject (see *Ä* I. 26-7). At least, when the subject is not form and content, the arguments are not philosophical. The relationship between these two much-abused categories is indeed the dominant theme of the lectures as a whole, and of the *Introduction* in particular, forming as it does the historical deduction of the Concept of art, and complementing the systematic deduction in the *Encyclopedia*.

The text uses the word 'deduction' only in the title of the final section of the *Introduction* (p. 83), and it may well stem from Hotho. It is harmless if it is taken to mean what is meant by reconstruction. The *Introduction* should leave us with an understanding of what distinguishes art from any other type of self-reflection such as religion or philosophy, so that when that is taken together with its systemic position, we will know what art is in categorial terms. If the theory is to be plausible, it must contain fundamental common-sense notions about what art is, so they are duly considered on their merits (*Ä* I. 40-82). The theory must then confront its more sophisticated rivals in order to justify itself, because if we are to accept it, it must be seen to be the best available, better than our intuitions and better than other theories. The examination of competing theories is therefore called the deduction proper (*Ä* I. 83-99). This historical deduction thus determines art as a mode of expression, whereas its necessary complement in the *Encyclopedia* determines it as a form of human activity, its role as an institution.

The *Introduction* is a good example of reconstructive method in 'Realphilosophie'. Hegel's examination of common-sense views ('Gewöhnliche Vorstellungen von der Kunst') ensures that his theory covers the distinctions which people have generally wished to make in calling something 'art', and also sifts out popular ideas which are incoherent, or in conflict with the facts. For example, the first basic factor considered is that art is a product of human activity. Hegel discusses the nature of this activity by showing the inadequacies of two conflicting popular notions, the notion that art can be learned, and the notion that it is the product of a peculiar and unique gift called 'genius'. Because not all highly skilled apprentices become great artists, and because many supremely talented artists study and develop their skills over a long period of time, both these notions are rejected as abstractions from the truth (*Ä* I. 44-7). The truth is the speculative synthesis of these dialectical views, a synthesis which is, as quite commonly in Hegel, indistinguishable from a reasonable, middle-of-the-road compromise.

The results of this section make common sense more sensible, and more universally acceptable. The ideas Hegel rejects are for the most part ones which had become popular, or indeed formed part of conventional wisdom, only in the late eighteenth century. He argues, for example, that art is for the senses, but rejects the idea that it is *only* for the senses, and is designed to arouse sensations, a doctrine he associates with Moses Mendelssohn ($\ddot{A}$ I. 52-4). Other rejected 'Vorstellungen' are the idea of a special aesthetic faculty or sense of beauty (pp. 54-5); that beauty is simply a matter of refined taste (ibid.); that art is, or should be, the imitation of nature (pp. 64-7); and the doctrine of moral didacticism, as we have already noted ($\ddot{A}$ I. 75-82; see 'Art as Absolute Spirit', above). The 'Vorstellungen' which Hegel takes up are that art is a human product in a sensuous medium, which is organized in such a way that it reflects the human mind, so forming the 'middle' between pure intellectual activity and natural sensuous material ($\ddot{A}$ I. 60). These are ideas lying deep in the history of thought about art, found in ancient and medieval times as well as in Hegel's own day. The speculative, categorial significance of them is to set up oppositions between art and nature, and art and conceptual thought, and to give a systematic position as the middle between mind and material. Hegel adds to these results a historical reconstruction of art's role in human affairs, acting as a surrogate for the *Encyclopedia* version, and concludes from it that when art is considered as an end in itself, its only purpose can be that of reflection. Hegel's concluding summary states that art is an end in itself which reconciles the opposition between mind and nature, by being the self-expression of mind in the form of a natural, sensuous medium. It is through art, and only through art, that *Truth* is revealed in a sensuous form ($\ddot{A}$ I. 82).

The rest of the *Introduction* works in the same way, but deals with specific writers and authorities. It confirms the above result that art is a middle between mind and sense, but differs in subjecting all the material to a categorial reinterpretation from the first. Hegel is concerned to show that everybody who discusses art always has recourse to two factors which can be understood as form and content. In other words, whatever anyone says, it can always be translated into a discussion of the two categories form and content and their relationship, and they are determinations of Thought from the *Logic of Essence*. Thus if Hegel succeeds in translating the discussion of art into a discussion of those two categories of Essence, he has translated 'Vorstellungen' into pure categories, and begun to do speculative philosophy, showing in the process that art can only be understood as a unity of form and content, the simplest and most fundamental categories in terms of which art can be discussed.

The relationship between form and content is the thread leading through the labyrinth of the *Introduction*, and its various twists and turns should be briefly sketched. The first example is the doctrine of the 'characteristic' propounded by the Berlin art historian Alois Hirt in an essay entitled 'Versuch über das Kunstschöne', which appeared in *Die Horen* in 1797. Hirt believed that the aim of art is to achieve the expression of something in a peculiar or distinctive way.[56] Hegel analyses Hirt's essay as a discussion of how a content, 'as e.g. a determinate sensation, situation, event, action, individual', is related to its form, 'the way in which the content is given expression', and seems to be correct in concluding: 'The abstract determination of the characteristic is thus concerned with the appropriateness with which the particular artistic form actually brings out the content it is to represent' (*Ä* I. 34). The element of manipulation in Hegel's procedure is that he chooses to discuss Hirt at all. He does so because he wishes to join in a discussion of Goethe's ideas about beauty in Johann Heinrich Meyer's *Geschichte der bildenden Künste bei den Griechen*, and defend the idea of the 'characteristic' adopted by his friend Hirt against Meyer's dismissal of it.[57] Meyer rejects it because he thought it had a nefarious effect on artists,[58] but Hegel claims that it is a complete misunderstanding to imagine that aesthetics is concerned to give prescriptive rules for artists, and that Hirt's idea contains a very important determination:

Nach der Bestimmung des Charakteristischen aber soll nur dasjenige mit in das Kunstwerk eintreten, was zur Erscheinung und wesentlich zum Ausdruck gerade nur dieses Inhalts gehört; denn nichts soll sich als müßig und überflüßig zeigen. (*Ä* I. 35.)

It should be noted that the determination of the characteristic admits to the work of art only such elements as are essential to the representation and expression of the specific content involved; for nothing should appear to be useless and superfluous.

Hirt is of interest, not simply because he distinguishes form and content, but because he specifies that their relationship must be one of identity: no element of the form can be inexpressive of the content, or it will be superfluous.

Hegel is able to develop this when he turns to the statement by Goethe which Meyer quotes: '"Der höchste Grundsatz der Alten war das *Bedeutende*, das höchste Resultat aber einer glücklichen *Behandlung* das *Schöne*"'–'"*Significance* was the Ancients' supreme principle, but the supreme result of a successful *treatment* was *Beauty*"' (*Ä* I. 36).[59] As is apparent from its context, Goethe means that the successful treatment of anything in art, no matter how disturbing, will result in beauty only if what is shown is significant, and significance was the criterion used by the Ancients for the inclusion of anything in art. Hegel once more interprets this as a statement about form and content, but this time identifies the content as–'something internal, a meaning', the meaning we are always seeking when we approach art (*Ä* I. 36). He then does something significant. He redescribes the relationship between form and content as that between body and soul, and adds:

Ebenso das menschliche Auge, das Gesicht, Fleisch, Haut, die ganze Gestalt läßt Geist, Seele durch sich hindurchscheinen, und immer ist hier die Bedeutung noch etwas Weiteres als das, was sich in der unmittelbaren Erscheinung zeigt. In dieser / Weise soll das Kunstwerk bedeutend sein ... (*Ä* I. 36–7).

In the same way the human eye, the face, flesh, skin, the whole form allows Spirit, soul to reflect itself through it, and in each case the meaning goes beyond what is shown by immediate appearance. It is in this way that a work of art is to convey meaning ...

This means that form is to content as body is to soul; the paradigm of the form of expression in art is the way in which human beings express themselves through their bodies. The body of a work of art is the material out of which its external form is made, and the soul it expresses in a non-verbal way is its meaning, 'an inner liveliness, feeling, soul, a content and Spirit' (*Ä* I. 37). Now, if we compare this description of 'content' with the one given in the case of Hirt, we find that it has changed from 'determinate sensation, situation, event, action, individual', which is a curious enough mixture, to the inner soul or meaning; that is, from the thematic material used by the artist, to the meaning or significance found in the work by an interpreter. So the content as thematic material, elsewhere called 'Stoff' (*Ä* I. 72), is formed into the body of physical material, and the result is a new content, the soul of the body, its meaning.[60] If the thematic material (content) enters the physical material (body) so as to infuse it all with significance, the result will be a meaning (soul) in complete identity with its expression.

Hegel now has all the elements he wants to build into his Concept of art, and he feels able to anticipate the result of his discussion of Kant and Schiller by saying that it confirms the role of art as a middle

between Spirit and Nature (*Ä* I. 83). Having summarized the argument
of the *Critique of Judgement*, Hegel concludes:

Dadurch ist im Kunstschönen der Gedanke verkörpert . . . so daß Natur
und Freiheit, Sinnlichkeit und Begriff in *Einem* ihr Recht und Befriedigung finden. (*Ä* I. 88.)

Thus fine art embodies thought . . . with the result that Nature and
Freedom, Sensuousness and Concept all come together, and are satisfied
in a *single* unity.

The form/content duality is here given new filling: 'form' is material,
nature, and sensuousness; 'content' is thought, freedom, and Concept.
This interpretation of content is new, for it is identical neither with
'theme' nor with 'meaning'. The result Hegel derives from Schiller
gives a further nuance: 'Das Schöne ist also . . . die Ineinsbildung des
Vernünftigen und Sinnlichen . . .'–'The Beautiful is thus the fusion
of the rational and the sensuous . . .' (*Ä* I. 91). Content can also be
described as 'the rational'. Clearly, if Hegel's usage is coherent, the
oppositions which he sets up must be functioning on different levels: at
the categorial level, art can be understood as the unity of mind and
nature, or of rational thought (Concept) and sensuous material (appearance); at the empirical level, it is the unity of a theme and its execution,
or a meaning and its expression. The full range of these oppositions will
be examined in the next chapter when the system of the arts and the
art-forms provide further levels. The form/content thread takes just one
more twist as the *Introduction* turns into the *Division* of the subject—
the content is called 'Idea' (*Ä* I. 100), and as actual, it forms the Ideal
(ibid. 105). It is the offspring of a double union: the union of mind and
nature, and of the human and the Divine, and forms the apex of the art
world, the centre and the highest point. Having conquered it, we can
survey the scene before going back through the arts and art-forms.

The Ideal is the Idea of Beauty, the result of the progressive integration of form and content until they become a distinction without a
difference. Hegel opens his account of 'the Ideal as such' by taking up
the body/soul motif, and says in effect that if the eye is the window of
the soul, a work of art turns all the points of its surface into eyes, 'zu
einem tausendäugigen Argus, damit die innere Seele und Geistigkeit an
allen Punkten gesehen werde'–'into a thousand-eyed Argus, so that the
inner soul and spirituality can be seen at every point' (*Ä* I. 203). The
work of art looks out at us from every point, allowing us to see into its
soul and discover its meaning. The external appearance is nothing but

the manifestation of the internal, every moment of the whole is significant and therefore necessary ($\ddot{A}$ I. 132). If we translate this into pure
determinations of thought, the determination of art as the locus of
Beauty is 'das sinnliche Scheinen der Idee'—'the sensuous reflection of
the Idea' ($\ddot{A}$ I. 151).[61]

This determination is the speculative abbreviation[62] of Hegel's
aesthetic theory, and should be treated as a formula which only derives
its meaning from the system of which it is the abbreviation. Hegel only
uses it once, but it has achieved a misleading degree of autonomy from
its context.[63] It combines the theoretical apparatus of the *Logic of
Essence* and the *Logic of Concept*, for it is there that 'Schein' and 'Idee'
respectively are worked out. The Idea is the unity of Concept and
reality, and the relationship between them is understood in terms of
Essence, as 'Scheinen'. The terms Hegel uses throughout to explain art
(form and content, inner and outer) are themselves determinations of
Essence (see *WL* II. 66-76, 150-5), so that the moments of the Idea
(Concept and reality) are related to each other as Essence is to 'Schein'.
The *Logic of Essence* gives the purely logical account of the body/soul
relation. It is worth noting that this parallel is not simply a metaphor
(for in that case it would be a 'Vorstellung'), but constitutes a claim
about how meaning is conveyed in art. It should be taken seriously at
face value. It does not ground the mode of expression in art, but expli-
cates it by giving an exact parallel, and in the same way, when body and
soul is being dealt with in the *Anthropology*, the body is described as
'das Kunstwerk der Seele'—'the work of art of the soul' (*Enz.* §411).
Both examples explicate each other, and the relation as such is
accounted for in *Essence*. So in art, content (Concept) is to form
(reality) as Essence is to 'Schein'. The content or Thought which is the
soul of the work, completely determines its form, so as to infuse it with
significance.

The text is guided towards the concept of 'Schein' from the very
first. After only a few pages, Hegel mentions that art is often identified
with illusion, and adds: 'Denn das Schöne hat sein Leben in dem *Scheine*'
—'For Beauty lives in *appearance*' ($\ddot{A}$ I. 17). 'Schein' is used here in its
usual sense of what is not real, and therefore illusory. However, Hegel
promptly takes this up, and defends the 'Schein' of art, because it is the
manifestation of Essence:

Doch der *Schein* selbst ist dem *Wesen* wesentlich, die Wahrheit wäre
nicht, wenn sie nicht schiene und erschiene, wenn sie nicht *für* Eines
wäre, *für* sich selbst sowohl als auch für den Geist überhaupt. ($\ddot{A}$ 1. 21.)

But *appearance* itself is essential to *Essence*, there would be no Truth, were it not to reveal itself and appear, were it not *for* a subject, *for* itself as well as for Spirit in general.

This is elaborated, and the illusion of art given a higher position than any other illusion, because it points beyond itself to the spiritual content it manifests, the truth it reveals (*Ä* I. 23). When the motif is taken up again, it is pushed towards paradox: the sensuous appearance of art is 'nur als Oberfläche und *Schein* des Sinnlichen'—'only as the surface and *appearance* of the sensuous' (*Ä* I. 60). It is just the illusion of being sensuous because in fact it is the expression of a spiritual content. In a successful work of art, its appearance as mere illusion is illusory—it is only when form and content are not in unity that it is 'ein Schein, der als bloßer Schein ausdrücklich gesetzt ist'—'an appearance which is expressly posited as mere appearance' (*Ä* I. 77). Art is 'Schein' because it is a human product and is more than it appears to be. Illusionistic art gains its interest from the fact that it has been made by an artist, whilst appearing to be real, and is therefore described by Hegel as Spirit's mockery of nature (*Ä* I. 215).

The Ideal is an example of the Idea, and as such is given a systemic location in the *Logic*. The Idea is the unity of Concept and reality, it is Concept as actual, and its immediate manifestation is as 'Life', the form in which subjectivity enters into unity with reality (i.e. the immediate union of Spirit and Nature; *WL* II. 412-13). The immediate form of Life is the living individual (*WL* II. 417-23). Hegel distinguishes the various relations between the subject (Spirit) and its embodiment which are to be treated in *Logic* under the title of 'Life', from other possible relations, and amongst them is the Ideal:

teils wird diese Einheit seiner [des Geistes] mit seiner lebendigen Körper— / lichkeit aus ihm selbst zum Ideal herausgeboren. Keine dieser Beziehungen auf den Geist geht das logische Leben an, und es ist hier weder als Mittel eines Geistes, noch als sein lebendiger Leib, noch als Moment des Ideals und der Schönheit zu betrachten (*WL* II. 415-16).

and also born out of this unity of Spirit with its embodiment, there is the Ideal. But none of these relations to Spirit is of concern in a purely logical consideration of Life, and in this context Spirit's embodiment will not be considered as a means, nor as its living body, nor as a moment of the Ideal and of Beauty.

This passage provides an anchor for the body/soul parallel, and distinguishes the Ideal from the logical Idea. The Idea of Beauty could be described as an eminent mode of the body/soul relationship, because the soul, Spirit, is actively forming its own body. Art and religion are ways in which the Idea gives itself an adequate form, and are ways in which it understands itself (*WL* II. 484). As a product of Thought, art is not only *itself* Idea, but is a *form of knowledge* of the Idea. And given that something is true in so far as it is Idea, art must both have Truth, and be a mode of knowing Truth. With this, we have reached the heart of the matter.

The thesis that art is Idea amounts broadly to two things. Firstly, it establishes that art is open to philosophical enquiry, that it falls within the province of 'Realphilosophe' (see *Ä* I. 127). This is the same as the claim that art is a rational object, and can only be understood philosophically (see 'What Could a Philosophy of Art Be?', above). Philosophy can reconstruct the Idea of art, that is, the Truth of art, by giving the determination which exhausts it (not a bundle of features which define it). True art will then be any instance which bears some relation to the Concept of art. The realization of the Concept of art is the Idea of art, which is the Ideal, or Beauty. Beauty is art's Ideal because it is the centre, the point of balance between the mind and the senses which only art can reach, and the instance to which the highest value is attached. It not only has the highest value, but is of exemplary excellence, because in it, form and content are completely identical, and excellence is itself something to which value is attached (though value may be attached on other grounds as well). Only philosophy can say what art is, and it therefore stands higher than art in systematic terms, because it can explain what art is in the process of understanding itself. Art can not only not say what philosophy is, it cannot say what it itself is, unless it moves away from its centre, and becomes theory. (As we shall see, Hegel believed that art had indeed developed so as to embody its own theory.)

Secondly, in determining art as Idea, philosophy has related art to itself. The identity between art and philosophy consists in their being Idea, which means that both are forms of systematic coherence. Philosophy is committed to the systematic coherence of pure Thought, which is the Idea of Truth. Art is committed to the systematic coherence of sensuous appearance, which is the Ideal of Beauty. Philosophy will be judged according to its Truth, and art will be judged according to its Beauty. In calling art and Beauty 'the sensuous reflection of the Idea', philosophy has shown it has something to say about art, and said it. By virtue of its own self-understanding as Idea, philosophy can understand art too (see *Ä* I. 83).

Thus from a speculative theoretical point of view, we see that Beauty and Truth are identical, in as much as both are Idea, a totality of systematically related moments. Truth is the complete articulation of reality by thought, in thought; Beauty is the complete articulation of reality by thought, in reality. Their difference is that Truth can only be thought, but Beauty appears to the senses. Concepts can be true, but only objects can be beautiful; a true Concept gives the exhaustive determination of its object, and a beautiful object is one which is exhaustively determined by thought.[64]

However, art is not just related to Truth by being explicable through the same categories. It is also an expression of Truth as Absolute Idea. Beauty involves coherence; Truth involves coherence and correspondence, but in the case of Absolute Spirit (as opposed to Logic), it is not correspondence to the way things are, but to the way things are believed to be (see 'Introduction'). The more a work of art reflects the beliefs of societies, and the more seriously held and substantial those beliefs are, the greater will be the value attached to the work. A work which articulates the central and essential beliefs of a community embodies its Truth, so that a member of the community is aware of his identity through reflection mediated by the work of art. This is the case when the work is a manifestation of the Divine. The Ideal is an epiphany.

The Ideal is the fullest possible realization of what art can be, but the relation to Truth, in the sense of Absolute Spirit, is present in all art. The beliefs reflected are the principles of ethical life as a whole, not just existential ones (though they are the most seriously held). So what Hegel has done is to relate the Idea of the Beautiful to the Idea of the True, and thereby to the Idea of the Good—to morality, in the widest philosophical sense, as the sphere of practical reason. The aesthetic is parasitic on the ethical, because art embodies values which are rooted in the ethical life of societies, and because it will be judged and evaluated according to norms which are not themselves aesthetic, but ethical. When value-judgements are passed on art, they are passed in the language of morals. If I call a work of art 'sentimental', the judgement can be challenged either by redescribing the work to show that it is not sentimental, or by saying that there is nothing wrong with sentimentality. The argument over the latter is not aesthetic, but ethical.[65]

The implications of the relationship between art and Truth in the sense of social norms and ethical values, can be briefly illustrated with reference to a remark made by Collingwood about Eliot. He says that in *The Waste Land*, Eliot had given expression to a widespread feeling

of spiritual and social decay, a commonly held view.[66] This means that
The Waste Land can be understood as Absolute Spirit, in as much as it
mediates self-reflection. If Collingwood is correct in supposing that the
feelings it expresses were widespread, then the poem reflects seriously
held, substantial beliefs of a society, and will therefore have value
attached to it by being called a 'serious' or 'substantial' work of art. It
will not for that reason alone have artistic excellence, for excellence is a
function of the integration of form and content into a unity of systematic coherence, which is to say that it is a function of Beauty, not of
Truth. But it is nevertheless the case that a substantial work of low
artistic merit may have more value attached to it than a less weighty
one of high excellence, though there are reasons to believe that a work
cannot be trivial and of high excellence. The poem has its value, whether
or not the beliefs it reflects were valid or justified. Artistic Truth is not
a matter of validity (as Logical Truth is), but a matter of reflecting
beliefs. The truth of the beliefs is irrelevant, for as the content of
Absolute Spirit, they will often form the ultimate ground for judging
the validity of other tenets, so that their truth cannot be questioned.
Eliot may have spread, or even created, feelings of decay through his
poem, but this is irrelevant as far as its role as Absolute Spirit is concerned.[67] The values and beliefs reflected change from society to society
and throughout history, so it follows that a society which does not
share Eliot's sense of decay may find *The Waste Land* uninteresting, or
hard to understand, but it will be aware of its seriousness, just as we are
aware of the seriousness of the Oedipus plays, although we do not hold
people responsible for crimes they unknowingly commit. Because we
can see that Oedipus does feel guilt at discovering what he has done, so
much so that he blinds himself, we take him seriously. If Eliot's work is
substantial, it will be taken seriously even when it has become alien.
Through Absolute Spirit, the principle of history asserts itself—the
values which art reflects, and according to which it is judged, are subject to historical change.

To summarize, one could say that within Absolute Spirit, the difference between Beauty and Truth is one of commitment. The Idea of
Truth implies commitment to *saying* something about the way things
are; the Ideal of Beauty implies commitment to *showing* something
about the way things *appear to be*. And one could say that the beauty
of art is rooted in art's systematicity, and its truth is rooted in its historicity. These claims will be elaborated in the next chapter. Before
that, we should reflect briefly on what has been done so far.

Problems and Solutions

Hegel's result is the formula 'sinnliches Scheinen der Idee'–'sensuous reflection of the Idea', and as a result, it is empty without the process of reflection which it summarizes. At the end of the same paragraph in which it occurs, Hegel talks about the 'Scheinen des Begriffs'–'reflection of the Concept'–as well (*Ä* I. 152). This is quite consistent if we bear in mind the *Logic of Essence*. In a relation of Essence, each moment is reflected in its other, and their identity is constituted by their relation. The determining moment in this case is the content (i.e. Concept or Thought) and it constitutes itself by determining its other, the form (i.e. reality, the sensuous material). The form or appearance of the work of art is the form it is, only through its relation to the thought determining it, that is, it is the reflection or 'Scheinen' of Concept. The unity of the moments, their relation, is the work of art, or in purely categorial terms, Idea: the moments are distinct (for thought) but not different (in reality). The full determination of art would then be: Absolute Spirit in the form of the sensuous reflection of the Idea.

Because it is anchored in a theory of categorial determinacy, Hegel's aesthetic theory has several advantages over alternative ones. As the determiner of the form is defined logically, as Concept or Thought, we are not embarrassed by reference to the artist's intentions. The thought-content of the work is what the intepreter finds in it, as he tries to establish the significance of each moment by relating it to other moments, and the whole. Because he has a Logic, Hegel is also saved from the need to explain art by analogy, as, for example, Solger is forced to do. Solger claims that art is a unity of the universal and the particular, and then attempts to ground art in self-consciousness, because it too is an instance of such a unity.[68] Solger thus sets up parallels, and arbitrarily reinterprets them as Essence-relations, making one instance function as a principle and ground another, which is irrational. The parallels in Hegel, such as form/content and body/soul, are explicatory, not grounding, a refinement which obviates problems bedevilling modern aestheticians. Richard Wollheim, for example, wishes to use human facial and bodily expression as a parallel for artistic expression, but does not wish to mystify the world by attributing feelings to pieces of music.[69] One popular answer to this problem is to say that sad music is music which awakens sadness in its listeners, but this founders on the contingency of response. A sad piece of music will probably make its listeners feel happy at the aesthetic pleasure it gives them. It is certainly no more likely to make anyone feel sad than would the sight of a depressed human countenance, and if it belongs to the supporter of a rival football team which has just played mine, it would probably make me rejoice. Nelson Goodman tries to solve the difficulty by saying that although a painting can really be grey, it can only metaphorically be sad.[70] He knows this because he has decided, for reasons which are obscure, that only sentient beings and events can really be sad, and that in the case of art, sadness is 'to some extent contra-indicated'.[71] All he means is that paintings do not feel sad—it does not follow from that, that they do not really look sad, any more than it follows that an actor who does not feel sad cannot look sad, despite contra-indications. Hegel avoids all this by grounding both human and artistic expression in the *Logic*, and understanding subjectivity as a category. Art can then be sad as unmetaphorically as a human face, for it is not reduced to an analogy with what is arbitrarily taken to be the primary 'literal' instance.

The formula articulates two fundamental oppositions: art is a product of free subjectivity, and so stands in contrast with nature; and it is necessarily in a sensuous medium, and so stands in contrast with pure Thought. The first opposition means that clouds and trees are not works of art, and neither is a rock which is weathered into the shape of a Henry Moore. Animals can produce art only if they are considered to be free agents (i.e. subjects), and the answer to that question is not aesthetic.[72] At present, most of *Homo sapiens* do not recognize other species to be free agents capable of self-reflection, so for the time being at least, art is of people, by people, and for people.

The claim that art must be in a sensuous medium has been denied both in theory and in practice. It has been denied in theory by Croce and Collingwood, so if their explanations are incoherent, we would have reasons for accepting the claim. Croce adopts the dubious psychological premiss that creating a work of art is the act of mechanically copying a prior mental image, and then shifts from it in a *non sequitur* to the claim that beauty can have no physical existence.[73] However, this must be wrong, because he distinguishes art as a form-giving activity, and if art is mental, there is nothing to form.[74] Similarly, he understands aesthetic judgement to be the reproduction of the artist's vision in the mind of the recipient,[75] but this too would be impossible if his thesis were correct. Collingwood is less radical, arguing only that 'a work of art may be completely created when it has been created as a thing whose only place is in the artist's mind',[76] and his reasons are that a composer may have made up a tune without having written it down, and that as works of art are not bits of wood, canvas, and paint, they must be 'imaginary objects'.[77] The answer to Collingwood is that the composer's act is both logically and psychologically parasitic upon there being sound, and so he has not got the real tune in its genuine state, but is imagining what the real tune would sound like. The second reason he gives is a false conclusion from a correct premiss: because a work of art is not exhaustively described by a description of its natural physical properties, it does not follow that it can be separated from them.[78]

The claim that art involves physical appearance has also been challenged in practice by the emergence in the late sixties in the USA of 'concept art' or 'idea art'. These works 'frequently did not actually exist as objects. Rather, they remained ideas; frequently, what did exist was only some kind of documentation referring to the concept.'[79] A Juddian positivist would have to capitulate to this, but there is no reason why we should not argue, and say that this is a category error, that concept-artists do not know what they are doing. They think that they are producing art, but are doing something so radically different from what art has always been taken to be, that their claim makes no sense: if ideas can be art, the category 'art' breaks down. The motivation behind concept art was political and moral, to protest about the commercialism of the art world by producing works which could not be bought or sold. It might be understood as political action which involves the claim to be art, a claim which only gains potency if it is political. Once accepted as art, the acts become harmless, and the documents describing the ideas (which were themselves objects) took the place of works of art, and began to fetch high prices.

One might still wonder what the Ideal of Beauty has got to do with modern art, in which ugliness and dissonance play such an important role. In Hegel's theory, the degree of Beauty is the degree of aesthetic merit, and it may be felt that to use the word in this way is misleading.[80] Hegel's justification is that what he is discussing, the integration of mind and sense, has traditionally (since the fourth century BC) been called 'the Beautiful', so there is little reason to find another word. It should also be remembered by those who feel constrained to pay obeisance to ordinary usage, that the German word 'schön' has a wider range than 'beautiful'. 'Das ist eine schöne Arbeit', for example, means 'That's a fine piece of work'; 'Das hat er sehr schön gemacht' means 'He's made a good job of that'. It usually covers the fine execution of a task involving skill, so it is very appropriate for artistic quality. In Hegel, 'das Schöne' does not involve prettiness, but the degree to which each moment of a work of art displays significance, and how articulate the result is. Dissonant elements are explicitly included in it, particularly in modern art, as 'das Unschöne' (see *Ä* II. 105, 139, 153), and they are encompassed within the aegis of the Ideal if they are significant and expressive. If they are extraneous and arbitrary, they are merely ugly. Dissonant elements can only have a dissonant effect if they are related to the others in a meaningful way.[81] A similar integration of ugliness into Beauty is found in Rosenkranz's *Ästhetik des Häßlichen* of 1853. The ugly is not a moment of Beauty, as in Hegel, but is co-ordinated with it, ('the ugly is inseparable from the Concept of the Beautiful')[82], and then subordinated to it ('subject to the general laws of the Beautiful')[83]. Hegel himself, it might be added, had a low tolerance level as far as dissonance was concerned, and shows relatively little skill in discovering how it could be a significant contribution to the expressiveness of a work.

I have been arguing that the Ideal must be understood as an apex, a central summit. But we should, before following through the two principles of the systematicity and historicity of art, consider what happens at the limits, the fuzzy edges of the art world which have been extended so far since Hegel's day. Maybe concept art is a mistake; but almost any object can find its way into a gallery, and claim to be art. In fact, lots of objects seem to fall under the category of the sensuous reflection of the Idea without being put in the Tate. Take forks, for example. Roger Scruton has analysed a modern Swedish fork design and the old 'fiddle-pattern' fork from an aesthetic point of view, and argued that they even reflect ethical substance. He suggests that to praise the modern fork for its '"clean", "functional" lines' is an aesthetic judgement, for from a utilitarian point of view, the older design, which may seem to have an '"ornate" or "heavy" quality' is superior, being better balanced, and having narrower, longer prongs.[84] This fork is also full of aesthetic subtlety, reproducing as it does the proportions of a classical column, with a base and capital, topped by a frieze of prongs. Regardless of its function, the fork can be regarded as a work of art, and a preference for one of the forks is also, Scruton claims, a preference for a form of life, and therefore reflects the self-understanding of the subject:

The two forks bear the insignia of contrasting life-styles—the pursuit of uncluttered function (not as a fact but as a symbol) and the leisured movement which despite its superficial contempt for function arrives rather more naturally at its aim. In choosing between the forms on aesthetic grounds one will also declare allegiance to one or other style of life . . .[85]

This illustrates the Hegelian thesis that the aesthetic is parasitic on the moral, that the values appealed to in aesthetic judgement and the values reflected by works of art are rooted in ethical life, in 'Sittlichkeit'. Scruton has analysed the forks as works of art, relating all the moments of them (the length and width of the prongs, the stem, the base, the weight) to each other, and establishing their significance, the thought they embody. Are they, then, works of art?

Suppose we were to put the forks in the Tate Gallery, or give them to someone like Carl André, who has a large enough price on his head to qualify as an artist, and make him do so. They would then be something to which value is attached (a few thousand pounds), and be part of the institution of art. In Hegelian terms, we can explain the difference between Scruton's forks, which are not art, and the Tate gallery forks, which are, as a categorial shift in the level of reflection: a shift from Objective to Absolute Spirit. The normal forks are a product of ethical life, and embody its values, as would any other manifestation of it. But the Tate forks are removed from the practical context of ethical life, and by being presented as art, become a reflection *upon* its values, not just a reflection *of* them. The forks gain significance because they are looked at with an interpretative attitude.

The argument of this chapter has now come full circle, because having abandoned the question of the aesthetic attitude, we have now returned to it. The difference between forks which are art and forks which are not art is a difference in the way in which they are regarded, not in the forks themselves. By saying what it is to be a work of art, Hegel has said what it is to consider something to be a work of art. He has reconstructed a mode of discourse through a consideration of the object of that discourse. Philosophy does not, and can never, tell us whether or not example x is a work of art, because to do so requires judgement, and judgement is empirical. All we learn from aesthetics is what we will have judged something to be if we judge it to be art. This does not decide controversial cases, but determines what the argument ought to be about. Aesthetic judgement and the aesthetic attitude are grounded by a philosophy of art.

However, that is not quite all a philosophy of art does. It also liberates us from unquestioning acceptance of positive facts. If the forks ever do turn up in the Tate, the Hegelian theory does give us grounds to accept that they are art, but it also gives us grounds for writing to *The Times* to complain that they are a worthless work of art. The reason is that there is no necessity to embody the reflection they do in the form of art, because Scruton has said it all already in a theoretical work on aesthetics. The form of art is merely a shell around a general observation which can be made in ordinary life and articulated quite adequately in a few sentences of prose. The forks merely serve the function of drawing attention to a change in life-styles and the values of society, and the desires of those who manipulate society. Forks in the Tate are a piece of moral and political didacticism, the occasion of reflection upon an abstract, universal claim, and if that is so, 'then what is figurative and sensuous is just a superfluous piece of external decoration, and the work is broken apart, its form and content no longer fused together' (*Ä* I. 77). The claim to be art would be a purely formal one, and its justification would be formal. The real question is whether the object should be valued or not; whether in admiring it, we are not admiring a decaying corpse; whether in searching for its meaning we are not staring into glazed eyes. If aesthetics can help us to distinguish the soulless bodies and the mummies from the thousand-eyed *panoptes*, then it may still have some claim on our attention.

2

THE SYSTEMATICS OF ART

Having seen how art is located within Hegel's system, our task now is to look at the systematic frameworks in terms of which it is then explicated. The Ideal gives the universal determination of art, and, in accordance with the structure of a philosophical Concept, it must also be considered as particular and individual. Given the nature of philosophical science, Hegel cannot organize his material in any way he finds convenient, but must present it so as to show the inner necessity of the object under consideration (see *Ä* I. 26). This means that the arrangement of the text itself should develop the necessary differences of the Concept of art. The issue ought to be decided by nothing more than the table of contents, but unfortunately both philological and theoretical problems are raised.

The Moments of Concept

The *Introduction* to the *Aesthetics* is an analysis of 'Vorstellungen' about art, from which the Concept of art is reconstructed. The *Division* (*Einteilung*) is where one would expect an immanent account of what is specifically Hegelian to begin, and Hegel indeed distinguishes it from the preliminaries of the *Introduction*, whilst confusingly adding that it is still in the *Introduction*, with the purpose of providing 'eine Übersicht . . . für die Vorstellung' (*Ä* I. 100). This phrase suggests that what follows will present the division of Concept in a way congenial to picturing thought, and this is indeed not far from the truth, as will be seen in due course.[1] We ought, however, to be dealing with the philosophical issue of the relationship between form and content, and dealing with it in purely conceptual terms. We wish to know how the moments of the Concept of art are to be determined.

Hegel specifies the rationale for the division as the successive stages in the development of content, which result in different forms of art (Gestaltungen der Kunst) (*Ä* I. 103). He then says that this development has two aspects. The first seems to be the development of content as something universal, but determinate:

Erstens nämlich ist diese Entwicklung selbst eine *geistige* und *allgemeine*, indem die Stufenfolge bestimmter *Weltanschauungen* als des bestimmten, aber umfassenden Bewußtseins des Natürlichen, Menschlichen und Göttlichen sich künstlerisch gestaltet (ibid.).

In the first instance, this development is itself *spiritual* and *universal*, in that the progression of determinate '*Weltanschauungen*', the determinate but all-embracing awareness of things natural, human and divine is given artistic expression.

One recognizes here the different contents of Absolute Spirit, the various differences in human self-understanding. But if there is development, if there are determinate differences, how can they be universal, rather than particular? Presumably because they are all-embracing, but they are only all-embracing for each particular stage, not from the point of view of art itself, which is what is at stake. It is only the second aspect which Hegel calls particular, the development of form (die bestimmten Weisen des sinnlichen Kunstdaseins) giving 'die *besonderen Künste*'–'the *particular arts*' (ibid.). The moment of particularity is therefore the differences in the material formed into art, resulting in the various arts themselves, such as architecture, painting, music, and so on. We further learn that the two aspects, the successive stages of content and form, have 'ein näheres Verhältnis und geheimes Zusammenstimmen'–'a closer relationship and a hidden accord' (*Ä* I. 104). Hegel was not usually one to treasure secrets, so this remark is enough to arouse suspicion. Suspicion grows as one realizes that the third moment of Concept, individuality, has disappeared. Unperturbed, the text promptly conjures it into existence with the lapidary comment: 'Vollständig jedoch teilt sich unsere Wissenschaft in drei Hauptglieder'–'However, the complete division of our science involves three main elements', and determines the Ideal itself as universal, a progression of 'Gestaltungsformen' (presumably the 'Weltanschauungen' of the previous page) as particular, and the arts themselves as individual (ibid.). No reason is given for calling differences in content particular and differences in form individual. Above all, we cannot tell whether we should believe the text when it calls the arts particular or when it calls them individual, and on that point it remains confused: the third part of the lectures is entitled 'Das System der Einzelnen Künste'–'The System of the Individual Arts', but the opening paragraph on architecture refers three times to the particular arts ('wird zu einer *besonderen* Kunst', 'Mit der Besonderheit aber', 'in dem Kreis der besonderen Künste'– *Ä* II. 266). Elsewhere, however, the role of individuality is taken over by the work of art itself. The third part opens by declaring its intention to deal with actual works of art, and continues:

Denn erst durch diese letzte Gestaltung ist das Kunstwerk wahrhaft konkret, ein zugleich reales, in sich abgeschlossenes, einzelnes Individuum (*Ä* II. 245).

For it is only in this final mode that the work of art is truly concrete, a real, autonomous, single individual.

So we have the art-forms and the arts as candidates for particularity, and the arts and works of art in competition for the place of individuality. The textual problem is complicated by the fact that some of the lecture notes from earlier years divided the *Aesthetics* into only two parts, whereas later ones have the familiar division into three finally adopted by Hotho.[2] As the text does not make it clear what Hegel actually meant, it is worth leaving it on one side and recurring to first principles in order to establish what he could, or indeed ought, to have done.

Clues may be gained from a comparison with the *Philosophy of Religion*, an area of 'Realphilosophie' as close to aesthetics as one can get. There the moment of universality is the Concept of religion as such, which corresponds to the Concept of art. The particular is the treatment of determinate religions, a systematic typology of some ten historical religions, arranged according to the adequacy with which they realize the universal Concept. The moment of individuality is filled by 'revealed religion' (Christianity), which realizes the Concept of religion (see *Werke* 16 and 17). If the *Aesthetics* were to follow this pattern, there would be two possibilities: either the arts as particular, leading up to sculpture as individual because it realizes the Ideal; or the art-forms (the 'Weltanschauungen') as particular, with the one corresponding to the Ideal, the classical art-form, as individual. In addition to this, one could imagine a double division into the arts and the art-forms as particularity, with works of art as individual, for clearly they must fit in somewhere.

This results in two main problems; the claims of both the arts and the art-forms to be particular, and the need to account for the concrete works themselves. They are an embarrassment, for on the one hand, they have very strong claims to fill the role of individuality, as only they are irreducible realizations of the Concept of art; but on the other hand, it is not possible for philosophy to say anything about them in speculative tone of voice, because they are empirical, contingent, and can only be discussed by means of judgement (see $\ddot{A}$ II. 263-5). They are the object of the first-order discourse of history and art-criticism which philosophy is reconstructing. Hegel is obliged to discuss them, but when he does, he will not be doing philosophy alone. The theoretical problems of the division of the subject stem from the fact that the *Aesthetics* is very heterogeneous, involving various theoretical levels and several distinct modes of discourse. All would be well if they were more disciplined, but they tend all to start talking at once.

By making the system as a whole the basis of a decision, it may be possible to turn the cacophony into harmony. The system points fairly unambiguously in one direction: the paradigm of the particular is Nature, the realm of spatio-temporal difference, implying that art is particular in so far as it is natural, and determinate with respect to space and time: the realm of individuality is Spirit, which deals not with spatio-temporal determinacy but with its more concrete form, socio-historical determinacy, implying that art is individual in so far as it is produced in a specific society at a specific time. The particularity of the Concept of art would then be the various arts themselves: sculpture is the organizing of material in space, painting forms colour in two dimensions, music forms sound in time. The arts are particular. An account of 'Weltanschauungen' would accordingly be an account of individuality, and thereby a solution to the problem of what to do with works of art. It is works of art, concrete instances, which are the realization of the Concept of art as individuals: 'music' is a particular art, and is as much 'the sensuous reflection of the Idea' as art itself is, but only Mozart's 'Jupiter' Symphony (for example) is a realization of art through the particular form of music, and is the sensuous reflection of the Idea as individual. However, all philosophy can say about the 'Jupiter' Symphony is that it is individual, and explain how it is by giving an account of the socio-historical determinacy of art. It will deal with society and history as factors, and illustrate social and historical differences by using works of art as examples.

If philosophy tries to do more than that, it is talking the language of history and art-criticism, and this is a type of theoretical ventriloquism dear to Hegel's heart. He devotes a lot of attention to filling out his systemic categories with historical material, and passing judgement on a wide variety of works, in order to illustrate philosophical points.

He is quite clear that he is not doing art-history or criticism for their own sake, but in order to show 'die wesentlichen allgemeinen Gesichtspunkte der Sache und deren Beziehung auf die Idee des Schönen in ihrer Realisation im Sinnlichen der Kunst'—'the basic general aspects of the matter, and how they relate to the Idea of Beauty in its realization in the sensuous medium of art' (*Ä* II. 265). His purpose is to make clear what he takes the consequences of his theory to be, by showing what a historian or critic might say on the basis of it; in other words, he gives examples of the first-order discourse his theory has reconstructed. One of the things which will be of interest in examining such examples in Part Two will therefore be whether the theory allows alternative examples, and how acceptable we find the critic and historian Hegel compared to the philosopher.

To sum up the discussion of the moments of Concept, we can set up a stricter division of the *Aesthetics* as follows:

universality: the Ideal, the determination of art

particularity: the arts, as spatio-temporally different

individuality: the socio-historical factors involved in actual works of art, with real examples.

This is not what the text actually gives us, for it presents the art-forms as particular and the arts as individual, so this suggestion is an unashamed recommendation that systemic rationality dictate over philological uncertainty. However, support for it is forthcoming from an unexpected quarter, from the only commentator to have seen the theoretical problem involved, Christian Hermann Weisse. He observes that:

die Kategorien der Besonderheit und der Einzelheit mit offenbarer Willkür vertheilt sind, indem mit gleichem, ja mit noch größerem Rechte die in Raum, Zeit und sinnlichem Material unterschiedenen Arten und Gattungen der Kunst als das *Besondere*, die Hineingestaltung des Welt- und Völkergeistes aber . . . als *Einzelheit* hätte gefaßt werden können . . .[3]

the use of the categories of particularity and individuality is clearly arbitrary, for there are equal, indeed more compelling reasons for regarding the art-types and genres which differ along the dimensions of space, time, and physical material as the *particular*, and the expression of human and national self-understanding . . . as *individual*.

He continues by noting that the moments of particularity and individuality ought to be developed out of the Concept of art itself, and that

although Hegel makes gestures in that direction, the development is
lacking, having been sacrificed to the 'hidden accord' of the arts and
art-forms.[4] Once again, one must agree. The problem is the doctrine of
the art-forms, one of those suggestive notions which distract attention
from Hegel's more substantial, but sober, virtues. Despite the mention
of 'Weltanschauungen', it is far from clear what the art-forms actually are.

Hegel ought to show that the art-forms are the necessary differences
within the Concept of art. This is his attempt to do so:

Ihren Ursprung finden diese Formen in der unterschiedenen Art, die Idee
als Inhalt zu erfassen, wodurch eine Unterschiedenheit der Gestaltung,
in welcher sie erscheint, bedingt ist. Die Kunstformen sind deshalb nichts
als die verschiedenen Verhältnisse von Inhalt und Gestalt, Verhältnisse,
welche aus der Idee selbst hervorgehen und dadurch den wahren Einteil-
ungsgrund dieser Sphäre geben. Denn die Einteilung muß immer in *dem*
Begriffe liegen, dessen Besonderung und Einteilung sie ist. (*Ä* I. 107.)

These forms have their origin in the various ways of understanding the
Idea as content, which conditions a difference in the form in which it
appears. The art-forms are thus nothing other than the different relationships between content and form, relationships which proceed from the
Idea itself, and therefore provide the true rationale for the division of
this sphere. For the division and particularization of a Concept must
always be immanent to *that* Concept alone.

It looks at first as if one thing is being said here, for that is how the text
wishes to be understood. In fact, it is saying two things, and they are
incompatible. The first sentence states that the art-forms are different
forms of content, which condition differences in form (Gestaltung). In
other words, the content varies because the Idea is understood in different ways, and each different content goes along with a different form in
which it appears. The form and the content are always in unity, because
the content changes, and the form changes along with it. But then the
second sentence concludes from this that the art-forms are different
relationships between form and content. So on the one hand, content
changes, and on the other hand, the relationship between form and
content changes. There is thus a dual derivation of the art-forms, and it
is presented as a unitary one because, as the third sentence states, it is
supposed to proceed from the Concept of art. It does not.

This can best be explained after reviewing the art-forms which Hegel
tries to derive from the Concept. There are three: the symbolic, the
classical, and the romantic. The *symbolic* art-form is the product of a

content which is indeterminate and alien to its form, because the content and form do not exhaust each other's determinacy. This lies in the nature of the symbol. The symbol is distinguished from the sign, in that a sign has no intrinsic relation to the meaning it designates. A sign is an arbitrary signifier, related to a signified meaning by convention. A symbol, however, does bear some non-arbitrary relation to its meaning (its content), but the relationship is indeterminate. For example, a lion is a symbol of strength because a lion actually possesses strength, so that it, as signifier, bears some relationship to what it signifies. But the relationship is indeterminate because a lion is many other things besides strong, and many other things besides lions have strength. Although it is not arbitrary that a lion should signify strength, there is no necessity that it signify strength rather than, say, regality or hunting prowess, and no necessity that strength be signified by a lion rather than, say, a bear or an ox. The relationship between the form (signifier) of a symbol and its content (signified) is indeterminate, because it is not apparent exactly what the content is from the form, for they do not exhaust each other's determinacy. Symbolic art will therefore be enigmatic, for its meaning is indeterminate, the form and content in only partial unity. The primary example of symbolic art is, according to Hegel, that of the ancient East, especially Egypt.[5] In the *classical* art-form this indifference between form and content is overcome, so that a fully determinate content is completely shown in its corresponding form. The meaning is not enigmatic, but clear, and is such that it can only be the meaning it is if it appears in concrete form to the senses; it is part of the meaning of the content to be form. The paradigm of classical art is that of Ancient Greece.[6] With the *romantic* art-form[7], form and content part company once more, but in this case because the content is fully determinate, and is determined as inimical to sensuous manifestation. There is more to the content than art can show. It is described as self-conscious interiority, and identified with Christian art up to and including the early nineteenth century. The content is determinate, but its determinacy is not exhausted by its form; the signified is richer than the signifier, and is thus alien to its form.[8]

If we now consider what the relationships between form and content are in these three cases, we will discover two: identity (the usual terms are 'Angemessenheit' and 'Entsprechen') in the case of classical art, and difference in the case of the other two. The form is a result of the content, and so belongs along with it, in each case, regardless of whether they 'correspond' or not. The difference between symbolic and romantic art is not the relationship between form and content, but the content itself: in symbolic art it is indeterminate, and therefore takes on arbitrary forms; in romantic art it is determinate in such a way that it likewise takes on arbitrary forms. The reason why Hegel tries to suggest that the art-forms are simply different relationships between form and content, is that they would then permit of derivation from the Concept of art, because the difference between them would be logical. But if one considers the Concept of art purely a priori, all one can say is that its moments (Concept and reality, that is, content and form) either correspond or do not correspond. To say *how* they fail to correspond entails considering not the relationship, but the relata, the nature of form and content in themselves. The real theoretical significance of this is that although there must be at least two art-forms, there is no reason why there should be only three. Recalling once more the structure of the *Philosophy of Religion*, there is no reason why Hegel should not place the classical art-form at the end as a telos, in the same way in which Christianity functions as telos, and lead up to it with a succession of ten art-forms showing a progressive integration of form and content. He does not do so because the doctrine of the art-forms is itself an example of theoretical heterogeneity, mixing systematic issues, which Hegel advertises ostentatiously, with history and sociology, and they all get in each other's way.

The art-forms have been taken to be different philosophies which determine art,[9] different 'visions' which it embodies,[10] and, more sensibly, different understandings of subjectivity,[11] and sociological categories.[12] It is also fairly clear that they have something to do with religion, though it is not clear what, and that they have a systematic and historical function.

One can begin by stating that as the art-forms are differences in the content of art, they are differences in the content of Absolute Spirit, and thus different products of self-reflection, in the most general sense. This is why Hegel calls them 'Weltanschauungen'—they are sets of beliefs. This being so, one wonders again why there should be only three. Surely there is a need to distinguish, for example, the eighteenth century from the thirteenth, but both are covered by the romantic art-form. It may be that religion is uppermost in Hegel's mind, for he seems to treat post-Roman times as a unity because they are Christian. However, this cannot be the reason, for various religions, such as Indian, Egyptian, and Persian, are included together in the symbolic art-form. So, assuming for the present that the doctrine is coherent, it must be based upon features shared by all the ancient religions mentioned, which distinguishes them from the whole of Western culture since the Roman Empire, and the features must be such that they result in different forms of art, or it would make no sense to talk about 'art-forms' at all. This is the point at which historical and systematic factors collide. As differences in content, or as 'Weltanschauungen', the art-forms are historical cultural unities; but as differences in the relationship between form and content, they are different modes of representation, which result in systematically distinct forms of art. As we have seen, Hegel does his utmost to equate them, but at one point he is forced to make the distinction which cracks open the whole theory. The third chapter of the section on symbolic art is called 'Die bewußte Symbolik der vergleichenden Kunstform'—'The conscious symbolism of the comparative art-form', and whereas the rest of the section is ordered historically, this chapter is systematic—it deals precisely with a certain art-form, regardless of where or when it emerged. Thus when discussing the riddle, Hegel says that it is an oriental form, but adds that it plays a major role in Scandinavia and Germany as well as the Middle East, in the Middle Ages (Ä I. 510). It is the allegory, the next type of symbolic representation, which wrings the ultimate concession from him:

Die Allegorie gehört überhaupt weniger der antiken als der mittelalterlichen romantischen Kunst an, wenn sie auch als Allegorie nichts eigentlich Romantisches ist. (Ä I. 514.)

The allegory in general belongs not so much to ancient art as to the romantic art of the Middle Ages, although as allegory it is not really romantic.

So we have a symbolic art-form which occurs principally in medieval romantic art—although it is not really romantic. Hegel fights a desperate rearguard action to defend this odd pronouncement, but all he does is to say why the allegory was used so much in the Middle Ages. This merely confirms that the mode of representation is common to the symbolic and romantic art-forms: that, as forms of art, based on the relationship between form and content, they are identical, and that it is only as 'Weltanschauungen' that they are distinct.

The art-forms are thus covering various degrees of specificity. They account for differences in sets of beliefs in general, certain of which are essential to the self-understanding and identity of the subject, and certain of these essential beliefs affect the mode of representation in art. The issues covered by the art-forms are distinct, but related, which is why Hegel sounds so convincing a lot of the time. They are related as instances of the category 'Idea'.

The term 'Idea' designates the relation between an inner content and its external manifestation, a soul and a body. Man is Idea, the Divine is Idea, and art is Idea. In as much as they are Idea, there is a structural relation between man's self-understanding, his understanding of the Divine, and the mode of representation in art, and it is this which Hegel means to articulate in the doctrine of the art-forms. He then mixes it up with the question of 'Weltanschauungen', which is plausible because the systematic problem of representation depends upon certain elements of general ideology. This is best clarified with reference to the examples he gives.

The Greeks expressed their essential beliefs through religion, and reflected their conception of their own identity in their gods. They conceived of the Divine as they conceived of subjectivity in general— as essentially embodied. Even the souls in Hades are not disembodied. In consequence, the Greeks could show their gods, and thereby what they themselves essentially were, in the form of art. They understood the Idea as an indissoluble unity, so the relationship between its two moments (Concept and reality—inner and outer—content and form) was one of identity, be it as a god, a man, or as art. A Christian, however, understands the Idea as a contingent unity. The Divine is essentially dis-embodied, and the essence of man is his soul, which will live on after his body has decayed. God cannot now be represented in art, he can only be symbolized through some convention, and man can no longer show what he essentially is in art—his identity is articulated through religion, which knows more than art can show. As the relationship between the moments of the Idea is contingent, the content of art is only con-tingently related to its form, so the mode of artistic representation will be symbolic. Romantic art is thus unrestricted in its subject-matter and the forms it can take on, because the form/content relationship is con-tingent. Now at this point the argument must shift in order to account for the differences between the ideological unity 'symbolic art' and the ideological unity 'romantic art'. Because the Ancient Egyptian, for example, has an unclear, indeterminate understanding of the Divine, and thus of his own identity, his art is abstract. The Christian, on the other hand, has a determinate understanding of God, who has revealed Himself through Christ and the Scriptures, and of his own identity. Because of the doctrinal differences between Egyptian and Christian religions, and the different ethical norms which they determine, the content of art will differ. A good example of this is Hegel's justification of realism, which (he believes) is characteristic of romantic art, but not of symbolic art. This 'Heimatlichkeit im Gewöhnlichen' as he calls it (Ä II. 146) is a necessary element of romantic art because of the content of Christian beliefs:

Dies Äußere ferner *muß* in die Gestalt der Gewöhnlichkeit, des empirisch Menschlichen eintreten, da hier Gott selber in das endliche, zeitliche Dasein hinabsteigt, um den absoluten Gegensatz, der im Begriff des Absoluten liegt, zu vermitteln und auszusöhnen (Ä II. 145).

This externality *must* take on the form of the everyday, of what is empirical and human, for in the case of romantic art God Himself descends into finite, temporal existence in order to mediate and reconcile the absolute opposition which lies in the Concept of the Absolute.

Subjectivity as such cannot appear in art, so it expresses itself indirectly through almost any form. It must express itself through contingent, finite forms, because God Himself entered into the finite form of a man, and thus, in the figure of Christ, hallowed the empirical, and rendered the real world worthy of artistic representation.

It is now possible to see that if we opt for theoretical rigour, the heterogeneous doctrine of the art-forms must be dismembered, and the spoils divided between the moments of universality and individuality. The question of representation concerns the logical relationship between form and content, and is a universal issue. The rest concerns the parasitism of the aesthetic on the ethical, and art's role as Absolute Spirit, the role of embodying and articulating Truth. Once it has been established that art embodies beliefs, and that the beliefs differ through time, philosophical argument stops, and the rest should be left to the historian and the critic. In as much as Hegel adopts both those roles himself, his remarks should be taken as examples, not as principles. There is no reason why there should be just three distinct forms of self-understanding, and in practice Hegel subdivides the art-forms so as to account for the most obvious distinctions which have to be made. Interesting though the art-forms are, their interest is really just historical, for they show Hegel as a child of his time, constructing a triad on the model of 'Anfang, Blüte und Verfall' and encompassing the opposition of the ancients and the moderns; all conventional wisdom of his day.[13] What is uniquely his, is the treatment of form and content, which must now be examined in full.

Form and Content

It is one of Hegel's major theses that art must be understood as a unity
of form and content, and analysed in terms of them, so that to establish
their identity in a work of art is to establish that the work has quality.
The theme is a familiar one, as Hegel's *Introduction* showed, and tends
to be dismissed today, partly for that reason.[14] 'Form' and 'content'
can be used to refer to almost anything, it seems, and have become
meaningless clichés, or at best commonplaces which hark back to the
days of classicism, and the view is widespread that they should be dis-
carded. There is less reflection on why they can refer to almost anything, and why they are clichés. Hegel at least clears the ground by
explaining both things: they can refer to anything because they are
categories or determinations of thought from the *Logic of Essence*, in
terms of which reality is understood; and they are clichés because they
are unavoidable in a discussion of art. A term only becomes a cliché if a
lot of people have found it useful, so a cliché is unlikely to be completely unworthy of attention.

To understand the full implications of the issue, some reference
must be made to the results (if not the arguments) of the reconstruction
of 'form', 'content', and 'material' in the *Logic of Essence* (*WL* II. 66–76
and *Enz.* §§132–4). 'Material' is the name Hegel gives to what is form-
less in as much as it is indifferent to its form. Material does not lack any
form, it lacks determinate form, and is thus itself not determined by
any form, which is to say that it can be what it is regardless of its form.
'Content' is formed material, which is the content it is by virtue of being
the form it is, that is, form and content are not indifferent, but determine each other. Whilst not different, they are distinct, for as determinations of the same determinacy, form and content stand in contrast to
one another. It is thus possible to distinguish an aspect of something
which is merely formal as an aspect which could be altered without
altering content. This contrast is not between having form and having
no form at all, but between having form which is essential and form
which is inessential. Inessential form can alter without altering the
identity of content, which is to say that inessential form is indifferent
to content, not determined by it and therefore contingent. The case in
which there is no such indifference and in which form is totally determined by content, is the case in which form and content stand in an
absolute relation, a relation Hegel memorably describes as 'Umschlagen':
'so daß *der Inhalt* nichts ist als das *Umschlagen der Form* in Inhalt, und

die *Form* nichts *als Umschlagen des Inhalts* in Form'—'so that *content* is nothing but *the turning over of form* into content, and *form* nothing but the *turning over of content* into form' (*Enz*. §133). The first instance of categories exhibiting an absolute relation is the case of accidence and substance (*WL* II. 184–8). There is no more to substance (as content) than is manifested in its accidents (as form), and there are no accidents which are not accidents of substance. An account of substance is exhausted by an account of its accidents, that is, substance and accidence exhaust each other's determinacy. The reason why it is this pair of categories which are the first in the *Logic of Essence* to stand in an absolute relation is that such a relation is only possible if content is determinate and substantial. If content were abstract and indeterminate, it could have a corresponding form, but the form too would be accordingly indeterminate. This being so, it would be possible to alter the form to a large extent without altering the content; in other words, if the content and its appropriate form correspond, but are indeterminate, they must be relatively indifferent. For example, if we take 'animal life' as content, it has a vast number of forms, and can be correctly exemplified by a wide variety of different organisms because it is indeterminate. 'Dog' already has a far more restricted relationship to its forms, but it is not an absolute relation because there are so many species of dog. An absolute relation obtains between a content and form which determine each other uniquely: they are what they are through their relation, so that neither can be altered without altering the other. An absolute relation is only possible when a substantial content fully determines its form as its own manifestation, so that all form can be shown to be content, and this is how form and content are related in the Ideal of art. This is why Hegel distinguishes what he calls the 'formal' correspondence of content and form, when the one is merely a correct reflection of the other, from the identity of a concrete, substantial content with the form it determines (*Ä* I. 109), and observes that in certain art 'the *weakness of the form* stems from the *weakness of the content*' (*Ä* I. 105). It follows from this that although art may be of substantial content, and still a failure (through, for example, a lack of articulacy), it cannot be trivial and of high excellence.[15] We come back once more to an implication of the formula, and the parallel between Beauty and Truth: the content of art is Idea, which means that it shows systematic determinateness, each moment being related to other moments so that it must be thus and not otherwise, both determining them and determined by them.

To relate the identity of form and content to the question of artistic quality is a commonplace, but what is unique to Hegel is the luxury of grounding this in a theory of categories, and the ingenious way in which it is used on a series of different levels. In linking up Beauty and Truth, it links up art, society, and morality, and both relates and distinguishes the questions of artistic excellence and value. We can see how this works by tracing the input of various sets of contrasts between form and content, starting at the 'highest' level, and getting more specific.

Art itself is a *form* of Absolute Spirit, so its *content* is in the most general sense self-reflection. The eminent mode of self-reflection is reflection upon substantial beliefs, the ethical and religious principles which determine the subject's identity. The next level of specificity is the *form* in which art manifests itself, and this introduces the complication of the arts and the art-forms. The arts are *forms of the form* of art, which means the *material* it forms in order to produce a content. The art-forms are *forms of the content* of art, and are thereby forms of Absolute Spirit, to the extent that they can be understood as different 'Weltanschauungen', determinate sets of beliefs. (One could again say that art, religion, and philosophy are different forms of the form of Absolute Spirit, different modes of self-reflection; and the art-forms are forms of the content of Absolute Spirit, different products of self-reflection.) Within the art-forms, there are various sets of beliefs which provide *content* for art, such as mythologies, stories from the past, or ethical conventions such as romantic love. They are the *forms* in which the 'Weltanschauungen' express themselves, and provide material for the artist in the *form* of themes. To give a theme artistic *form* is to produce a work of art, and this form is then the expression of a *content* to which it uniquely belongs. It is the body of a soul from which it cannot be separated. On this final level of the work itself, one can only distinguish what is expressed from how it is expressed. The latter is simply what appears to the senses, and the former is the thought informing it. At this level, form and content stand in an absolute relation: the form is the content itself:

Diese rechte Form aber ist so wenig gegen den Inhalt gleichgültig, daß dieselbe vielmehr der Inhalt selbst ist. Ein Kunstwerk, welchem die rechte Form fehlt, ist eben darum kein rechtes, d.h. kein / wahres Kunstwerk . . . Wahrhafte Kunstwerke sind eben nur solche, deren Inhalt und Form sich als durchaus identisch erweisen. Man kann von der Ilias sagen, ihr Inhalt sei der Trojanische Krieg oder bestimmter der Zorn des Achill; damit haben wir alles und doch nur sehr wenig, denn was die Ilias zur Ilias macht, das ist die poetische Form, zu welcher jener Inhalt herausgebildet ist. Ebenso ist der Inhalt von *Romeo und Julia* der durch die Zwietracht ihrer Familien herbeigeführte Untergang zweier Liebenden; allein dies ist noch nicht Shakespeares unsterbliche Tragödie. (*Enz.* § 133, Zus.)

Far from being indifferent to content, the proper form is in fact the content itself. A work of art which does not have the proper form is for that very reason not a proper, i.e. not a true work of art . . . True works of art are precisely those whose content and form prove to be completely identical. One could say that the content of the Iliad is the Trojan War, or more specifically the wrath of Achilles; this says everything and nothing, for what makes the Iliad the Iliad is the poetic form which that content takes on. In the same way the content of *Romeo and Juliet* is the ruin of a pair of lovers through the feuding of their families; but this is a long way from being Shakespeare's immortal tragedy.

The poetic content is nothing other than the poetic form, which turns the thematic material into a web of meaning from which it cannot be separated.[16] At each level except the last, what had been considered as form is then itself considered as a content. If the role of the arts is excluded, for it is really a separate question, there is a continuous thread tying the work of art to the Ideal, which can be represented in tabular form.

	Content	Form
1.	Absolute Spirit	Art
2.	Art	Art-forms
3.	Art-forms	Mythology
4.	Mythology	Themes
5.	Theme	Treatment
6.	Thought	Expression of thought

At each level, the relationship can be more or less close. For form and content at any level to correspond would mean that they exhaust each other's determinacy, giving complete mutual inclusion. Starting on level 5, this would mean that the treatment articulated the whole significance of its theme, so that, to use Hegel's example, the *Iliad* shows us the full meaning of the wrath of Achilles. If then (level 4), the theme encompasses a whole mythology, the work has given full expression to a way of understanding experience which is familiar and of interest to a society, in the way that the *Iliad* recounts stories about the gods, and

represents the relationship between gods and men so as to be an auth-
oritative source of mythological material of interest to the Greek nation.
If the mythology corresponds to an art-form, it is not just an expression
of something of general interest, but of a 'Weltanschauung', the whole
substance of a community (level 3). This would mean that the gods in
Homer were not just a literary convention, but were taken seriously,
and played a central role in Greek ethical life. If this art-form corresponds to art itself (level 2), the substantial beliefs of the community
can be expressed only in art, and the Ideal of Beauty will be not only
the Ideal of art, but also the paradigm of the self-understanding of the
subject: Beauty will be the Truth of the individual subject and the
whole community. In that case (level 1), art is the only mode of self-
reflection which can properly articulate the identity of the subject and
the community, so that the Ideal is an expression of Truth, and the form
in which Truth must be expressed if it is to be complete. This would be
realized if, in reading or hearing the *Iliad*, the Greeks were confronted
with a work which they took as seriously as Christians take the Bible,
which showed them what and who they are completely and without
distortion, in a way only possible in art.

Levels 1 to 5 show how a work of art is mediated with ethical substance, with moral principles and religious beliefs. If there is correspondence at all these levels, there is a guarantee that the thought
content of the work on level 6 will be substantial. However, the thought
content may be substantial if all the levels mediating Absolute Spirit and
the work have broken down, and this will indeed be so in most cases.
Only the Ideal itself shows full mediation at all levels. For example,
romantic art breaks the chain of correspondence at levels 2 and 3:
although there are various generally accepted principles and conventions
embodied in art (such as courtly love), such conventions (which can be
included under the rubric of 'mythology') do not exhaust the 'Weltanschauung' of the art-form, and the art-form does not correspond to the
Ideal of Beauty or art. In romantic art, the Ideal of 'Kunstschönheit'–
'artistic beauty' is replaced by 'geistige Schönheit'–'spiritual beauty'
(*Ä* II. 156), so that although works of art can be beautiful by fulfilling
the criterion of form/content identity at other levels, art itself is not
beautiful, but encompasses 'das Unschöne' (for example *Ä* II. 105, 139,
153). This does not mean that romantic art is worse than classical art; it
means that it does not have so much value attached to it by society,
because it is not the ultimate form in which self-reflection is mediated.
The ultimate form is religion, and religion accordingly has a higher

value than art. For the Greeks (Hegel supposes) the Divine itself, the reflection of man's identity, was manifest in art, and only in art, that is, the Divine itself was beautiful, rather than purely spiritual. Thus only when there is correspondence at every level does art fufil its highest function, and have its greatest value. Once religion articulates Truth in such a way that it cannot be shown without distortion in art, art itself has lost value—but it has not for that reason lost quality.

Levels 1 to 5 account for the value attached to art by various societies at various times. Level 6 accounts for the aesthetic quality of works of art at all times. It is a necessary, but not a sufficient condition of a work having quality that it embody determinate thought. If it embodies substantial thought which is not mediated through the other levels (that is if levels 2 to 5 break down), it may or may not have value attached to it by virtue of the beliefs it expresses. The beliefs will not be universal ones, so certain limited groups or even individuals may attach supreme value to the work, and other groups or individuals attach no value to it at all. This is a result of the position of art in society, the nature of society itself, and the ethical base of human self-understanding; in other words, an alteration in the relationship between Beauty and Truth (as Absolute Spirit). There is nothing any artist can do about that.

What concerns the artist is what the aesthetician can understand as the categorial relationship between Beauty and Truth, their identity as Idea, that is, their systematicity. This is the same as the issue of quality, of the identity of form and content on level 6. What this means can be illustrated by an example drawn at random from Shakespeare, an unobstrusive line uttered by Iago towards the end of Act II, scene iii of *Othello*. Iago reveals his plans for Othello's ruin, and outlines the role to be played by Desdemona. He sums it up with three lines, the first of which runs: 'So will I turn her virtue into pitch' (l. 349). If it is regarded as an example of the sensuous reflection of the Idea, then it should show that it has poetic form by virtue of being fully determinate, so that no aspect of it can be changed without a loss of content. An analysis of its artistic qualities should involve showing how it fits into the whole play as a supporting element of a systematic structure which in turn determines the way the line itself is.

If we try to say what the line means, it looks prima facie as if Iago is restating the well-known phrase of turning virtue into vice. That is in fact precisely what he does not mean. Desdemona's moral qualities will be unaltered; her virtue will remain virtue, but through Iago's plan it will be turned to pitch. To turn virtue into pitch is to turn an abstract

moral quality into a substance which has a strong effect on the senses,
to three in particular: to smell, touch, and sight. Pitch has a pungent
smell, it is sticky, and it is black. Consideration of its context shows
that there are reasons determining the choice of 'pitch'. The stickiness
of pitch shows its function as a trap: Othello and Cassio will be stuck
to her, and left to struggle helplessly. The smell of pitch is in stark
contrast to the presentation of Desdemona, described by Cassio earlier
in the scene as 'a most fresh and delicate creature' (l. 20), and points to
the inversion which Iago will bring about. Its blackness links it with a
network of imagery running through the play: Othello is black, sin is
black, hell is black, night is black; Desdemona is white, purity is white,
innocence is white. The word's sensuous connotations and its associ-
ation with common life are in accord with Iago's imagery throughout,
imagery which is alien to Othello, who tends to be lofty and solemn
until Iago begins to establish power over him. Changing virtue into
pitch will be to move Desdemona from Othello's sphere to Iago's. The
word 'pitch' is richer in meaning than an alternative such as (bird)-
'lime' and sounds more effective than a closer rival such as 'tar', which
ends on a weak open vowel. The word order of the line disrupts the
natural speech rhythm which would have been achieved by 'So I will
turn . . .'. This alternative would emphasize the iambic rhythm, and
make the line trip along with a stress on 'I'. By writing 'So will I turn
. . .', Shakespeare makes the rhythm more reflective, and enriches the
meaning of 'So' and 'will': 'So' draws a conclusion, and adds the nuance
of 'in this way': 'will' is emphasized, and draws attention to the fact
that this is not just something Iago is going to do, but something he
wishes to do. (He attaches great importance to the power of the will;
see I. iii. 319 ff.) This would have been lost with 'shall'.

The reasons why the line is as it is are the thought-content behind it,
the content which is determining its form. Whether Shakespeare sat
down to work it all out, or wrote it instinctively because if 'felt right' is
irrelevant to the results. Some artists do the former (for instance
Flaubert), others, probably far fewer, are instinctive (for instance
Goethe). Some artists have rational instincts, others are very self-
conscious. The thought present in the result is all that matters. Making
the thought apparent is a theoretical activity, characteristic of philosophy and here engaged in by empirical art-critical discourse. The identity and difference of philosophy and art, that is of Truth and Beauty,
are common systematic rationality or coherence, and a different commitment to proof or validity: 'autonomous identity and structured

development' are common to art and philosophy, but philosophy gives explicit reasons for the way it is, whereas art 'does not go as far as to point things out explicitly' ($\ddot{A}$ III. 255). The line does not *mean* 'I'll turn her virtue into something which fits in with the imagery of the play'; it just does it.

If the analysis of the line is correct, or partly correct, it has established that it is of quality—what has been said above could not be true, and the line be bad poetry. 'Quality' here closely links the two senses of 'excellence' and 'what distinguishes something'. It is substantial poetry of some excellence, because it is distinct from anything else by virtue of being determinate. Art which is of high excellence must be individual. The more reasons there are for the form being as it is, the richer the content, the greater the systematic necessity of every moment. If the work shows absolute necessity, everything expresses something. The notion of absolute (that is, systematic) necessity is important, for it is distinguished in the *Logic* from real or relative necessity, which applies in the realm of nature (see *WL* II. 178-80). Real necessity is characteristic of bad works of art, for it is the necessity involved in realizing a limited aim. Hegel describes it in the *Aesthetics* as 'Zweckmäßigkeit', for it implies a teleological relationship between a specific end and a means ($\ddot{A}$ III. 253). No part of a work of art may function as a means. When this happens, we find an element being used for effect, or extraneous elements intruding for external reasons, or composition which follows a formula. The happy ending of many Hollywood films is an example of real necessity: it is part of a formula, with the specific end of making the audience happy (and increasing the box-office takings). We may enjoy such films, but if we are discriminating in our responses, we might realize in the enjoyment that the film is not a great work of art. A fine example of real necessity in literature is provided by the unknown author of these classic lines, written for the Diamond Jubilee of Queen Victoria in 1897:

> Hail our great Queen in her regalia;
> One foot in Canada, the other in Australia.[17]

The poor man needed a rhyme, with the result that one wonders how Victoria's legs could have stretched so far. By switching from a line about the actual appearance of the Queen, to an image, with no time for reflection, the poem makes the metaphorical feet attach themselves stubbornly to the Royal personage, her legs stuck to the globe by a rich rhyme worthy of W. S. Gilbert. Far from determining each other, the

two lines get disastrously in each other's way, and 'Australia', or perhaps 'regalia' has its sole *raison d'être* in the need to rhyme with its un-
willing partner. The bathos depends on its being read in a certain way,
as a serious poem. If it were to be read as a comic or satirical poem, its
significance would change. Excellence is a function of the returns on
hermeneutic investment; a fine work of art is one which makes a lot of
sense, and shows a high degree of coherence if it is read in a certain way,
and it may be that coherence is there, but has not been found. The
familiar case of the abused and misunderstood masterpiece is a case of
a work demanding new ways of reading, hearing, or seeing, which are
not discovered until long after its first appearance. (Atonal music, for
example, was long considered 'difficult' because of its dissonance,
despite the fact that late Romantic music of similar or greater dissonance was popular. The real reason for the comparative difficulty of
atonal music is the incoherence which seems to, or does, result from the
lack of tonality's organizing principles.) By changing the interpretative
framework used to understand a work, we may succeed in discovering
possible qualities in it. If something seems to be ridiculous if read liter-
ally, for example, it may make better sense if read as ironic, unless
there are elements in it which cannot be fitted into the system if it is
ironic.

What is revealed by interpretation as the determiner of form is
Thought (Concept), not an idea or representation. The model for a
work of art is therefore not the symbol, which is the presentation of a
general meaning, but an appearance which is its own meaning, like a
Greek god. The symbol shows mere affinity between form and content, and is thus a deficient mode of artistic representation.[18] Artistic
representation is an eminent mode of symbolism which overcomes the
indifference between form and content attaching to the symbol, and
this is how Hegel understands the gods of Homer:

Wird nun von solchen in sich freien Subjekten ein allgemeiner Begriff
als deren Bedeutung abstrahiert und neben das Besondere als Erklärung
der ganzen individuellen Erscheinung gestellt, so ist das unberücksichtigt
gelassen und zerstört, was an diesen Gestalten das Kunstgemäße ist.
(*Ä* I. 406.)

If a universal concept is abstracted from these autonomous free subjects, and put forward alongside their particularity as a meaning which
explains the whole individual phenomenon, then the very thing which
makes these figures objects of art is left unaccounted for and destroyed.

To interpret art in order to arrive at meanings is to treat it as symbolic.

This will indeed be justified in most cases, as both the symbolic and romantic art-forms are dominated by a symbolic mode of representation. The classical Ideal, however,

hat zu ihrem Inneren die freie, *selbstständige* Bedeutung, d.i. nicht eine Bedeutung von irgend etwas, sondern das *sich selbst Bedeutende* und damit auch *sich selber Deutende*. Dies ist das *Geistige*, welches überhaupt sich selbst zum Gegenstande seiner macht. (*Ä* II. 13.)

is free *independent* meaning in itself, in other words, it does not contain the meaning of something, but is *its own meaning* and thus also *its own interpretation*. This is so because it is *Spirit*, and Spirit always makes itself its own object.

A statue of a Greek god is a paradigm of the mode of representation unique to art. It is a function of its meaning that it appear to the senses in the form it does, and the form in which it appears is its meaning. It is not only a paradigm of excellence, but is invested with the highest value accorded to art, because it is an object of veneration through which man realizes his identity with the Divine, and is shown what he is. To account for this, art's highest function, is not to show a 'classical bias' but simply to provide a complete theory of art. And it is a consequence of a consideration of all art at all times, which avoids bias by imposing no restrictions on the material, that from the point of view of its highest function, art is now a thing of the past.

The End of Art

In his own major work on aesthetics, published five years before the first volume of Hotho's edition of Hegel's lectures appeared, Christian Hermann Weisse adds a long and somewhat polemical footnote to the effect that Hegel's pupils were putting it about that art would be absorbed into philosophy, and that the new dawn of artistic production in Germany was in fact the onset of twilight.[19] In his review eight years later, Weisse again comments that Hegel's followers tended to talk about the end of art, and adds that this could hardly have been Hegel's own opinion.[20] Weisse documents the origins of the doctrine of 'the end of art', a phrase which never occurs in the *Aesthetics*, in the loose talk of those who heard Hegel lecture. There has always been some awareness of the issue, but it has only recently entered the forefront of debate, producing a spate of articles since the 1950s.[21] The opinions about what Hegel's opinion really was fall very roughly into three groups: those

who think he was wrong; those who think he was only partly wrong,
or that his system can be saved despite itself; and those who think
he had an important insight, not about the end of art, but about its
future.

1 *The 'funeral oration' thesis*

This is the thesis that art is coming to its end because it has been taken
over by philosophy: if we have philosophy, we do not need art. These
commentators are critical towards Hegel, and usually claim that he
regards art as philosophy made pretty, and that the doctrine is the result
of an incoherent system. Examples are Croce, Glockner, Litt, and in
more recent years, Wolandt and Bubner.

Croce believes that the whole tendency of the *Aesthetics* is anti-
artistic, and describes it as a 'funeral oration' (*un elogio funebre*) on
art.[22] Glockner accuses Hegel of giving it 'an all too "fixed" position in
the development of Concept', and says that he is wrong to say that art
will come to an end because it is not some sort of imperfect philosophy.[23] Litt shares this view, pointing out that art is autonomous and
cannot be eliminated in a higher dialectical synthesis.[24] Wolandt understands Hegel to be claiming that art as such is 'an epoch in the development of Spirit', and that because he makes the mistake of looking at
the whole of culture from the point of view of the development of
consciousness: 'Die Kunst bleibt auf dem Wege zum Begriff als eine
gebundene, den Begriff ans Sinnliche fesselnde Phase zurück'—'Art is
left behind on the path leading to Concept, as a phase shackling it to the
senses'.[25] Bubner says much the same: 'Philosophie löst Kunst ab und
verweist sie in eine vergangene Phase der Entwicklungsgeschichte des
Geistes'—'Philosophy takes over from art and consigns it to a past phase
in the history of Spirit's development', and adds in a footnote that if
Hegel granted art a future, it was as permanent Biedermeier.[26]

The main recurrent motifs of the funeral oration are that art is
reduced to imperfect philosophy, and that Hegel is forced to say that it
has been overtaken because of the dictates of his system.

2 *Insights and illusions, and salvage attempts*

Athanas Stoikov and Christoph Helferich think that Hegel has insights
despite his system. Stoikov praises his view of Shakespeare and Dutch
genre painting, gained in spite of the pan-logism of the system and the
subordination of everything to Spirit.[27] Helferich says that although
Hegel thought that art could only express the Truth of one epoch, he

sees that what really happens is an alteration in its relationship to reality.[28]

Karsten Harries, on the other hand, believes that Hegel is right on his own terms, but we must go beyond him. He sees the *Aesthetics* to contain three fundamental theses which he states as follows: '1) Genuine art transcends our conceptual grasp. 2) Art reveals reality; it is tied to truth. 3) Truth demands transparency; only what can be comprehended is real.'[29] The consequence of this, Harries argues, is that art can only yield truth if it is translated into the medium of thought. Our reflective culture accordingly fails to grant art the importance it once had, because we are too cerebral to take its sensuous character seriously, and we turn art into a mere diversion. Harries believes that the only way out is to step beyond Western culture, a possibility revealed by Heidegger. The truth of what Hegel shows proves that his position is wrong.

Jörn Rüsen and Willi Oelmüller try to salvage insights from the illusions by using Hegel as a springboard for their own ideas. Rüsen interprets Hegel as saying that art is autonomous in the modern world, and that it is no longer beautiful, but can remain true by virtue of this lack of beauty and its implied 'negativity'.[30] Rüsen then constructs a theory about art as a 'meta-theoretische Manifestation von Vernunft'– 'metatheoretical manifestation of reason',[31] and suggests, with the help of judiciously selected quotations, that it is found in Hegel. Oelmüller understands Hegel to be saying three things: one is about the history of religion and representation, to the effect that Christianity shows truths art cannot show; a second is about modern society, to the effect that it can no longer be shown as a totality; and the third is about art, to the effect that it is degenerating.[32] Oelmüller concludes that an immanent reading of Hegel can hold out little hope for art, but believes that the lectures contain the seeds of a theory of modern art which is better than the systematic one. He constructs the theory by sorting out Hegel's remarks about 'free' art, and claiming that they apply to modern art, showing that 'dies alles ist für Hegel kein Symptom des Verlusts der Mitte, sondern einer prinzipiell erst in der Moderne ermöglichten freien Kunst'–'for Hegel all this is not a symptom of the loss of the centre, but of a free art which is only made possible in principle in the modern world'.[33] This is close to a thesis which has actually been expounded, not by Hegel, as we shall see, but by Weisse.

3 *The future of art*

The largest group is composed of those who read the doctrine that art is in some sense a thing of the past as a prediction about art's future, usually referring to the development of art since Hegel's death to support him. There is no unanimity in the results, the essentials of which are as follows:

Bröcker   — art is subjective.[34]
Gadamer   — art is no longer a manifestation of the Divine, and has therefore become 'Reflexionskunst'.[35]
Heller   — the history of art shows it to be engaged in a 'journey into the interior'. Modern art shows interiority.[36]
Henrich   — there will be no future Utopia of art; it is reflective, free to use all historical forms, and it is partial.[37]
Hofstadter   — art is to show up its own falsity by destroying beauty in the medium of beauty.[38]
Jähnig   — art no longer reflects our highest interests.[39]
Kuhn   — art is no longer religious and the artist is deracinated (entheimatet).[40]
Patočka   — art has become a speciality.[41]
Wagner   — art shows a loss of substance, an increase in subjectivity and in the importance of technique.[42]
Wiehl   — the interest in art is no longer religious, but philosophical.[43]

There are in addition two analyses of what Hegel has to say about the art of his own day which do not attempt to read predictions into him. T. J. Reed places Hegel's account of the end of the romantic art-form in the context of the discussion of conscious processes in literary production conducted by Lessing, Schiller, and Friedrich Schlegel.[44] Otto Pöggeler examines Hegel's critique of the Romantics and their use of irony, concluding that it is a critique of subjectivity.[45]

Various attitudes to the 'end of art' complex have been reviewed by Werner Koepsel, who himself puts forward the view that the doctrine is contradictory: at one point (*Ä* I. 24) Hegel seems to say that art is no longer a need, and at another point—and, one might add, in a different context—(*Ä* I. 255) he seems to say that it is.[46] The resolution, it is suggested, is not to be found in Heidegger, or in revising Hegel, but in believing Adorno.[47]

This brief survey, which covers the main positions, but makes no claim to completeness, is enough to make one wonder not only about what Hegel said, but what he said it about. It is not clear whether he is talking about art, or artists, or society; the past, the present, or the future. Most options appear to be open. He has been understood to be claiming that art is autonomous in the modern world, and that it is the slave of philosophy; that it is only true when it is beautiful, and only true when it is ugly. Whatever Hegel means by calling art a thing of the past, his idea is clearly complex, and concerns several things.

It might be mentioned at the outset what it does not concern. It does not concern the future, because philosophy reconstructs the actual by examining what has been and what is, so it cannot predict: the owl of Minerva flies at dusk. Nevertheless, it is obvious that if it has analysed a seed which has since grown into a tree, it may be directly relevant to the present; it might tell us what sort of a tree it is, but we cannot expect to learn how long its branches are. The other thing it does not, or should not concern, is Hegel's taste, his likes and dislikes. He twice dismisses complaints about how dreadful modern art is, and lamentations about the state of society—he is concerned solely with establishing what is the case, and leaves the judgement of it to others (see *Ä* I. 24 and *Ä* II. 234).

We have in fact already noted the points at which art comes to an end. It ends where purely conceptual thought begins, where 'Poesie der Vorstellung'—'the poetry of representation' becomes 'Prosa des Denkens'—'the prose of thought' (*Ä* I. 123 and *Ä* III. 234). Art ends when it goes beyond its own limits. Comedy constitutes another limit when it becomes absolute, for if nothing can be taken seriously, art is deprived of its material, and is replaced by the jokes of nihilists (*Ä* III. 572-3). These limits are systematic, and the reason why the phrase 'end of art' gained currency is that Hegel reinterprets them historically, suggesting that they have in fact been reached in the art of his contemporaries.

The first element in this thematic complex concerns the content of Absolute Spirit and the problem of representation:

Nur ein gewisser Kreis und Stufe der Wahrheit ist fähig, im Elemente des Kunstwerks dargestellt zu werden; es muß noch in ihrer eigenen Bestimmung liegen, zu dem Sinnlichen herauszugehen und in demselben sich adäquat sein zu können, um echter Inhalt für die Kunst zu sein. (*A* I. 23.)

Only a certain sphere of Truth, at a certain stage, is open to representation in a work of art; its own determination must require it to take on a sensuous form in which it is fully adequate to itself in order for it to be a fitting content for art.

This is Hegel's starting-point, a logical one lying deep in the theory. Truth, understood as beliefs with the status of principles, and encompassing the Absolute or the Divine, can only be shown in art if it is in its determination that it should appear to the senses. This is the case when form and content correspond on levels 1 and 2, as seen above, and Hegel believes that this condition was fulfilled in ancient Greece, when the principles governing human life were embodied in gods who had human form. They could be adequately represented without any distortion in art, and only in art—art was the mode of mediating self-reflection which uniquely corresponded to the Greeks' conception of Truth (see *Ä* I. 140). Whether Hegel was right about this has never really been questioned. He tends to write as if art and religion were identical in ancient Greece, though in the *Aesthetics* he no longer uses the dubious title 'Kunstreligion' which plays a prominent role in the early *Phenomenology* (*PhG* 490-520). The Greeks distinguished art from religion, having religious rites which did not involve works of art, and likewise producing a large amount of secular art. However, it would be very ungenerous to criticize Hegel on these grounds. His main point is that the gods were represented fully and without distortion in art, and this is surely true; the gold and ivory statue of Zeus by the artist Phidias, which stood in the centre of the temple at Olympus, was the object of worship, and is said to have added something to accepted religion.[48] In Christianity, this would be impossible. Christianity needs art too, for the purposes of communication, and in order to portray the life of Christ, but the use of art by the Church brings with it theological problems (witness the iconoclasts) which could not arise for the Greeks, because the Christian God is pure Spirit, and only appears in part of His nature, as the Son. Art cannot contribute to religion, because Beauty is no longer the form in which Truth is manifest:

Ist es aber das Bewußtsein der *Wahrheit*, worum es sich handelt, so ist die *Schönheit* der Erscheinung und die Darstellung das Nebensächliche und Gleichgültigere, denn die Wahrheit ist auch unabhängig von der Kunst für das Bewußtsein vorhanden. (*Ä* II. 149.)

If, however, it is the consciousness of Truth which is at stake, the *beauty* of its appearance, and its representation, are a secondary, less important consideration, for Truth is available to consciousness independently of art.

This is a crucial distinction: Christian art does not communicate new truths, it just takes over and conveys in its own way truths which are known independently of art from the Scriptures and Church teaching. With the coming of Christianity, art had already ceased to fulfil its highest function.

Hegel has now moved from the systematic question of representation to the historical question of the differences between religions. His theory demands that he give an actual instance of art being the form in which the highest beliefs of a community are expressed, but it does not demand that the Greeks provide that example. Nor does it demand that the next art-form be Christian. There are many other religions, including many older ones, which have a determinate conception of a deity inimical to artistic representation. This is where the multiple role of the art-forms makes itself felt, for what in one role should be an exemplificatory instance, functions as a principle in another role: as a particular conception of the Divine, Greek religion and Christianity are examples, which could be unrelated and need not be unique; but as 'Weltanschauungen' they are sets of principles and are not just examples of a mode of representation, but uniquely constitute the very substance of the art-form. Various cultures are selected and placed in a line which is chronological, and has systematic significance.

Hegel pays no heed to his theory's lack of pedigree, for it enables him to understand his own time. As we have inherited the Christian tradition, so the limitations inherent in artistic representation determine the position of art in modern culture: 'Uns gilt die Kunst nicht mehr als die höchste Weise, in welcher die Wahrheit sich Existenz verschafft'—'For us, art is no longer the highest way in which Truth manifests itself' ($\ddot{A}$ I. 141). So however we may feel about it, art no longer fulfils our spiritual needs in the way it, and it alone, has fulfilled those of other cultures ($\ddot{A}$ I. 24), and this fact is not contingent, but a result of the development of art itself ($\ddot{A}$ II. 234). The development of Christian culture was such that art was driven ever further from its own centre between the mind and the senses:

als aber der Trieb des Wissens und Forschens und das Bedürfnis innerer Geistigkeit die Reformation hervortrieben, ward auch die religiöse Vorstellung von dem sinnlichen Elemente abgerufen und auf die Innerlichkeit des Gemüts und Denkens zurückgeführt. In dieser Weise besteht das *Nach* der Kunst darin, daß dem Geist das Bedürfnis einwohnt, sich nur in seinem eigenen Innern als der wahren Form für die Wahrheit zu befriedigen. (Ä I. 142.)

but as the drive to knowledge and enquiry and the need for inner spirituality gave rise to the Reformation, religious thinking too was drawn away from the element of the senses, and led back to the interiority of the mind and thought. In this way what comes *after* art is Spirit's endemic need to satisfy itself in its own interior as the real form for Truth.

In tracing this historical development further, we have moved down to levels 3 and 4: because God is pure Spirit and cannot be represented, the material taken up by art alters too over time, and especially after the Reformation shows less interest in the world of the senses. This had to happen, because of Spirit's drive to knowledge. Hegel expresses this as if it were a psychological or anthropological fact that man has a 'Wissenstrieb', but on examination, it turns out to be a function of the principle of history, the principle of non-repetition. Once some content has been made clear and understood, it is dropped:

Ist aber der vollkommene Inhalt vollkommen in Kunstgestalten hervorgetreten, so wendet sich der weiterblickende Geist von dieser Objektivität in sein Inneres zurück und stößt sie von sich fort. Solch eine Zeit ist die unsrige. Man kann wohl hoffen, daß die Kunst immer mehr steigen und sich vollenden werde, aber ihre Form hat aufgehört, das höchste Bedürfnis des Geistes zu sein. (Ibid.)

But once the perfect content has achieved perfect expression in figures of art, Spirit, looking onward, rejects this objectivity and turns away from it back into its own interior. Such an age is our own. One can indeed hope that art will forever continue to reach new heights of perfection, but its form has ceased to be the highest need of Spirit.

Once Spirit has fully investigated something, it moves on to something new, as if to avoid getting bored, and we have got bored with what art has to tell us. Art may continue to flourish, but it will not be a need of Spirit, because the need of Spirit is to know itself, and art has nothing new to say. There is no way of increasing and deepening the self-understanding we already have in the form of art.

Spirit's recurrent boredom and drive to escape it is a function of the principle of history. The activity of Spirit is gaining self-knowledge, and any knowledge-gaining activity is such that it alters the relationship between the knowing subject and the object of its knowledge. A known object has, from the point of view of the subject, changed from what it was before, which means that the activity of gaining knowledge is historical: it alters the context of its own possibility. As Spirit is engaged in self-knowledge, it alters itself through being what it is, and is there-fore essentially historical. Through being what it is, it always necessarily changes through time, and can never repeat itself, or continue to do the same thing. Doing something a second time is necessarily different from doing it a first time, so doing it once means that it can never be done again—whatever is done will be new. Thus Hegel continues:

Mögen wir die griechischen Götterbilder noch so vortrefflich finden und Gottvater, Christus, Maria noch so würdig und vollendet dargestellt sehen—es hilft nichts, unser Knie beugen wir doch nicht mehr. (Ibid.)

No matter how admirable we may find the statues of the Greek gods, and no matter how impressive and accomplished representations of God, Christ, and Mary may be—it is of no avail, we still do not fall on bended knee.

And, one might add, even if we did bend our knee in devotion as we used to, it would be a different act, the devotion would not be the same; it would be self-conscious. Once Spirit knows something, it cannot for-get: consciousness cannot be put into reverse.

We have now moved from the modes of representation possible in different religions to cultural history, and have come to the subject of the public, to Hegel's 'we'. The 'end of art' is as much to do with us as with art, as much to do with our conception of Truth and our values, as with Beauty. We have replaced a devotional attitude to art with an atti-tude of critical reflection:

wir sind darüber hinaus, Werke der Kunst göttlich zu verehren und sie anbeten zu können; der Eindruck, den sie machen, ist besonnenerer Art, und was durch sie in uns erregt wird, bedarf noch eines höheren Prüf-steins und anderweitiger Bewährung. Der Gedanke und die Reflexion hat die schöne Kunst überflügelt. (Ä I. 24.)

we are past being able to venerate works of art because of their divinity and to worship them; the impression they make is more circumspect, and we need a higher touchstone, some further check on what they arouse in us. Fine art has been overtaken by thought and reflection.

The modern public is reflective, and no longer accepts a work of art without thought, but judges it, and measures what it expresses against other knowledge available from outside art (see Ä I. 25-6, and 'What Could a Philosophy of Art Be?' chapter 1 above). The pious Greek could not judge what he was shown about the gods by Homer or Phidias, for there was no higher authority than artists like them. When art was

challenged by Platonic philosophy, this situation began to change.
The Christian still worships a statue of the Virgin, but he knows about
her and her significance from the Church, not from art. He is already
in a position to judge what he sees. The Lutheran, however, worships
no images. Truth for him is only available through thought, the image
is fundamentally flawed. The public of the early nineteenth century
has become so reflective and critical, that it has distance towards
everything. Nothing is sacred; nothing is bound to be accepted without
justification, which is why the modern public needs a philosophy of art.
We are interested in judging art aesthetically and evaluating its success,
and we do not believe what it says without assessing it on the basis of
external information. Art is only one mode of reflection, and our self-
awareness is so broad, that art cannot fill it.

This state of affairs inevitably also affects the practising artist, who
cannot isolate himself from the reflective culture in which he lives, and
is 'infected by it, and led to introduce more conscious thoughts into his
work' (*Ä* I. 25). This has two consequences: art itself will contain more
conscious thought, and, because of the distance between the artist and
any ethical principles, there will be no particular themes suggesting
themselves as peculiarly appropriate for artistic treatment. Old ones
have been exhausted, so new ones must be found, 'Denn Interesse
findet nur bei frischer Tätigkeit statt. Der Geist arbeitet sich nur so
lange in den Gegenständen herum, solange noch ein Geheimes, Nicht-
offenbares darin ist. Dies ist der Fall, solange der Stoff noch identisch
mit uns ist'—'For interest is only sustained by fresh activity. Spirit only
continues to work its way around things as long as there is something
mysterious and inexplicit in them. This is the case as long as the material
is identical with us'. (*Ä* II. 234.) The artist in a reflective age could still
deal with an old content, but then his only genuine purpose would be
ironic: 'das wahrhafte Bedürfnis, ihn wieder aufzunehmen, erwacht nur
mit dem Bedürfnis, sich *gegen* den bisher allein gültigen Gehalt zu
kehren'—'the need to take it up again only really arises with the need
to turn *against* a content which had hitherto enjoyed unique validity'
(ibid.). The artist finds a role as a rebel, trying to do the opposite of
what was done before. But it is only one possibility—form and content
have in fact become a *tabula rasa*:

Das Gebundensein an einen besonderen Gehalt und eine nur für diesen
Stoff passende Art der Darstellung ist für den heutigen Künstler etwas
Vergangenes und die Kunst dadurch ein freies Instrument geworden,
das er nach Maßgabe seiner subjektiven Geschicklichkeit in bezug auf

jeden Inhalt, welcher Art er auch sei, gleichmäßig handhaben kann . . .
jeder Stoff darf ihm gleichgültig sein, wenn er nur dem formellen
Gesetz, überhaupt schön und einer künstlerischen Darstellung fähig
zu sein, nicht widerspricht. Es gibt heutigentags keinen Stoff, der an
und für sich über dieser Relativität stände, und wenn er auch darüber
erhaben ist, so ist doch wenigstens kein absolutes Bedürfnis vorhanden,
daß er von der *Kunst* zur Darstellung gebracht werde. (*Ä* II. 235.)

For the artist of today, being tied to a particular content and a manner
of representation which is uniquely suited to that content is a thing of
the past, and thus it is that art has become a free instrument which he
can bring to bear equally on any content, whatever its nature, as his
personal skills permit . . . the material he takes can be a matter of indifference to him, providing only that it does not contradict the formal
law of somehow being beautiful and open to artistic treatment. These
days there is no material which in and of itself escapes this relativity,
and even if it does, there is no compelling need that it should find expression in *art*.

This is the final stage in the development of romantic art, which established a diremption between form and content in its thematic material:
the two worlds of inner subjectivity and external objectivity. As long
as they are mediated, so that subjectivity expresses itself through some
external form, there will be romantic art, no matter how varied and
contingent its manifestations may seem to be (see *Ä* II. 138–40 and 'The
Moments of Concept', chapter 2 above). However, when they part company altogether, romantic art comes to an end:

Dadurch erhalten wir als Endpunkt des Romantischen überhaupt die
Zufälligkeit des Äußeren wie des Inneren und ein Auseinanderfallen
dieser Seiten, durch welches die Kunst sich selbst aufhebt und die
Notwendigkeit für das Bewußtsein zeigt, sich höhere Formen, als
die Kunst sie zu bieten imstande ist, für das Erfassen des Wahren zu
erwerben. (*A* II. 142.)

Thus as the end-point of the romantic art-form, we arrive at the complete arbitrariness of both the external and internal aspects of art, and
the dissolution of both of them, whereby art sublates itself and shows
consciousness that for the understanding of Truth, it is necessary to
turn to forms higher than those which art can offer.

The two separated aspects are pure objectivity, in the form of the
naturalistic portrayal of reality in all its contingency, and the pure
subjectivity of humour (*Ä* II. 198). With the end of the romantic art-
form, there is complete dissolution of the relationship between form
and content on all levels but the last, and there is therefore no specific

art-form providing new forms and new contents, just a return to the mysteries of symbolic art with its indeterminacy. No themes demand any specific treatment; there is no mythology to provide thematic material; there is no accepted 'Weltanschauung' to ground a mythology in communal life: there is just art and works of art, with no mediating levels to erode the contingency between them. The value of art will depend on what it does with its chosen material, and it can do anything with it, as long as it makes it interesting to somebody. It will please a public either as a technical *tour de force* or as the purveyor of a message which the public finds agreeable when it has interpreted it out of its shell. This point is not just the end of art, but the end of aesthetics too, for there is nothing more to be said about form and content. They stand in no necessary relation, so philosophy can say nothing more about art.

Before proceeding, what Hegel has said can be summarized as a series of theses:

1. When the Divine is understood to be such that it can be represented in art, and only in art, art fulfils its highest function. (Systematic claim about representation.)
2. With Christianity it ceased to do so, and could only reflect truth already known in religious form. (Socio-historical claim.)
3. This had to happen because of the principle of non-repetition. (Principle of the philosophy of history.)
4. It led to a steady increase in reflection and a growth in self-awareness reaching a peak in the late eighteenth century, when society was no longer able to identify itself with past beliefs. (Historical observation.)
5. This state of affairs has the following effects:
   - on art: it provides only parfial and derivative means of self-knowledge;
   - on us, the public: we judge works critically and assess their truth-content against other knowledge we have;
   - on artists: they are not identical with any material, so face the problem both of what to treat and how;
   - on the works they produce: they are self-conscious, formal innovations on familiar material.

This reinforces the point that the doctrine of the 'end of art' is a complex of theses which are related but about different things. It is a good example of the heterogeneity of the *Aesthetics* at work, and its reception is typical of the confusion this heterogeneity has understandably caused.

There is a problem in all this, though, and it lies in the ambiguity of Hegel's doctrine that art, religion, and philosophy have the same content. It is this which lends plausibility to the picture sometimes presented of the modern artist picking up crumbs of wisdom dropped from the table of the philosopher, and cooking them up in an exotic stew, giving old spiritual contents the spice of a novel sensuous form. One strand of Hegel's thought is certainly that art is played out, and that any new contribution to man's self-understanding can only come in conceptual terms, terms he tends to equate with philosophy. He ought not to do so, for conceptual reflection is only philosophical when it is a priori and systematic, but apart from that, one might hesitate over his verdict on art. If he is right, then Proust and Kafka, Wagner and Schönberg, Van Gogh and Cézanne, have not given articulation to anything new, nor anything which could not have been put another way: *Der Prozess* would merely be the diverting and virtuosic form in which a few ideas are presented, ideas best put clearly in purely conceptual terms. Not a few people will find this consequence unacceptable, or absurd. It comes from a subtle *non sequitur* in the theory, and goes back to the belief Hegel had that we first get to know a content through our senses, and then come to understand the same content through thought. What his historical observations show is that religion and intellectual reflection have contents which cannot be shown in art. He slides from this, to the claim that they can take over what has been shown in art, so that the only mode of reflection viable today is conceptual. Art may have become less important, contain more thought itself, and be the object of critical judgement; it does not follow from that that its role can be usurped, and absorbed in thought. If there ever were things which could only be conveyed through art, there always will be.

Hegel is consistent in giving modern art a psychological justification, by saying that although its content may be old, we retain a desire for the 'the Truth of art' (Kunstwahrheit) provided by making truth available to 'feeling and picturing thought' (Vorstellung) (*Ä* II. 239). Those who wish to feel the content, to have it present to their senses, will wish to have art, but they will not learn from it. This is the one disturbing element in an analysis which otherwise carries striking conviction. He is surely right that what has been done once cannot be done again, that we cannot become Greeks, artists cannot become Catholic 'in order to settle their sensibilities' (*Ä* II. 236), and that we demand a reflection of our present interests in art: 'Only the present is fresh, the rest is dull and stale' (*Ä* II. 238). It is surely also true that the two sides of romantic art have led to the expansion of art to the expression of every human interest without restriction, that the only subject of art is the 'Humanus',[49] the feelings and experiences of the artist himself to whom nothing human is alien (*Ä* II. 238), and encompassing the whole expanse of the external world as well as the full depths of the interior one.

In view of this, why should one not regard modern art as liberating itself from the shackles of religion, and reaching its full potential by embodying more thought than before? We are fortunate to have an able exponent of just that view in Weisse. His *System der Ästhetik* of 1830 is a philosophy of art which undertakes to do what Hegel does. It contains, within a similar theoretical framework, an interpretation of modern art directly opposed to Hegel's, so one of them must be wrong, and if their theories are rational it must be possible to say why. Weisse's case is certainly not weak—after all, as he points out,[50] the period which is supposed to witness the end of art was one of intense artistic activity in Germany, almost unprecedented in its extent and quality.

Weisse, like Hegel, has three art-forms, which he calls 'Ideals': the classical, the romantic, and the modern. The latter is the summit of the development, for it contains the Concept of Beauty as a moment, and is thus *'der seiner selbst bewußte Begriff der Schönheit selbst*, d.h. das Wissen um, oder die Einsicht in die Idee der Schönheit in ihrem vollen Umfange'—*'the self aware Concept of Beauty itself*, i.e. the knowledge of, or insight into the Idea of Beauty, in all that it encompasses' (pp. 304–5). He criticizes what one can take to be a Hegelian position, claiming that it is external to art and tries to reduce it to philosophy. All it can grasp of art, he says, is 'die in ihr verhüllte Wahrheit'—'the truth hidden in it', and he contrasts this with his own determination of Beauty as 'die aufgehobene Wahrheit . . . wobei es freilich eine Forderung der Wahrheit selbst bleibt, daß die Form ihres reinen Erkennens auch in dieser ihr jenseitiger Sphäre sich erhalte und bewähre' —'sublated Truth . . . whilst it remains a prerequisite of Truth itself, that even in this realm beyond it, the form of its pure cognition should be preserved and confirmed' (p. 305).[51] The modern Ideal is the realization of the norm of Beauty for two reasons: it is pure and it is universal. It is pure because it shows Beauty as such, purely aesthetically, without any religious element intruding (the phenomenon noted by Hegel, *Ä* II. 237);

and it is universal because it is totally unrestricted in its range, so that anything which can be beautiful is made beautiful (the phenomenon noted by Hegel, *Ä* II. 235; Weisse, pp. 306-7). Thus only modern art is free and autonomous; art was not a necessity in classical and romantic times, for it was then only used to externalize and preserve mythology. Only in an age of self-consciousness can art develop the full possibilities which attach to it as art, and be free (pp. 318-20).

Weisse is the man Willi Oelmüller would like Hegel to be (see 'The End of Art': 'Insights and illusions' above). He sees exactly what Hegel sees, but interprets it with attractive optimism. This means that the facts are the same in both cases, and the disagreement theoretical. There are two competing frameworks of explanation, and unless reasons can be found for choosing between them, both should be rejected as arbitrary personal opinions of no further interest. The reasons must be theoretical, and it is fortunate that as both theories are of the same type, the same rationale applies to both. And according to that rationale, it seems to me to be fairly clear that Weisse is wrong, being guilty of two philosophical errors: he conflates theory and practice, and he confuses a categorial totality with an empirical aggregate.

Although Weisse puts up a smoke-screen by so prominently accusing Hegel of mixing up Beauty and Truth, his unexplained notion of 'sublated Truth' should not blind us to the fact that he is the one who does so. The modern Ideal is not the Concept of Beauty, but the mixture of the Concept of Beauty and the Concept of Truth. If the modern Ideal is self-conscious Beauty, it is Beauty and the theory of Beauty together, a mixture of art and aesthetics. Weisse elevates self-conscious works of art to the status of norms for all art, in the belief that they are pure. As is apparent from the terms with which Weisse himself has to describe them, they are not pure, but theoretical, and not free of any extraneous elements, but shackled to philosophy as an ingredient. Weisse demands of artisitic practice that it contain its own theory, and then calls this hybrid, characteristic of modern art, the realization of the Concept of art. He has shifted the centre towards philosophy, by making practice the unity of theory and practice.

His second mistake is to confuse the existence of limitless diversity with the attainment of a totality of determinations. The realization of the Concept of art is that instance which completely exhausts its determinacy, and so realizes the full potential of art. What Weisse calls 'universality', however, is a very large number of very diverse instances of something, a quantitative aggregate. What he ought to be showing is that each of these instances in itself contains something earlier instances did not have, and is thus a more complete realization of the Concept of art. Instead of looking for the instance which realizes a totality of determinations, Weisse sees an increasing number of instances becoming increasingly diverse, but they can never be a totality, only a set of instances, the limits of which are constantly expanding.

Weisse's mistakes show what happens when a philosopher regresses from systematic thought to 'Vorstellung' and replaces thought with images. The notion that art is 'unfree' when it derives its material from religion in such a case. Excluding all religious and mythological contents from art on the grounds that they are not aesthetic is simply to fail to account for all the forms and contents of art and to restrict arbitrarily the account. But dealing with religious themes does not make art unfree —that is an image. It restricts the choices available to artists, which does not make them unfree either, it just helps them to take a decision about their theme which they always have to take anyway, and guarantees that their theme be substantial and of concern to others. The Hegelian theory is more powerful and more sophisticated; it is able to explain everything Weisse can, and more.

Hegel's conclusion is that art in the modern world is a formal need, not a need of Spirit: there are just new forms, not new contents. There are examples of art from the twentieth century which call this in question, and we have seen that it is the result of a theoretical equivocation. Setting that on one side, we have a powerful and provocative reading of modernity, in which the owl of Minerva on its evening flight seems to have understood what the next day would bring. Hegel was not predicting, but the course taken by art since 1830 does strikingly confirm a lot of his observations. He was not the only one to make them, but it would be fair to regard the *Aesthetics* as the culmination of the reflection on the nature of modern art over the previous fifty years.

If one were to invent a motto to cover what Hegel diagnoses as the end of the romantic art-form, the most appropriate would be 'reflective subjectivity'. The subjectivity which arose with the onset of the romantic art-form has, at its close, become self-aware, self-orientated, and lacking in any allegiance to universally accepted ethical principles. The role of the artist in society has become problematic, for it is not clear what need art fulfils. Hegel contrasts the honour in which Athenian society held Pindar with the shoddy treatment meted out to Klopstock by his publisher (*Ä* III. 441. The example points the difference between Greek 'Sittlichkeit' and modern civil society as the realm of political economy, in which he who pays calls the tune.) The question had become acute by the end of the eighteenth century. In 1781 Mozart left the employment of the Archbishop of Salzburg in an attempt to live independently, and died a pauper ten years later. At the same time, Goethe had completed *Tasso*, one of the first literary works of art to thematize the situation of the artist, a theme which was to become an obsession. As art becomes self-aware, so it thematizes itself, a tendency found in Sterne, and continuing into the present. The artist is an outsider, and so the normal citizen, the bourgeois identified with social substance and accepted ethical principles, becomes a figure of envy or disdain. The artist is either an ambivalent figure (as in Thomas Mann) or superior to others (George, Mallarmé), or inferior (Kafka).

As no particular contents are poetic, everything is potentially art, but everything is equally inimical to it. If it is not possible to represent anything of substance as embodied in reality, art finds its fundamental task of relating Concept and reality rendered difficult if not impossible. The theoretical contrast between art and reality which has always been valid has become a real opposition.[52] If the world is unpoetic, one can either affirm the break, which leads to abstraction, fantasy, and the doctrine of 'l'art pour l'art'; or seek to overcome it by either transforming the banal world into art (as Baudelaire did with his idea of the artist as the alchemist turning the slime of the great city into gold) and thus making art determine reality, or by relying on pure representation, and reflecting the banality of the world in art (naturalism, contemporary super-realism) and thus making reality determine art. The inner world and outer world run their separate courses, the former ending in the late poetry of Paul Celan, the latter in political commitment which places art at the service of the demands of the real. Those who succeed in so mediating these two extremes that they express something universal through their personal, subjective concerns have the status of modern classics (for example Eliot, Mann, Kafka). Hegel describes another sort of mediation which he found exemplified in Rückert and in Goethe's *Divan* as 'objective humour', a type of irony he valued highly, in which the subject succeeds in investing an object with significance ($\ddot{A}$ II. 240). The simple act of representation is enough to lend something interest if it is skilfully done, showing Spirit enjoying a technical triumph of virtuosity over nature ($\ddot{A}$ I. 215–16). Hegel rejects only the form of irony which he regards as having no significant results because it is pure subjectivity, the 'virtuosity of an ironic–artistic life as a *divine genius*, for whom all and sundry are but fleeting shadows' ($\ddot{A}$ I. 95), something he

identifies, rightly or wrongly, with the Romantics.[53] The ironic humour
found in Sterne, on the other hand, is praised ($\ddot{A}$ II. 231). Irony attaches
itself not just to contents but also to forms, as the artist picks out any
attractive form in his 'musée imaginaire', the 'stock of images, procedures, earlier art-forms' ($\ddot{A}$ II. 235) at his disposal, a phenomenon familiar today from the patchwork technique used by Eliot, or Stravinsky's
use of different styles. Hegel makes it clear that the lack of determinate
forms and contents was a problem for the artist. He reports: 'One complaint in particular which one often hears these days, is how difficult it
is to find the sort of material needed for appropriate backgrounds and
situations' ($\ddot{A}$ I. 281). If there is no generally accepted mythology, one
can either try to create one, as Wagner did, or place one's faith exclusively in form, producing 'absolute' art like Mallarmé or Flaubert (who
expressed the wish to write a book about nothing, held together by
nothing but its style), or one can consciously rebel against older forms,
creating a 'permanent revolution'[54] in which something must be new in
order to have any interest. The pursuit of the new and the flight from
boredom itself became a major theme in the nineteenth century (for
instance, in Baudelaire and Huysmans), as art reflected typically on its
own state, even creating an ethos based on art—the Dandy or aesthete,
who, be he Baudelaire or Wilde, reverses the relationship between the
aesthetic and the ethical, and derives the latter from the former.[55] If we
look around a gallery of modern art today, we will find that the trends
Hegel diagnosed have reached a logical conclusion, so that art has turned
into objects, concepts, theories, and happenings. To be art is to make a
claim, the claim that an object or event has meaning. The meaning will
only be apparent to those initiates familiar with the theory behind it,
which is the real soul of the work. The interest of piles of bricks and
heaps of dung in the Tate Gallery is not artistic, but theoretical. The
object is banal; what matters is the interpretation it occasions by virtue
of claiming (by its position in a gallery) to be part of the institution
'art'. Like the Sphinx and the pyramids, Carl André's bricks sit enig-
matically awaiting their interpreter to reveal the soul they contain, its
indeterminate symbolic essence. The end of romantic art is a return to
symbolic art, and all Hegel's theory can do is to iterate itself, for what
matters is not the object, but how the subject interprets it. Thus the
theorist returns to the aesthetic attitude, to Kant's aesthetic judgement,
which is indifferent to its object.[56]

Despite the clear temptation to revise Hegel's analysis in order to
bring it up to date, there have been few serious attempts to develop his

theory into the present.[57] It diagnoses a loss of centre: the links between the work of art and the Ideal are disrupted, art and society enter into a new and problematic relationship, Beauty has a contingent relationship to Truth, which has itself become particular and problematic. But art also moves away from its position as the 'middle' between the mind and the senses, becoming increasingly reflective and theoretical on the one hand, or losing all spiritual significance on the other.[58] That centre is the meeting point of two axes: one is classicism, the central art-form; the other is sculpture, the centre of the arts. To see why sculpture should be the centre we need to examine what Hegel calls the individual arts, and what I have argued should be called the particular arts, the Concept of art in its second moment.

The System of the Arts

Hegel calls the system of the arts a totality ($\ddot{A}$ I. 123), so he must reconstruct them on the basis of a systematic principle, showing why there are the arts there are, and why there are only those. Such speculations have a long and chequered history, their results usually depending on the status of the various arts at different times. Kant still allowed himself to pass judgement on their respective value,[59] but this is something from which Hegel ought to refrain. He must derive the arts from the Concept of art itself, and in considering other attempts, he rejects the diverse principles they use, such as the material of the arts of their relationship to space and time, as abstract ($\ddot{A}$ I. 123).[60] Instead, he deduces them from the art-forms ($\ddot{A}$ I. 124), with results which Weisse called an 'embarrassment', adding that no Hegelian could be so devout as to overlook 'das . . . in sich selbst Haltlose und Willkürliche dieser Anordnung'—'the . . . internal untenability and arbitrariness of this arrangement'.[61] It is hard to disagree.

The very procedure is peculiar. On the one hand, Hegel tries to deduce the moment of individuality (as he sometimes thinks) from the moment of particularity, which is dialectically aberrant: both should be differences in the Concept of art as such. On the other hand, Hegel gives no reasoned deduction at all, but an image—a 'Vorstellung'. He describes the 'world of the arts' built around the god in his temple, worshipped by a community in verse and music ($\ddot{A}$ I. 115-23). It may be awareness of this which lies behind Hegel's use of the phrase 'Übersicht . . . für die Vorstellung' to describe the *Einteilung* (see 'The Moments of Concept' above). The rationale behind the image is to show the statue of the god as the middle, and the rationale behind the use of the art-forms is Hegel's little secret, the correspondence of each art-form with certain arts. Architecture is symbolic, sculpture is classical, painting and music are romantic, and literature corresponds to all three in equal measure. Literature thereby disrupts the schema, as does the fact that painting and music are indistinguishable—that alone is enough to show that the art-forms cannot be the final ground of the differences between the arts. The best Hegel might reasonably hope for is the independent deduction of arts and art-forms and the subsequent observation that there is a parallel in their content. As it is, he maps systematics on to history, producing paradoxes which were first remarked upon by Rosenkranz. For example, architecture is supposed to be symbolic, but it transpires that the realization of its Concept is classical architecture.[62]

Frank Dietrich Wagner has attempted to lend some coherence to Hegel's system of the arts by taking the progression from externality to internality as the ordering principle, with a steady increase in determinacy from architecture to literature, the former being the most abstract, and the latter the most concrete.[63] The problem with this is music: music is very 'inward' (it is non-spatial) but also very abstract. Wagner admits this, but pleads for what he calls a 'change in perspective' brought about because Hegel was concerned to do justice to all aspects of the arts.[64] That is to concede the point, however. The arts cannot be ordered in a line, for there is no single principle from which they can be reconstructed. Hegel's system of the arts pushes a realm of plural determinacy into a linear progression.

The system of the arts ought to give an account of the forms of the material in which art is realized, so that it derives from the Concept of art, and is complete. Hegel's system is obviously incomplete—dance, for example, which was often included in the eighteenth century,[65] is given a perfunctory dismissal as an imperfect 'hybrid', a transitional form which does not exemplify a determination of the Concept ($\ddot{A}$ II. 262-3). It is far from clear what dance is a transition from or transition to; and one is forced to conclude that Hegel is weakly rationalizing his desire to be rid of the subject of dance, of which he had a low opinion ($\ddot{A}$ III. 518). That is no reason to exclude it from art. As Paul Kristeller has shown (note 60), Hegel inherited the five arts he deals with from a particular tradition. They are not a theoretical totality, and in choosing them, Hegel was a son of his time.

It may nevertheless be possible to achieve greater rigour within the

framework of his theory. It follows from the Concept of art that in its
moment of particularity art is spatio-temporally different. Now whereas
there is no limit to the material art could use, there are only a limited
numbers of ways in which it can be determinate with respect to space
and time, so something a priori might be said about that. All the arts
exist through time, but some of them are indifferent to it, and some are
determinate with respect to it. The same applies to space, in two or
three dimensions. It is possible to display all the various possibilities as
shown in the first diagram.

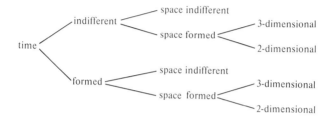

The result is six ways of forming space and time. This means that there
are at least six arts which are distinct from one another by virtue of
their spatio-temporal determinacy. There may well be other distinctions
one would wish to make, but there are certainly these. It is apparent,
for example, that if we reconstruct the arts with the aid of this schema,
naming the six nodes, some of the nodes will have several names. Architecture and sculpture are both indifferent to time, and form space in
three dimensions. This in itself is enough to show that there can be
no a priori reconstruction of the arts based on a single principle, and
spatio-temporality is the only principle which can be derived directly
from the Concept of art as the sensuous reflection of the Idea. Of particular interest is the bottom node, and the forming of time and two-
dimensional space. The forming of space in two dimensions gives
pictures, and if the pictures are also determinate with respect to time,
they must change in it: in other words, there is an art which uses moving
pictures as a medium. The reconstruction is shown in the second
diagram, on the following page.

Film has always been a possible art, with a dignity of its own,
although of course the technical means to produce it have only been

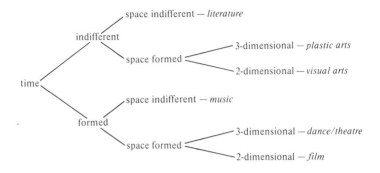

available in this century. Holography has now added the third dimension to film, so that from the spatio-temporal point of view holograms are placed alongside dance and the theatre. They will probably be regarded as a type of film because of the techniques they are able to employ, so one should beware of putting too much emphasis on space and time. However, the schema does vindicate dance as an art which cannot be regarded as a combination of any others, as Hegel suggests. It can also explain a few phenomena which have often been observed. As literature as such is indifferent to space and time, it can be given temporal concretion by being read aloud, or full concretion by being filmed or put on in the theatre. This brings with it greater vividness, but a loss of suggestiveness as space and time are made determinate. It likewise shows why the arts which are temporally determinate can involve music, and the others cannot. There can be no musical accompaniment to a statue, any music played would be 'also going on'. But in the early days of film, a pianist was required to make use of the temporal dimension which was flowing on unused; people had the feeling that in a purely silent film, something was missing. The fascination of mime is that this missing element is not filled in.

Hegel makes some attempt to distinguish the arts by reference to the senses they affect ($\ddot{A}$ II. 254) and also to their material ($\ddot{A}$ II. 259–61). Both are implications of their spatio-temporal determinacy and are thus otiose: for example, painting is two-dimensional, so it appeals to the eye and its material is light; music is purely temporal, so can only use

sounds which appeal to the ear, and so on. The progression from externality to interiority is also an implication of the space-time relations—
the most external arts are the most determinate in spatio-temporal
terms, and with the loss of a dimension goes an increase in interiority,
taking us from the plastic arts to the visual arts, through music to literature.[66] The problem in Hegel's progression is that he equates an increase
in interiority (that is, the loss of a dimension) with an increase in spiritual or intellectual content, and here once more it is music which
disturbs the progression, by being very interior, but lacking determinate
intellectual content. Hegel regards music as verging on triviality, as will
be seen in the next chapter. The correspondence with certain art-forms
is a result of the progression from symbolic externality, through classicism to romantic interiority, which provides a rough parallel. Hegel
draws metaphysical conclusions from this parallel, and tries to say
something a priori about the richness, range, and quality of the arts at
different times, an attempt which is theoretically illegitimate, and a
poor substitute for the complex empirical explanations of the phenomenon which can only be provided by historians. Examples of this will
be found in the next chapter.

What remains to be considered here is the role of sculpture as the
'middle'. Hegel is explicit about this:

Als diese Darstellung des Ideals in seiner dem inneren, wesentlichen
Gehalt dennoch schlechthin gemäßen Äußerlichkeit sind die Skulptur-
bilder der Griechen die Ideale an und für sich, die für sich seienden,
ewigen Gestalten, der Mittelpunkt der plastischen klassischen Schönheit
(*Ä* II. 92).

As this representation of the Ideal in the external form which totally
corresponds to its essential inner content, the sculptural works of the
Greeks are the Ideals in and for themselves, figures which are for themselves and eternal, the middle-point of plastic classical beauty.

This is a theoretical claim, and clearly has nothing to do with Hegel's
personal preferences. He seems himself to have been far more interested
in literature than sculpture, and remarks at one point that it is hard to
appreciate classical Greek sculpture because it is not congenial to
modern taste (*Ä* III. 17).[67] Hegel's view of sculpture lies deep in the
theory as a consequence of his Concept of Beauty and its relation to
Truth. It is a view which is as much ethical as aesthetic, and as much
about man as about art. If Hegel had a vision, this was it:

Die *Mitte*, das eigentlich gediegene Zentrum, bildet hier die Darstellung des *Absoluten*, des Gottes selbst als Gottes, in seiner *Selbstständigkeit* für sich noch nicht zur Bewegung und Differenz entwickelt und zur Handlung und Besonderung seiner fortgehend, sondern in sich abgeschlossen in großartiger Ruhe und Stille. (*Ä* II. 257.)

The *middle*, the true solid centre, is formed here by the representation of the *Absolute*, of the god himself as god, in his *autonomy* for himself, not yet developed into movement and difference nor particularizing himself through action, but complete in himself, in magnificent calm and quiet.

The final words echo Winckelmann's famous phrase 'edle Einfalt und stille Größe'.[68] It is a vision of man at home in the world, of the soul resting in a body to which it uniquely belongs, and through which it manifests itself (cf. *Ä* I. 115). The Divine does not enter the world to suffer in it and leave it, but to enjoy its pleasures and remain. It is mind entering material to create art.

Sculpture is the complete forming of three-dimensional space, so that organic, and not just geometrical forms can be represented. It can therefore represent individuality, and is the first art in which the human subject can be represented in the full spatiality in which he in fact is, in his full physical presence. Sculpture is also indifferent to time, so it can show the human figure removed from transience and given universality by being fixed in a position free of any context or particular situation, as potential activity. In sculpture, therefore, mind forms matter so as to represent that agent which is its own material embodiment— man; and it represents him in his universality as unchanging. It is thus a representation of the principle of which it is an instance, the art which shows what art is, by showing what man is: the unity of body and soul. By being man's literal self-reflection, sculpture is art's self-reflection: the sculpted human figure both is itself, and represents, what both man and art are—the unity of body and soul, of Concept and reality.

This is of course a particular view of the world of art, which arose under particular cultural and intellectual circumstances in Germany at the beginning of the last century. It soon gave way to a view of art orientated around music rather than sculpture, a view which gained dominance through the writings of the Romantics, Schopenhauer, and Nietzsche, and echoed as far abroad as Pater and the French symbolist poets.[69] Hegel would not only not have been disturbed by this, he would have been able to say 'I told you so.' Modernity has moved away from the centre, and naturally finds the subjective art of music more to its taste, for it is looking for pure interiority. In a sense,

Schopenhauer and Nietzsche confirm Hegel by opposing him.

That does not eliminate the particularity of the Hegelian centre. Behind it there is a 'we' of reflective, critical, educated people who believe they have good taste because their taste is rational. They and their descendants, the journalists, academics, and critics who influence the norms of taste today, are prepared to reject certain artistic products because they are not self-reflective as modern art should be, and call them 'Kitsch'.[70] Kitsch is characterized by all the things Hegel rejects: arbitrariness, the loss of substance, the erosion of individuality by repetition, and the inappropriateness of form and content. Accordingly, it does not reflect the self-understanding of modern intellectuals, and by their rational criteria it is bad art. However, the lost centre was also a moral centre, and in a society which is no longer a small, tightly knit organic whole like ancient Athens, but a vast, sprawling, complex, pluralist conglomerate like the societies of the industrial West today, there are only particular views. Hermann Broch was therefore quite right to say that in condemning kitsch, one is condemning the 'Kitsch-Mensch' who actively likes, seeks out, and buys bad art.[71] It will be difficult to prove to him that he is wrong, because he will not accept the criteria by which he is judged. Tell him the film bringing tears to his eyes is sentimental, and he will say that he is sentimental; tell him his garden gnomes are childishly inappropriate, and he will say he is childish, and add in both cases that there is nothing wrong with that. The aesthetic is parasitic upon the ethical, Beauty is Beauty only with reference to a certain conception of Truth, a set of values and beliefs, and a form of life. We have lost the centre, and may not regret it, but what has been lost is a form of social life as much as a form of art. Whatever we may think of the Ideal centre, whether we yearn for it or are bored by it, respect it or think it an irrelevance, Apollo's message to us is clear and uncompromisingly consistent; 'Du mußt dein Leben ändern.'

Part Two:
INSTANCES

Er meinte, wenn die Philosophie es sich zur Pflicht mache, auch auf die
Sachen und Gegenstände, welche sie behandelt, Rücksicht zu nehmen,
so dürfte sie um so wirksamer werden, je mehr sie freilich auch mit den
Empirikern zu tun bekomme; nur werde immer die Frage entstehen, ob
es zugleich möglich sei, ein großer Forscher und Beobachter und auch
ein bedeutender Verallgemeinerer und Zusammenfasser zu sein . . . Er
traue Hegel zwar sehr viel Kenntnisse in der Natur wie in der Geschichte
zu, ob aber seine philosophischen Gedanken sich nicht immer nach den
neuen Entdeckungen, die man doch stets machen würde, modifizieren
müßten und dadurch selber ihr Kategorisches verlören, könne er zu
fragen nicht unterlassen.

Goethe, as reported by Eduard Gans, from a conversation of
28 August 1827.

3

FROM ARCHITECTURE TO MUSIC: OPENING UP THE INTERIOR

To complete our account of Hegel's theory of art, we have now to consider how he gives the determination of each of the five particular arts in his system, and how he uses examples to illustrate his principles. This will mean examining Hegel as a historian and critic, as philosophical discourse cannot instantiate principles, it can only say what an instance would be (see 'The Moments of Concept', chapter 2 above). It has been suggested that such was Hegel's incompetence in matters of empirical judgement, it is not worth while undertaking this task.[1] This view is too simple, if only because it naïvely assumes that we are in a position to pass judgement on his judgements. Rather than finding out whether Hegel was progressive enough to anticipate the conventional wisdom of the late twentieth century, I will try to establish why he said what he did, and whether, on the basis of his principles, he could have said anything else; in other words, the attempt will be made to see where theory ends and judgement begins, and whether the theory provides a satisfactory rationale for the judgements.

This chapter will follow the succession of the arts from architecture to music as expounded in the third part of the *Aesthetics*, the *System der einzelnen Künste*. This maps out a journey into the interior with the gradual elimination of spatial dimensions (see 'The System of the Arts', chapter 2 above). The first problem is why architecture should be the first of the arts.

Architecture

The first question Hegel faces in the system of the arts is how his discussion is to begin, and the first thing he says about that is what it means for architecture to be the first of the arts:

so muß dies nicht nur den Sinn haben, daß sich die Architektur als diejenige Kunst hinstelle, welche sich durch die Begriffsbestimmung als die zuerst zu betrachtende ergebe, sondern es muß sich ebensosehr zeigen, daß sie auch als die der *Existenz* nach erste Kunst abzuhandeln sei (*Ä* II. 266).

this should not simply be taken to mean that architecture is to be dealt with first because of its determination; it must equally well be shown that it comes first because it was the first art to *exist*.

One might suppose this to mean that architecture is not just the art to come first systematically, by virtue of being the most external and abstract, but was also the first actually to come into existence. However, the next sentence, whilst affirming that the beginning will be 'dem Begriffe und der Realität zufolge'–'according to its Concept and reality', asserts that the matter can be decided without reference to 'das empirisch Geschichtliche'–'empirical history'. So it seems that when Hegel claims that architecture was the first art to come into existence, he does not mean anything historical. That being so, it is far from clear what he does mean, and far from clear why the question of existence should matter at all.

In the next paragraph it is dropped, and the issue of a systematic starting-point is taken up. Hegel does not want to use an anecdote or 'Vorstellung' about the beginning of art such as the famous one in Pliny[2] which explains the origins of painting with a story about a girl tracing her lover's shadow (*Ä* II. 267). This story is not historical, but neither is it systematic. Hegel needs to find the point at which man organizes the material of nature so as to imbue it with significance, making it into a work of art (ibid.). This would indeed be a systematic starting-point, but again Hegel adds that it is found with architecture, 'welche ihre erste Ausbildung früher gefunden hat als die Skulptur oder Malerei und Musik'–'which first developed earlier than sculpture or painting and music' (ibid.). The explanation of Hegel's equivocations thus appears to be that he typically equates a systematic beginning with a historical one, the equation bedevilling the whole of 'Realphilosophie'.

The deduction of the Concept of architecture as the beginning of art takes a circuitous route. Hegel takes the house and the temple to be the simplest forms of building, and then says that both are merely means to an end which lies outside art, the satisfaction of basic human needs (*Ä* II. 268). The house serves man, the temple serves a god. He then argues that because of this separation of end and means, neither the house nor the temple can be the beginning of art, for two reasons: the separation implies a relation, and therefore mediation, whereas a beginning must be immediate; and art can only be an end in itself. The beginning must therefore be found in works which go behind the means/ end distinction, by having their ends in themselves, like sculptures, and he accordingly calls the type of independent architecture he has in mind 'unorganische Skulptur'–'inorganic sculpture' ($\ddot{A}$ II. 270). As the meaning of these works can only be indicated symbolically, architecture is a symbolic art ($\ddot{A}$ II. 269).

There are two major problems with all this. First of all, it is very dubious whether the means/end distinction is valid in the case of architecture, for it is distinguished from the other arts precisely in being functional. The purpose of a building is fully relevant to its aesthetic appraisal, for what may be a good church may not be a good railway station, and Hegel tacitly admits this by his use of the house and the temple as basic types, a distinction which is functional.[3] The function of a building is not irrelevant to its design. Secondly, by starting with sculptural architecture, Hegel produces three paradoxes: he pushes the whole of architecture away from its centre towards sculpture; he begins with what, on his own terms, he ought to end with–architecture which is half-way towards sculpture and thus a transition to it; and it transpires that although architecture as such is supposed to be symbolic, the Concept of architecture is only realized in classicism–only classical architecture is really symbolic![4]

The rationale for the division of the subject is the means/end relation. We are to begin with independent architecture which is an end in itself and without a function; the second type is the diremption of end and means in purely functional building; the third is the synthesis of the two, a type as independent and sculptural as the first, but which is also functional ($\ddot{A}$ II. 270-1). The illustrations of these types are Egyptian, Greek, and Gothic, so that they follow the real chronological order. What follows is mainly cultural history, ordered according to a systematic rationale which collapses from the very outset.

Hegel begins with independent symbolic architecture, which is an end in itself, and therefore without any function. He promptly admits that it does have a function, the religious one of being a unifying point for a nation, and this is, furthermore, the very same function shared by classical and romantic architecture. In each case Hegel argues that the aesthetic qualities of the buildings are related to their function and the beliefs of the communities which erect them, so the distinctions he is trying to make are eliminated. The division of the section on symbolic architecture also highlights the inadequacy of his placing of it: only three pages are devoted to 'works built to unify nations' ($\ddot{A}$ II. 276-8);

the rest is divided between 'works which are half-way between architecture and sculpture' (pp. 279-88) and 'the transition to classical architecture' (pp. 288-302). Most of the examples he gives are not works of architecture at all, but statues (he repeatedly uses the term 'Memnonstatuen', for example on p. 281) which indicates that although architecture is symbolic, symbolic architecture is half-sculptural. True architecture (die eigentliche Architektur) is classical ($\ddot{A}$ II. 296, 298), so that although its fundamental character is symbolic (p. 271), the Concept of architecture is only realized in classical art (p. 303). This incoherence results from Hegel's desire to map the arts on to art-forms, and make history and systematics correspond.

The account of symbolic architecture is filled up with summaries of authorities, prominent amongst whom is Herodotus, and is consequently of little interest. Most of Hegel's reporting appears to be accurate, but he does seem to confuse Herodotus' reports on the temples of Bel at Is and at Babylon (compare $\ddot{A}$ II. 277-8 with Herodotus, *The Histories*, Book I, 181-4). Hegel had the misfortune to die just before the publication of Champollion's *Grammaire égyptienne* and *Dictionnaire égyptien* in 1832, so he espouses a view of Egyptian culture as a religion dominated by mystery, a view far more plausible before Champollion deciphered the Rosetta stone than it is today. The only explorers Hegel mentions are the adventurers Denon and Belzoni who were active at the turn of the century ($\ddot{A}$ II. 293, 300). Serious Egyptology did not begin until the expedition led by Richard Lepsius in 1842, and scientific excavation not until the expeditions of W. M. F. Petrie in the 1880s.[5]

One thing which interests Hegel a good deal about the ancient Egyptians is the idea, found in Herodotus (Book II, 122), that they were the first to believe in the immortality of the soul, and this leads him on to discuss the pyramid. He reinterprets the separation of body and soul in architectural terms, the pyramid being the body enclosing the mummy inside it, which is its soul. He links this with his semiotic image, calling the soul the meaning and the body the sign, and this provides a transition to the classical temple, which is the functional house around the soul of the god within ($\ddot{A}$ II. 291-2, 296-8).[6] The beauty of classical architecture is said to consist in the appropriateness with which it fulfils its function, a function which is made manifest in all its forms, but is external to it ($\ddot{A}$ II. 302-3). If it is indeed the case that classical architecture 'clearly reflects its single end through all its forms', one wonders how Hegel can simultaneously say that it is an end 'which it does not have in itself' (ibid.). He lends some plausibility to his description by juxtaposing several images: end and means are reinterpreted as meaning and expression and as signified and signifier. The soul of the temple is the god inside it, which is its end and its meaning (see *Ä* II. 268, 303-4). One might therefore describe classical architecture as follows:

der Mittelpunkt der Verehrung ist ein Subjekt, ein individueller Gegenstand, der für sich selbst bedeutend erscheint und sich selber ausdrückt, unterschieden von seiner Behausung, die somit als bloß dienende Hülle konstruiert wird (*Ä* II. 292).

the central point of worship is a subject, an individual object, which has meaning in itself and expresses itself, and which is distinct from its dwelling, constructed merely as an ancillary covering.

This would be an accurate description of the statue of the god standing independently of the building, the only function of which is to house it. In fact, it is Hegel's description of the Egyptian houses of the dead. The distinctions he tries to make are artificial, for the end/means relation is the same in every case, and the distinction between symbolic and classical architecture collapses.

At the heart of the problem lies the semiotic interpretation of the pyramid which offers Hegel an equivocation he is able, wittingly or unwittingly, to exploit. The pyramid is a sign, because what is inside it (the mummy) is completely unrelated to its external appearance (the pyramid itself); in other words, there is complete indifference between signifier and signified. As a sign, the pyramid has a meaning, which is: to be the alien external body of a soul. Its meaning is therefore: to be a sign; so the pyramid is the sign of its own meaning. However, this implies that its meaning and its appearance are not indifferent, but related, and in that case, the pyramid is not just a sign but a symbol. By virtue of being the specific sign it is, it is the symbol of what it is to be a sign at all. Because of this, Hegel is able at one time to stress the indifference between signifier and signified and treat the pyramid as a sign, which is what he does when discussing it as a work of architecture (the stone construction bears no relation to the mummy inside it); and at another time he stresses the identity of signifier and signified, treating the pyramid as a symbol, and says that it has its end in itself (because it is its own meaning). The paradoxes do not end here, for Hegel draws attention to the fact that the soul of the pyramid is not a soul at all, but a dead body (*Ä* II. 292). The pyramid is in fact a body around a body, a sign without a meaning, a 'significant' whose 'signifié' is absent.[7]

The dual role of the pyramid means that as a sign it is in fact the paradigm of classical architecture, the functional house ($\ddot{A}$ II. 305-6); but of course it is also a symbol, so it cannot be classical. The final twist to the series of paradoxes is that the real difference between the pyramid and the classical temple is that the purpose of the former is not apparent from its form, whereas the purpose of the temple (allegedly) is (pp. 302-3). If that is so, it would be a reason to say that classical, not symbolic, architecture has its end in itself, an end which is apparent from its appearance. And indeed this is precisely what Hegel is at pains to emphasize. The classical temple is not merely functional, but 'a totality complete in itself' (p. 303), the proportions of the classical column are 'immanent' to it (p. 312), and Roman villas and palaces are criticized for being dominated by functionality so that beauty is merely decorative (p. 305). One might characterize the results of Hegel's deliberations on classical architecture by saying:

So erweisen sich denn diese Gotteshäuser und Bauwerke überhaupt für den Kultus und anderweitigen Gebrauch ... als schlechthin zweckgemäß, aber ihr eigentlicher Charakter liegt gerade darin, über jeden bestimmten Zweck fortzugehen und als in sich abgeschlossen für sich dazusein. ($\ddot{A}$ II. 331.)

So these temples and buildings can be seen to be perfectly suitable for religious practice and other uses . . . but their true character consists precisely in going beyond every specific end, and standing complete for themselves.

These words, however, apply to romantic (Gothic) architecture. There is furthermore no reason why they should not apply to symbolic architecture too. The whole section on architecture, which is prima facie quite coherent, is probably the most fundamentally confused in the whole of the *Aesthetics*, and the equivocations continue with the notion of 'Zweckmäßigkeit' which serves as a motto for classical building.

Hegel's use of 'Zweckmäßigkeit' covers two senses. One is the sense of 'appropriateness', and refers to the appearance of a building, the aesthetic effect of its internal teleology. This is no more than a limited case of the notion of systematic coherence Hegel uses to explain aesthetic excellence in general: each element of the building should look appropriate in relation to the other elements. The other sense is that of 'purposiveness', and this does not refer to the appearance of a building, but to the appropriateness with which the building as a whole fulfils its function. Hegel links these two senses by an argument he never states, but which must run like this: the classical temple is purely purposive, so it fulfils its function as a house of a god with complete appropriateness; therefore, each element of the temple is designed to fulfil a function, and does so appropriately (that is, each element is fully determined by its structural function); therefore, the building as a whole, and each of its elements, looks appropriate and has a satisfying aesthetic effect. Each step is a *non sequitur*. Nothing about the elements of a temple follows from the functionality of the whole—the criticism of Roman architecture was precisely that it is 'useful' but without internal coherence. And even if each element is structurally necessary, it does not follow that the building will look harmonious. For example, if one is using a very strong material, it may be possible to use very thin columns to support a weight, but the result may look unstable, even though it is not.

In characterizing Greek architecture, Hegel slides from one of these things to another, and contradicts himself in doing so, as for example in his account of the column. Whereas the function of a wall is to support and enclose, he observes, the column has the unique function of supporting ($\ddot{A}$ II. 309–10).[8] The height and thickness of columns will therefore be dependent on the weight they bear, and they must be seen to be of the appropriate dimensions: 'den Anblick der Zweckmäßigkeit gewähre[n]' (p. 310), meaning that it must look right to the observer. Because the column's length is not arbitrary, it lies within its Concept to begin and end at certain points, and for this reason it is given a base and capital, distinguishing it from a stake or post (ibid.). What Hegel is demanding here is not, despite his protestations, functionality, but the appearance of functionality as an aesthetic effect. The column would, on Hegel's account, still be 'zweckmäßig' without a base and capital if it supported the weight it was designed to carry; it would lack only the appearance of functionality. Hegel's argument about functions reduces the base and capital to decorations of the column to emphasize its carrying function; the irony is that the capital had an important structural function, acting as a bracket to concentrate the load of the entablature on the column.[9] By using 'Zweckmäßigkeit' to designate aesthetic effects, Hegel undermines his reading of Greek architecture as 'zweckmäßig' in the sense of 'purposive'. The roof is another example: Hegel says that in southern climes, where it does not rain, roofs could be flat, but the Greeks pitched theirs in order to make it clear that the function of a roof is to be carried without carrying anything itself (Ä II. 314). Needless to say, the sun does not always shine in Greece, and roofs were indeed pitched to allow rain-water to flow off. Hegel seems prepared to go to great lengths in order to show that the function of each aspect of the building plays no role at all, and that the Greeks were concerned solely with how it looked. 'Zweck-mäßigkeit' as 'appropriateness' is what counts, and it loses touch with its second meaning of 'purposiveness'. His case could be much stronger, but often, as here, he misses the true structural function. Engaged columns (columns attached to a wall) are rejected because walls support and enclose, and columns only support, and so, despite their extensive use from early times, they are dismissed for a priori reasons which are spectacularly bad:

dennoch aber sind Halbsäulen schlechthin widerlich, weil dadurch zweierlei *entgegengesetzte* Zwecke ohne innere Notwendigkeit neben-einanderstehen und sich mit einander *vermischen* (Ä II. 316).

but nevertheless half columns are offensive in principle, because they allow two *opposed* purposes to come together without any inner necessity, and be *mixed* with each other.

Of course, the purposes are by no means opposed—they are just differ-ent. If Hegel's argument were correct, walls, which enclose and carry, ought to be offensive too. Once more, the Greeks used engaged columns structurally, to narrow a span, as well as for mock colonnades.[10] Hegel quotes the young Goethe's *Von deutscher Baukunst* in support, unaware that Goethe changed his mind later when he saw some engaged columns in Palladio's villas at Vicenza. Though resistant, Goethe allows his eye to be cajoled, typically allowing the evidence of his senses to triumph over doctrine.[11] It is also typical that Hegel is dogmatic when his argu-ment is bad, as if he knew it. Had he followed through the principle of purposiveness, it might have occurred to him that engaged columns can have a specific function.

As in the case of symbolic architecture, most of Hegel's descriptions are derived from sources, in this case mainly Vitruvius and Hirt.[12] His conception of classicism is entirely Greek, with no mention of the Renaissance, and no reference to theorists as important as Bramante, Alberti, and Palladio. Nor does he exploit and develop points which have theoretical significance. He mentions, for example, that both architecture and music rely on 'a harmony of relationships, which are derived from numbers' (Ä II. 305–6). The connection between these two arts and mathematics is very ancient, and has played an important role in architectural theory and practice, so it is surprising and regrettable that Hegel does not have more to say on the matter.[13] His reference to eurhythmy is similarly lapidary. He simply mentions 'eine geheime Eurhythmie, welche der richtige Sinn der Griechen vornehmlich heraus-gefunden hat . . .'—'a mysterious eurhythmy, discovered above all by the sound instincts of the Greeks' ($\ddot{A}$ II. 306). This statement fits in with Hegel's belief, common at the time, that the Greeks were an instinctual people, but far from being a secret discovered intuitively, eurhythmy was one of the six cardinal principles of ancient architecture, and was derived from the precise observation and measurement of the human body. The description of these principles and their relation to the human form is one of the most celebrated passages in Vitruvius, of which Hegel can hardly have been ignorant.[14] Despite this evidence, the desire to see the Greeks as penetrating by instinct things which are mysterious to us was too strong for him.

Hegel never went to Egypt, Greece, or even Rome, but in describing the Gothic cathedral as the pre-eminent example of romantic architec-ture, he could speak from first-hand experience. He refers to no auth-orities, and although what he says is very general, he does mention some individual works, in contrast to the section on classicism.[15] His eyes are those of a layman, but he shows how far the understanding of Gothic has come since the eighteenth century, when the style was scorned. It is striking how much more interesting and illuminating Hegel is when he does rely on himself rather than authorities.

Hegel describes the exterior of the cathedral as combining a single upward movement with detailed particularization of the surface, and refers to the general effect as one of eurhythmy, which indicates how loosely he understood the term ($\ddot{A}$ II. 331-2).[16] The interior is designed to exclude nature, even to the extent of having stained glass to trans-form natural light ($\ddot{A}$ II. 333).[17] The result is a world in which the in-dividual can turn in on himself, and reflect at the same time on the magnificence of the house of God.[18] In contrast to classical style, there is no emphasis on the supporting function of columns; instead they soar upwards to enclose space like the trees of a forest ($\ddot{A}$ II. 335). The materiality of the stone is almost eliminated through the decorations and windows, and the thinness and precision of the walls and columns ($\ddot{A}$ II. 345-6). The cathedral was not just the place where the individual could find 'composure of mind', but was also the centre of communal life and day-to-day business, the focal point of ethical substance ($\ddot{A}$ II. 340-1).

Hegel is able to recognize how the elements of Gothic style fit together and cohere. He relates the various elements of the style so that their significance is shown, and it is possible to appreciate the aesthetic effect of the whole. Almost everything he points out has become a commonplace in writing about the great cathedrals, but in the 1820s he had few precedents.[19] The historical significance of this section on architecture is that the classical and Gothic styles are placed alongside each other and their differences described without being evaluated. Consider the observation that in Gothic the eye is led upwards, whereas in the case of a Greek temple it is not ($\ddot{A}$ II. 333). This describes a difference in the buildings, without an attempt to show that one is better, and for Hegel to be wrong about the presence or absence of upward movement would be comparable to mistaking a circle for a triangle. Elements can be related in different ways, which is why interpretations and explanations are different. Evaluations, based on ethical values, are notoriously variable. But there is a degree of cognition involved in understanding art which gives a rational foundation to the discourse of art-criticism. The well-known puzzle shape which looks like a duck or a rabbit depending on how it is seen and understood, shows amongst other things how difficult it would be to see it as a cat. Hegel's description of the Gothic cathedral, unscholarly as it is, gives some idea of what genuine aesthetic description could be.

Sculpture

The move from architecture to sculpture is the move from mechanics to biology, from the inorganic to the organic, but within all three dimensions of space:

Die Skulptur im allgemeinen faßt das Wunder auf, daß der Geist dem ganz Materiellen sich einbildet und diese Äußerlichkeit so formiert, daß er in ihr sich selber gegenwärtig wird und die gemäße Gestalt seines eigenen Inneren darin erkennt ($\ddot{A}$ II. 362).

Sculpture in general shows the miracle of Spirit entering what is purely material, and forming this externality in such a way that Spirit is present to itself in it, recognizing in such externality the appropriate form for its own inner nature.

Sculpture is in fact distinguished from architecture in Hegel's account solely by its capacity to represent organic forms, which is why the geometrical pyramid is not sculpture. It is apparent from the section on architecture that he does not properly distinguish the two, as he equates having an end in itself with looking like a statue. It is curious to note that although Hegel never mentions the position of buildings as a matter of any importance, he does mention its relevance to works of sculpture ($\ddot{A}$ II. 352). The surroundings of a temple or cathedral are certainly as important to its aesthetic effect as is the position of a sculpture, and furthermore, a building cannot be moved. Hegel's reason for referring to the matter may be his regret that C. F. Tieck's Apollo, which he had seen and admired in the atelier, could not be properly appreciated in position on the 'Schauspielhaus' in Berlin. He contrasts it with Schadow's famous Victory on the Brandenburg Gate, which he says was designed more carefully with its intended position in mind, and given simpler, bolder outlines than the Apollo ($\ddot{A}$ II. 435–6).

In distinguishing sculpture from painting, Hegel argues that it is relatively abstract, and introduces the idea that sculpture should be colourless, because it shows only the form of the human body:

ihre Formen erhalten keine Mannigfaltigkeit von partikularisierten Farben und Bewegungen. Dies ist aber kein zufälliger Mangel, sondern ein durch den Begriff der Kunst selbst gesetzte Beschränkung des Materials und der Darstellungsweise. ($\ddot{A}$ II. 355.)

its forms are without the internal differentiation which comes from particularized colours and movements. This is no chance defect, but a limitation of the material and manner of representation posited by the Concept of art itself.

This is Hegel's main systematic claim, and it is expounded in a systematic context before he tries to instantiate it. He is out to say what is sculptural about sculpture, and the leitmotiv of his account is the lack of particularization through colour and movement. The centre of sculpture is a human figure which is colourless, motionless, and sightless—a headless marble torso in fact.

Hegel's attitude to colour is peculiar, as his arguments slide from systematic to empirical ones. He states first of all that as sculpture reveals forms to the eye through pure light unmixed with darkness, it will be colourless ($\ddot{A}$ II. 356). This strange statement becomes comprehensible against the background of Goethe's theory of colour, to which Hegel was deeply attached, and which explains colours as the mixing of light and dark. That apart, sculpture cannot appeal to pure light, for if it is three-dimensional it will involve shadows. As Hegel elaborates his point, things become clearer; what he objects

to is the use of paint. He does not say this first of all, but simply
states:

Das Skulpturbild ist im ganzen einfarbig, aus weißem Marmor gefertigt,
nicht aus vielfarbig buntem. (*Ä* II. 358.)

The sculpted figure is entirely of one colour, being made of white,
rather than variegated coloured marble.

The status of this claim is unclear, but it cannot be empirical. Hegel
well knew that the Greeks, not to mention medieval and Baroque
sculptors, produced many polychromatic works, amongst which were
some of Phidias' most celebrated masterpieces. In confronting this fact,
Hegel makes it clear that what he really wants to do is to exclude the
painterly use of colour from the Concept of sculpture:

Gegen die bloße Einfarbigkeit des Marmors lassen sich freilich nicht
nur die vielen Statuen aus Erz, sondern mehr noch die größten und
vortrefflichsten Werke anführen, welche, wie z.B. der Zeus des Phidias,
mehrfarbig waren. Doch von solcher äußersten Abstraktion der Farb-
losigkeit ist auch nicht die Rede; Elfenbein und Gold aber sind immer
noch kein malerischer Gebrauch von Farben. (*Ä* II. 359.)

Examples can be adduced against plain marble, including not only the
many statues in bronze, but some of the greatest and finest works, such
as the Zeus of Phidias, which were polychromatic. But what is at issue
is not the extreme abstraction of colourlessness; adding ivory and gold
is still not to use colours like a painter.

This claim is systematic. Hegel wishes to avoid pushing sculpture too
far towards painting, and says no more than that a sculpture can be
perfectly satisfying without the use of colour as a painter uses it, because
what is sculptural is the organization of forms, not the colouring of
surfaces. The separateness of the two activities is confirmed by the division of labour customary in ancient Greece: Pliny tells how Praxiteles
most valued those works of his which had been painted by Nikias,
showing how the sculpting and painting of figures were quite distinct
activities.[20] However, the theoretical requirement that sculpture be distinguished from painting is also interpreted empirically, as if the Greeks
did not paint their statuary out of a desire to mark off systematic
limits. The ideal of white marble is in fact a Renaissance conception
thoroughly alien to the Greeks, who painted their stone figures, used
tinted marble, and gilded their more numerous bronzes.[21]

   The blindness of sculpture is connected with its lack of colour,
for the eye is an organ which is differentiated purely by colour, and

therefore poses a problem for the sculptor.[22] Hegel has his own reasons for keeping sculpture sightless: as the eye is a short-cut to the soul's interior, it cannot appear in sculpture which is only the first milestone along that road—every point of the sculpted surface is an eye, so the illusion of a real eye on the figure would be a distraction (*Ä* II. 357). The minimal systematic claim being made here is that sculpture does not need the detail of the eye, and can in this respect be contrasted with painting: a portrait painting with blank eyes would have a peculiar and disturbing effect, whereas a portrait bust would not.[23] There are numerous examples of sculptures from all times in which the eyes are left blank. However, there are also many examples of the eyes being painted on, and the Greeks usually either did this, or inset them with gems and precious metals, as Hegel is well aware (*Ä* II. 388). He dismisses this fact with the observation that these techniques are not enough to lend the eyes the intensity of full expression, and then insists on what he wants with the sort of dogmatism which has got him a bad name. He shifts levels by deducing empirical facts from theoretical principles:

Wir können es deshalb hier als ausgemacht ansehen, daß an den wahrhaften klassischen und freien Statuen und Büsten, die aus dem Altertum auf uns gekommen sind, der Augenstern sowie der geistige Ausdruck des Blicks fehlt . . . Und dieses Seelenvollste muß die Skulptur entbehren . . . Die Skulptur hat die Totalität der äußerlichen Gestalt zum Zweck . . . so daß ihr die Zurückführung auf den einen einfachen Seelenpunkt und die Augenblicklichkeit des Blicks nicht erlaubt ist. (*Ä* II. 389–90.)

For our purposes we can thus regard it as settled that all the true, classical, and free statues and busts which have come down to us from Antiquity are without pupils, and lack any expression of spirituality in their gaze . . . And this, the clearest expression of the soul, sculpture has to do without . . . The purpose of sculpture is the totality of the external figure . . . so that it cannot allow itself to reveal the soul at just one single point or fix a momentary glance.

This is an example of level confusion, whereby an a priori principle becomes an empirical prescription: we move from the idea that sculpture does not need to detail the eye to the assertion that the Greeks did not in fact allow themselves this superfluous detail in their 'truly classical' works. Hegel wants things to be like that because it fits in with his belief about cultural history: the Greeks were not spiritual and interior enough to put eyes into their statues, only Christians could have thought of doing so, because only they have the requisite souls.

However, having expressed his beliefs, Hegel elaborates his original systematic point—'entbehrt die Skulptur nicht nur nichts durch die Blicklosigkeit ihrer Gestalten' ('not only does sculpture not lose anything because of the sightlessness of its figures')—by adding a further one: 'sondern sie *muß* ihrem ganzen Standpunkte nach diese Art des Seelenausdrucks fehlen lassen'—'but by virtue of its whole position, it *must* leave out this sort of inner expression' (*Ä* II. 390). This suggests that the 'muß' does not mean 'should', but 'cannot help'; in other words, whatever the sculptor does, the eyes of a sculpture will lack something because they are in principle sightless. The significance of this can again be seen by comparing sculpture with painting. A painter can represent the play of light on the eye and use it to convey a wide variety of emotions, so that the viewer can be made to feel that he is making eye-contact with a portrait. The sculptor cannot do this, which is why Greek sculptors used a convention of body positions to indicate emotions.[24] Statues invariably stare whether eyes are carved or not, because the effects of light on the eyeball cannot be represented sculpturally. Wittkower has pointed out that the expression achieved through a carved eye is one of determination and will-power, and Michelangelo and Bernini used it accordingly, otherwise leaving the eyeball blank.[25] When Hegel does not draw conclusions about empirical facts from his principles, the systematic points he makes usually make sense.

What Hegel has to say about the movement of figures seems to single out the position associated with Polyklitos as the 'middle'. He picks out the upright posture of humans as the best for sculpture because it shows the body subject to the will, and goes on to reject the stiff, straight arm and leg position of the early archaic 'kouroi' for a similar reason—they show no 'spiritual determination from within' (*Ä* II. 398). The movement must be enough to individualize, but, in the case of the gods, not so much as to disturb their calm. Hegel has room for two specifications: the gods should be involved in some action peculiar to them, either beginning or ending a movement, so that they look as if they could stay in that position for ever; and more human figures can be frozen in the middle of some action, showing 'fleeting moments captured from nature, and given permanence by the sculptor' (*Ä* II. 432; cf. *Ä* I. 262-6, *Ä* II. 396-401). The middle would then be a figure which is 'establishing a point of balance',[26] and this fits the pose most often used by Polyklitos in the fifth century BC. On the one side of the ideal are the hieratic figures of the archaic period, and on the other the sometimes dynamic figures of the later Hellenistic style.

Hegel identifies sculpture almost exclusively with the ancient Greeks. That he does so is a result of the doctrine of the art-forms, and one can distinguish three lines of thought: first, as we have already seen, the belief that Greek religion gave sculpture a privileged role; second, the idea that Greek culture in general gave particular encouragement to sculpture; and third, that the quality and quantity of their production was, as a result, unique. The classical art-form is the sculptural art-form *par excellence*, an idea which can be traced through Hegel's use of the word 'plastisch'.

'Plastisch' is the key to Hegel's vision of Greece, and he uses it in an ethical sense to characterize a human ideal. Pericles, Phidias, Plato, Sophocles, Thucydides, Xenophon, and Socrates are 'plastisch', that is to say 'universal and yet individual':

ideale Künstler ihrer selbst, Individuen aus *einem* Guß, Kunstwerke, die wie unsterbliche todlose Götterbilder dastehen, an welchen nichts Zeitliches und Todwürdiges ist (*Ä* II. 374).

ideal artists of themselves, individuals of *one* mould, works of art, standing like immortal, deathless images of the gods, beyond the reach of death and temporality.

The term 'aus einem Guß' is taken from metal casting, it being a mark of particular skill to be able to cast a bronze statue in one piece without the need for further work with the chisel (cf. *Ä* II. 441–2). The one other case in which Hegel uses a similar expression is in referring to Murillo's beggar boys: they are 'Menschen aus *einem* Stück, ohne Verdrießlichkeit und Unfrieden in sich . . . zufrieden und selig fast wie die olympischen Götter'—'of *one* piece, without moroseness, and at peace with themselves . . . happy and contented almost like the Olympian gods' (*Ä* I. 224). Being 'plastisch' or 'aus einem Guß' means being complete and three-dimensional, as opposed to the fragmented, one-dimensional modern,[27] being at home in the world as opposed to being alienated, and standing fully behind everything one does. It is a moral ideal which Hegel admires, and finds in modern times only in Goethe, above all, Goethe as portrayed by Rauch (*Ä* II. 84–5; Hegel probably knew the bronze copy of Rauch's portrait bust displayed in Berlin in 1822). Goethe is in Hegel's eyes a modern Greek, linked to them through his classicism, but more importantly through his instinctual creative psychology: the Greeks are repeatedly said to possess 'Sinn' or 'großen Sinn', and Goethe is the only non-Greek to whom this is attributed (compare *Ä* I. 264 with 257). Hegel had no way of knowing whether the men he mentions were as he says they were—about Phidias, for example, next to nothing is known—so in characterizing them as he does he is expressing a belief about Greek culture: it is how he would like them to have been. The connection with the art of sculpture is obscure. Hegel's list consists of artists, philosophers, and historians he admires. Some portraits of them have come down to us, but most Greek statues used athletes as models, and Hegel mentions them only as an afterthought (p. 374).

The other problem with Hegel's observation, if we wish to take it seriously, is that if modern Europe can produce a Goethe, it ought also to produce sculpture. However, Hegel links Greek culture with the quality and quantity of works produced, contrasting Greece with modern Prussia. In the face of such evidence, he says,

müssen wir in das größte Erstaunen geraten und zugeben, daß der Kunstsinn der Skulptur ein eigener Trieb und Instinkt des Geistes sei, der gerade in solchem Maße und solcher Verbreitung nur zu *einer* Zeit unter *einem* Volke existieren konnte (*Ä* II. 442).

we can but express our astonishment, and admit that the artistic sense which produces sculpture is one of Spirit's peculiar instinctive drives, which could be present to such a degree and such an extent at only *one* time amongst *one* people.

Once and once only can there be such a wealth of sculpture, because only once does it fulfil the needs of self-knowledge. Now it is one thing to argue that the significance of Greek sculpture is unique, but it is quite another to say that it is necessarily superior in quality and greater in volume that the sculpture of any other age or society. That is historicist metaphysics, deducing empirical facts from an a priori linear progression which ignores the enormous output of, for example, the late Middle Ages or the Renaissance. But what Hegel is expressing is the more modest insight that 'such an insatiable appetite for the nude is unlikely to recur. It arose from a fusion of beliefs, traditions and impulses very remote from our age of essence and specialisation.'[28] The difference between this and what Hegel himself says highlights the weakness in his understanding of Greek culture. What was unique about the Greeks was not a passion for sculpture, but a passion for the nude, an admiration for the human body which manifested itself amongst other things in sculpture. The inspiration for their work came from young athletes, not intellectuals, and Winckelmann has probably come closer to the truth about this than did Hegel.[29]

Qualifying Hegel, one might reasonably say that no other culture has produced sculptures of nude male figures to the extent that the Greeks did, although individuals like Michelangelo have made the male nude the main form of their work. Hegel only refers to him as an example of religious Christian sculpture, a curious choice, and the choice of work is more than curious. In 1822, on a journey through the Netherlands, Hegel made a special visit to Breda in order to see the tomb of the Count of Nassau, which he believed to be by Michelangelo, and he describes it with great enthusiasm ($\ddot{A}$ II. 460). Ernst Gombrich has taken it to be indicative of Hegel's ignorance of the arts that he was taken in by the attribution to Michelangelo, which he calls a 'Küster-märlein', an old wive's tale, told to visitors by the church sexton.[30] It is unfair to generalize from this case without bearing in mind the general state of expert opinion of the time, but it is striking how restricted Hegel's examples are. He uses first-hand observation whenever he can, but the only non-Greek examples given are from Berlin, Nuremberg, and the Low Countries, and the scanty treatment of other styles may be due to ignorance. The assertion that because of its greater spirituality Christian sculpture shows more of the characteristics of painting ($\ddot{A}$ II. 459) does not inspire confidence—whatever it means, it hardly fits twelfth- or thirteenth-century Gothic.

In describing the classical ideal, Hegel draws heavily on Winckelmann and pays him tribute, but adds that the discovery of the Aigina marbles and the pieces Lord Elgin had transported to Britain between 1803 and 1812 had led to some revision of views, and in particular drawn attention to an earlier phase of Greek sculpture characterized by greater severity ($\ddot{A}$ II. 378-9). Hegel accepted a model of stylistic development which goes back to Vasari, was adopted by Winckelmann, and had become a commonplace in the early nineteenth century, the model of growth, flowering, and withering. Arts, epochs, and styles have a period of groping imperfection, reach a peak, and decline into decadence, and Hegel uses the terms 'streng', 'ideal', and 'angenehm' or 'gefällig' for these periods, which he introduces as a perfectly usual set of distinctions ($\ddot{A}$ II. 246-7).[31] As far as one can ascertain from his descriptions, Hegel regards the move from 'streng' to 'ideal' as correspondent with the changes which took place from the sixth to the fifth centuries BC, and 'gefällig' as characteristic of Hellenistic work. The word dominating the first general description of the ideal style is 'lebendig', which, with its cognates, occurs some half a dozen times over two pages ($\ddot{A}$ II. 380-1), and presumably refers to the works from Aigina (500–480 BC) and the Parthenon (477–433 BC). The distinction of the fifth century was indeed to develop carving technique so that the stylization of archaic sculpture could be relaxed, and greater naturalism achieved. Figures no longer had four sides, but were fully rounded and naturalistic, so that it looked as if life had been breathed into stone. One example Hegel gives is a horse's head, almost certainly the horse of Selene from the eastern pediment of the Parthenon (**Plate I**), and what he draws attention to is the way in which a geometrical conception of form has given way to an organic one. The result, he says, is the feeling that every feature of the head fits in with every other feature, and this is what he calls 'der geistige Hauch der Beseelung'—'spiritual life being breathed into it' (*Ä* II. 381). The soul is reflected by every point of the surface, every moment of which is related to every other—in other words, it is 'the sensuous reflection of the idea' as individual.

It is interesting to note the praise Hegel lavishes on a horse's head, for the ideal Greek head is said to be beautiful because it eliminates nature from its features and emphasizes what is uniquely human about man. The figure of beauty is an intellectual, the impractical animal, whose features are engulfed by his brain. What Hegel finds significant about the Greek profile is that it links the (practical) nose to the (theoretical) forehead, so that instead of a protruding animal snout, we have a nose which is a cerebral excrescence (*Ä* II. 383-6). The nose as such should disappear because it is merely natural, and Hegel goes on to give details of its shape:

Eine scharfe Nase mit dünnen Flügeln sind wir z.B. mit einem scharfen Verstande in Zusammenhang zu bringen gewohnt, während uns eine breite und herabhängende oder tierisch aufgestülpte auf Sinnlichkeit, Dummheit und Brutalität überhaupt deutet (*Ä* II. 393).

We usually associate a sharp, narrow nose with a sharp mind, whereas a broad, drooping one, or a snub nose like an animal's, indicates sensuality, brutality, and stupidity.

The only element of truth in all this is that people with large, snout-like noses are not generally regarded as models of beauty. It does not follow that being beautiful is equivalent to having a high IQ. Hegel's example is particularly unfortunate, in that Socrates, the most spiritual Greek of all who heralded the new principle of individuality, was famous for his ugliness, and especially his flat, snub nose.[32] But the argument itself is peculiar, in dividing up the body into theoretical or human, and practical or natural parts. 'Non-natural' seems to be equated with intellectual activity, so the forehead emerges as the most important feature of the face. In fact, most expression is conveyed through the lower half of the face and the eyes, not the forehead, but there is in any case no part of the body which is not both natural and practical. Legs have no theoretical function, so on Hegel's account a legless torso should be more beautiful than a full-length figure. What Hegel has done is to confuse two things: he confuses human beauty and artistic beauty, so that it is not clear whether he is talking about people or statues; and he confuses intellect with expressiveness. He noticed, following Winckelmann, that a lot of the sculptures have a withdrawn, reflective air to them, and this is in part due to the deeply sunk eyes under a prominent forehead (*Ä* II. 392). This is a particular expression, not in itself the result of a desire to emphasize intellectuality. The shape of the head, and the straight line joining nose and forehead which is the most salient characteristic of the 'Greek profile' are probably the result of the Greek passion for geometric order. Its regularity was the product of a long period of experimentation in which sculptors tried to find the correct proportions for the head, and it remained highly stylized throughout the fifth century. Once a balance had been found between all the features of the face, the model established itself as a model of beauty, but in practice it was abandoned as increasing degrees of naturalism became technically possible. The ideal head is the mid-point between geometric and naturalistic styles.

Hegel's descriptions of clothing reveal similar prejudices, above all his opposition to sensuality, which he again projects on to the Greeks themselves. He points out, with charming innocence, that most of the nude figures are male, whereas the female ones, which might be suspected of sensuality, are usually clothed (*Ä* II. 402). The possibility of homo-erotic interest, well documented though it is, does not occur to him; most female figures were clothed for religious reasons.[33] We are told once more that the Greeks covered up organs which only have a natural function, such as those which are used for digestion (*Ä* II. 405). The human digestive organs are of course internal, and could not possibly appear on a sculpted figure unless it were disembowelled. The absurdity of the remark suggests that it could be an embarrassed way of referring to the genitals.[34] Hegel knew that many statues were naked, at all events, he claims, 'not out of indifference towards the spiritual, but out of indifference towards the merely sensual nature of lust' (*Ä* II. 404), which is probably an exact reversal of the truth. Hegel is more accurate is saying finally that the older more dignified gods were clothed, and the younger ones naked (*Ä* II. 406).

In turning to the question of what sort of clothing is used, Hegel quickly rejects modern dress as unsuitable, as it merely serves to conceal the organic forms of the body, and looks like stretched-out bags with stiff folds ($\ddot{A}$ II. 406-7; cf. $\ddot{A}$ I. 218-19). The clothing should reveal the significant things such as the position of the body, and can be used to cover up the 'merely natural', so he concludes, paradoxically, that the best sort of clothing is like a piece of architecture, quite independent of the body, with a form of its own ($\ddot{A}$ II. 407-8). This is half of the truth. The drapery of classical fifth-century gods, such as those on the Parthenon, does have mass of its own when it gathers in swirls at the edges of the figures, but its main effect is to heighten their sensuality, something to which Hegel is blind, which is at least consistent.[35] The justification of Hegel's attitude can be found in the tradition of Kantian thought which insists on the 'disinterestedness' of aesthetic contemplation, a tradition first challenged directly by Nietzsche, though the example of Heinse shows that, although widespread, it had never been universally accepted.[36] But it also forms part of a pattern within Hegel's thought: expression is equated with having meaning (recalling Goethe's use of 'das Bedeutende'), and having meaning is equated with being intellectual. Thus the seat of the brain can be expressive, but the nose can not. The theme of Beauty and Truth is here given an odd twist, as the aesthetic is pushed towards the theoretical in human beauty, and physical presence only admitted to be aesthetically significant if it is encompassed by the brain. It is the transfer of a categorial relation on to the empirical level, an example of level confusion typical of the text.

The examples of actual works of sculpture which Hegel gives are in general disappointing, as he mentions only the best-known sculptures of the Greeks, and tends to praise what was customarily praised. Amongst those mentioned more than once are the Medici Venus, Apollo Belvedere, and the Laocoön and Niobe groups, and he once refers to the Dioscuri on Monte Cavallo in Rome.[37] He follows contemporary opinion in being reserved about the Medici Venus and Apollo Belvedere, saying that they are later than Winckelmann had believed, and show too much decadence to be ideal ($\ddot{A}$ II. 431-2), though he seems to admire the Venus (p. 185). The Laocoön is also said to be mannered (p. 435). This group was the most discussed piece of ancient sculpture during Hegel's lifetime, and it has suffered a loss of status even more severe than that of the other two classic models, the Venus and Apollo.[38] His approach to it is interesting, for he seems to be tired of the discussion the work provoked, and to have little time for those engaged in it ($\ddot{A}$ II. 434).[39] In his description of it, two things are emphasized: it is said to show pain and exertion without being grotesque or ugly; and the suffering it shows is alleged to be quite different from that found in Christian art ($\ddot{A}$ II. 434; III, 42-3, 50).[40] This is linked to a general point about the expression of emotion in Greek art, and in sculpture. The expressive limitations of sculpture compared to painting ($\ddot{A}$ II. 163) are put in parallel with the qualities of the Greek ideal. Of the Medici Venus, for example, we are told the following:

Ebenso haben wir in der Mediceischen Venus wohl ein plastisches Bild der Liebe, gegen dessen Zierlichkeit und schöne Ausarbeitung der Gestalt sich nichts sagen läßt; der Ausdruck der Innerlichkeit aber, wie die romantische Kunst ihn erfordert, fehlt durchaus ($\ddot{A}$ II. 185).

Thus the Medici Venus gives us a sculpted image of love whose grace and fine finish are beyond criticism; but it totally lacks that expression of inner warmth which is indispensable in romantic art.

Likewise, Laocoön is said to show nobility in bearing pain, but this is just cold resignation, without the reconciled serenity in the face of suffering which can be achieved in romantic art ($\ddot{A}$ III. 42-3). In this passage, Hegel does not describe the work, but speculates about what is going on inside the dying priest, on the basis of what he knows about Greek and Christian religion rather than what he can see in the work. There is no way in which Hegel can know whether Laocoön is triumphing over death or is just resigned, nor does it matter as far as the work of art is concerned. However, there is a difference in expression between Greek and Christian art, the Greeks usually dispensing with the display of emotion on the face, and tending to avoid ugliness of the sort common in medieval art (although centaurs on the Parthenon frieze do have distorted faces–they were the Greeks' enemies). The reason for this may be partly technical, but there is some reason to suppose that it was conscious. For example, they used a number of conventional bodily configurations to show certain feelings: the position of Laocoön's right arm behind his head (it was at first wrongly restored, and Hegel would have known it with this arm outstretched) was understood to show that he was in pain. Another example Hegel gives shows the same thing: the Niobid in Rome, whose arm gropes for the arrow in her back, has features of composed calm.[41]

    It is this calm which separates the Ideal from us. Greek art embodies a different moral ideal, a different understanding of subjectivity, which has room for stoic nobility, and lends the gods a 'trace of melancholy' (*Ä* III. 42) which is the only awareness they show of the law of cold necessity to which they, as well as humans, are subject. But it does not encompass the depths of negativity explored in romantic art, a possibility opened up by Christ's Passion. The Christian understanding of subjectivity is more complete than the Greek one, because it is more determinate, so as man's understanding of Truth moves on, Beauty is left behind.[42] We now know more about suffering than the Greeks did, and demand that it be reflected in art, and so though the Ideal remains, taste has changed:

Dies ist der Grund, weshalb uns die Skulpturwerke der Alten zum Teil kalt lassen. Wir verweilen nicht lange dabei, oder unser Verweilen wird zu einem mehr gelehrten Studium der feinen Unterschiede der Gestalt und ihrer einzelnen Formen. Man kann es den Menschen nicht übelnehmen, wenn sie für die hohen Skulpturwerke nicht das hohe Interesse zeigen, das dieselben verdienen. Denn wir müssen es lernen, sie zu schätzen. (*Ä* III. 17.)

It is for this reason that the sculptures of the Ancients can leave us cold at times. They do not hold our attention for long, and if they do, it is more because we are interested in a scholarly study of the subtler features of the figure and its individual forms. One cannot blame people for not devoting to these great works the high interest that they deserve. For we have to learn how to appreciate them.

The value of Greek sculpture is unique, but it does not embody our truth. Our attitude to it is reflective and distanced. There will be a few people out of sympathy with their own time who will approach it with the passion it has always inspired in some; but for the most part, only scholars will understand it. The modern public demands a reflection of itself in art, and this requires a more ideal medium, the next milestone along the path to the interior:

Einheimischer wird uns deshalb sogleich bei der Malerei. In ihr nämlich bricht sich das Prinzip der endlichen und in sich unendlichen Subjektivität, das Prinzip unseres eigenen Daseins und Lebens, zum erstenmal Bahn, und wir sehen in ihren Gebilden das, was in uns selber wirkt und tätig ist. (Ibid.)

Thus it is that we immediately feel more at home with painting. For with painting the principle of finite subjectivity which is infinite in itself, the principle of our own life and existence, establishes itself for the first time, so that a painter's creations reveal to us something which is active in ourselves.

Painting

With painting, the goal of the journey into the interior becomes visible from afar, shining through the materiality yet to be penetrated. It is a romantic art because it exemplifies the principle of inner subjectivity dominating the romantic art-form, and this principle forms the starting-point for Hegel's theory of painting.

Subjectivity is mind as it is in itself, and objectivity means both external reality, and ethical substance or Truth ($\ddot{A}$ III. 11). The sculpture of a god unites subjectivity and objectivity in both senses of 'objectivity': the god as a subject appears in necessary unity with his body, and is as such the embodiment of the ethical substance of the community. Now, however, this unity dissolves. Within subjectivity itself, there is a diremption between the human and the Divine, for man is embodied and God is disembodied. God and man can therefore only achieve unity through mediation: God can embody himself (as he did in Christ) or man can become disembodied (as he does after his death when his soul goes to heaven; $\ddot{A}$ III. 12). Because subjectivity itself is not necessarily embodied, there is also a diremption between it and objectivity, so that any unity they achieve will likewise be mediated. The possibility is thus established for subject and object to be mediated in any way at all, as their unity is not given. Painting mediates them through the element of light, so that their unity is visible, and music (the other romantic art) mediates them through sound so that their unity is audible.

What this means is that painting can express feelings sculpture cannot show, because it is more interior. With painting, one dimension is lost, so there is an element of illusion added which broadens its range. As it uses colour, painting can also show greater detail, so that in practice is can represent anything in the visible world ($\ddot{A}$ III. 19-34). But the move from sculpture to painting is also a move from Greek to Christian religions, because the principle of painting corresponds to the principle of Christianity. So in fact there is a content which is especially suited to painting ($\ddot{A}$ III. 20). Hegel then passes from this discussion of principles to the empirical level, and claims that the best painting is Christian. He knows full well that painting enjoyed a very high status amongst the Greeks, and admits that although little has survived, it was probably of very high quality. However, he insists that the Greeks did not, and could not, develop painting 'to the level of truly pictorial accomplishment' achieved in the Middle Ages. He continues:

Dies Zurückbleiben der Malerei hinter der Skulptur ist bei den Alten an und für sich zu präsumieren, weil der eigentlichste Kern der griechischen Anschauung mehr als mit jeder anderen Kunst gerade mit dem Prinzip dessen zusammenstimmt, was die Skulptur irgend zu leisten imstande ist. ($\ddot{A}$ III. 20.)

One can in any case assume that the painting of the Ancients fell short of their sculpture, because the real core of the Greeks' outlook on life accords precisely with the principle of what sculpture, more than any other art, can achieve.

Passages like this show the unfortunate empirical consequences of the (theoretically illegitimate) deduction of the arts from the art-forms. What Hegel might defensibly wish to claim is that certain contents peculiar to Christianity cannot be expressed in sculpture, but only in painting, that is, that Christianity needs painting. In fact he says the reverse, that painting needs Christianity to reach its greatest heights, because their principles correspond. Of course, if we knew more about Greek painting we might decide that the principle of their culture was not really sculptural at all, because it may be that they did express inner feelings in their painting. Hegel's systematic argument about the limits of each of the arts disrupts his dubious cultural hermeneutics, for if no sculpture is in principle able to convey emotions as painting is, it is no surprise that Greek sculpture does not do so—perhaps Greek painting did. Nobody knows, as it has all been lost; one cannot appeal to principles in order to decide what it must have been like. Hegel ought to compare Greek and Christian sculpture, not Greek sculpture and Christian painting, as he usually does (for instance $\ddot{A}$ III. 50), for that just assumes what he wishes to prove. He can either argue systematically or do cultural history, but not both at the same time.

Despite claiming that the subject-matter of painting is unrestricted, Hegel tries to show that the representation of the Madonna and child is the subject which forms the centre of Christian art. God cannot be represented in art without distortion, he can only be symbolized in various ways, for example as Lord of Heaven or as Father of Mankind, but even so, never in his full nature (see $\ddot{A}$ III. 45-6). Christ can be shown in art, but the problem remains of how to convey his full nature by representing his divinity ($\ddot{A}$ III. 46-51). The motif of the Holy Family, however, allows an artist to show the essentials of Christian belief without distortion, and these essentials correspond to what Hegel means by 'inner subjectivity'. The interior world opened up by Christianity is one of feeling, the love of God for man—the Greek gods did not love mankind, they just had favourites and enemies amongst the heroes. It is interesting to note that Hegel spends some time describing specific feelings very precisely, on the basis of his knowledge of Christianity. For example, there is a detailed discussion of the love between mother and child, which Hegel assumes is portrayed in any painting of the Holy Family, as opposed to the love between siblings or between the sexes (*Ä* III. 41–5, 51–3).[43] The feelings are determinate, and known by any Christian, but cannot be conveyed in sculpture, which is why Christianity needs painting.

The section on painting as a whole is the first in which the empirical material is of real interest. Hegel believed that first-hand experience is especially important in the case of painting (*Ä* III. 108), and he shows less reliance on sources than before, with the exception of the final historical section, which is derived almost entirely from Karl Friedrich von Rumohr's *Italienische Forschungen*. Almost all his examples are of paintings he had seen himself, and he shows a striking readiness to use the first person, something he otherwise does very infrequently, and which usually has the effect of reducing the authority of what he says. Thus one finds expressions like 'I must confess, that for me at least . . .' (*Ä* III. 46).[44] This may indicate a lack of confidence on the part of someone who knew he was not a connoisseur, but did take a strong interest in the visual arts, gleaning what he could from the *Berliner Morgenblatt*.[45] It may also indicate that as the content of painting is subjectivity, only subjective judgements about what it expresses are possible. Often what appears to be ignorance on Hegel's part is due to the state of knowledge in the early nineteenth century, or indeed the different view of art history prevalent at the time. For example, he refers at one point to the age of Raphael, Correggio, and Rubens, whereas Rubens was born a century later (see *Ä* III. 39).[46] He probably does this because he thinks of the sixteenth and seventeenth centuries as a unity, and it serves as a reminder that the familiar distinction between Renaissance and Mannerist or Baroque was established after Hegel's death. Similarly, there is a case of false attribution. The picture of Jacob and Rachel in Dresden which Hegel calls a Giorgione is in fact by Jacopo Palma (Palma Vecchio), but again this was not known at the time. The work has the initials 'G B F' on it, and was assumed to be by Giorgione until this century.[47]

It was in general far more difficult to become familiar with art history in Hegel's day than it is now. There was no public gallery in Berlin until the opening of the Royal Gallery in the Lustgarten on 3 August 1830. Hegel travelled through the Netherlands, knew the Dresden Gallery, and the collection of Sulpiz and Melchior Boisserée, which contained important Dutch and German works. In Berlin, he had access to Edward Solly's collection, which was strong in the Italian schools up to Raphael and was in Berlin from 1821, and he may have known the 157 pictures owned by the Marquis Vincenzo Giustiniani which were on display in 1826.[48] Hegel's experience was thus limited very largely to Italian, Dutch, and German art, which may well explain why he divides art into the simplistic categories of ideal Italian and realistic Northern styles. Murillo is mentioned once, but Hegel would have had little opportunity to see Spanish work, as the Berlin Gallery only began to collect it in the 1830s.[49] He shows no knowledge at all of French or English art. In galleries of the time, whether public or private, paintings were usually arranged according to subject-matter, making it hard to follow historical developments, and Hegel complains about this (*Ä* III. 108–9), looking forward to the new Berlin Gallery as a new departure. His friend Hirt had in 1798 been the first to suggest displaying pictures according to school and period, a system at that time in force only in the Imperial Gallery in Vienna.[50] All this might be borne in mind before condemning Hegel's ignorance.

One distinguished art historian is indeed impressed by the discernment Hegel shows in revealing the insipidity of some of the work produced around 1820.[51] The so-called 'Düsseldorf school', led by the director of the Düsseldorf Academy, Wilhelm von Schadow (son of the famous sculptor Johann Gottfried Schadow), held an exhibition in Berlin in 1828. Hegel's comments on the exhibition are significant in several respects: they show his interest in contemporary art, his independence of judgement and, most importantly, his rejection of classicism in modern painting. He refers, for example, to a painting of Rinaldo and Armida (**Plate II**), which must be the one which the then twenty-three-year-old Carl Ferdinand Sohn painted especially for the exhibition. It seems to have been what the general public wanted, and the press praised its 'fresh and lively sensuality'.[52] Hegel mentions it whilst discussing the problems of giving an adequate treatment to literary subjects in painting—the motif is taken from Tasso (*Gerusalemme Liberata*, XVI. 18–19). He comments:

Gewöhnlich stellten die vorzüglichsten Gemälde je ein Liebespaar dar,

Romeo und Julia z.B., Rinaldo und Armida, ohne nähere Situation, so
daß jene Paare gar nichts tun und ausdrücken, als ineinander verliebt
zu sein, also sich zueinander hinzuneigen und recht verliebt einander
anzusehen, recht verliebt dreinzublicken. Da muß sich denn natürlich
der Hauptausdruck in Mund und Auge konzentrieren, und besonders
hat Rinaldo eine Stellung mit seinen langen Beinen, bei der er eigentlich,
so wie sie daliegen, nicht recht weiß, wo er mit hin soll. (*Ä* III. 91.)

The best pictures were usually of a pair of lovers, Romeo and Juliet for
example, or Rinaldo and Armida, but they were shown without any
definite context, with the result that they had nothing to do or express,
except to be in love with each other, which means that they lean
towards each other and look at each other with loving devotion, gaze
lovingly into each other's eyes. This being so, of course, the main focus
of expression has to be the mouth and eyes, and Rinaldo in particular,
with his long legs, is in such a position that he does not really seem to
know what to do with them, the way they lie there.

Hegel has seen the dangers inherent in the subject and the compositional
weakness of the painting. The centre of the composition is the top of
the pyramid formed by the two figures where their heads meet. Rinaldo
gazes up with the large eyes characteristic of Greek heads, and Armida
stares past him: the focal point of the painting is an expressive void.
Rinaldo's bare leg dominates the lower left-hand quarter, to no apparent
purpose. Sohn's technique is virtuosic, producing a perfect classical
study in Armida, with the head taken from Raphael, and the drapery
from late-fifth-century Greek goddesses. Had Hegel been a classicist in
the same way as Winckelmann, for whom the Greeks were a real, rather
than a theoretical, ideal, he would surely have found this to his taste.
Instead he rejects it as insipid, an example of what he elsewhere calls 'the
pallid physiognomies' which became popular with Mengs (*Ä* III. 76).
Despite all he owed to Winckelmann, this case shows that Hegel's advice
to artists would have been the opposite: 'Do *not* imitate the Greeks.'
'Only the present is fresh,' the philosopher of history can say, 'the rest
is dull and stale' (*Ä* II. 238).

   In this discussion of the use of literary subjects in art, Hegel takes
issue with Schadow himself, with the example of his painting of Mignon
(**Plate III**), also in the exhibition. Schadow recommended the use of
poetic subjects, and Hegel is in no doubt that he was wrong to do so.
His attempt to portray Mignon in a painting, he says, was misguided
from the first, for the interest of the character lies in her past experience
and her inner complexity, none of which can be shown in a painting
(*Ä* III. 92-3). As a result, Schadow's feeble, zither-plucking angel is

unrecognizable as Mignon, so that the reference to her which the painting is supposed to make is meaningless.

The ethical values Hegel draws on in such judgements are not con-
sistently applied. He rejects the cult of sensibility, and the sort of
sentimentality shown by the Düsseldorf school, or by Guido Reni,
as when he remarks on the way in which the sentimental gaze of
upturned eyes has been turned into a mannerism in his work ($\ddot{A}$ III.
57-8). In other cases, however, Hegel follows contemporary taste,
lavishing extravagant praise on Correggio's Mary Magdalen in Dresden,
and describing the work in detail:

> Sie ist die reuige Sünderin, aber man sieht es ihr an, daß es ihr mit der
> Sünde nicht Ernst ist, daß sie von Hause aus edel war und schlechter
> Leidenschaften und Handlungen nicht hat fähig sein können. So bleibt
> ihr tiefes, aber gehaltenes Insichgehen eine Rückkehr nur zu sich selbst,
> die keine momentane Situation, sondern ihre ganze Natur ist. In der
> gesamten Darstellung . . . hat deshalb der Künstler keine Spur von
> Reflexion auf einen der Umstände zurückgelassen, die auf Sünde und
> Schuld zurückdeuten könnten; sie ist dieser Zeiten unbewußt, nur
> vertieft in ihren jetzigen Zustand, und dieser Glaube, dies Sinnen,
> Versinken scheint ihr eigentlicher, ganzer Charakter zu sein. ($\ddot{A}$ III.
> 106-7.)

> She is shown as the repentant sinner, but one can tell that she is not
> seriously committed to sin, but has a noble disposition and could not
> have been capable of corrupt passions and actions. Thus her deep,
> sustained introversion is simply a return to herself, which is not just
> temporary, but involves her whole nature. So it is that nowhere in the
> picture has the artist . . . left a trace of reflection on any of the cir-
> cumstances which might point back to sin and guilt; unaware of these
> times, she is lost in her present state, and this faith, this rapt medi-
> tation, comes across as really being her whole character.

The nineteenth century became so aware of the eroticism of the work,
which Hegel could be relied upon to overlook, that it was commonly
regarded as a fake. A more recent verdict is that it 'struck a chord in the
man of feeling of the eighteenth century. The combination of sentimental religiosity and sensuality proved irresistible and gave rise to
extraordinary panegyrics (including Diderot's, in the *Salons* of 1763
and 1767) and innumerable copies.'[53] As the painting was destroyed in
1945, one cannot judge for oneself any more, but the reaction of others
suggests that Hegel was blind to things in it which he rejects elsewhere.
It is a mystery how Hegel can derive all the information he has about
her soul, her character, what she used to be like, her motivation, and

her present thoughts from any painting, least of all this one. His reaction to it may be due to his being influenced more than usual by the climate of contemporary taste.

The part of the section devoted to the historical development of painting is dominated by the contrasting of Italian and Dutch art, an opposition grounded in what Hegel sees as the consequences of the principle of painting. Painting can take up substantial religious subjects and treat them in a serious, ideal manner—the word 'plastisch' is used again in this context—so that the subject itself is admired; or it can represent any objects at all to reflect subjectivity, choosing totally insignificant ones, but rendering them significant through the representation itself, in which case it is the technique involved, the skill of the painter, which is more important ($\ddot{A}$ III. 35). The Italian schools produce painting of the former type, taking on the character of modern Greeks ($\ddot{A}$ III. 102), and the northern schools, identified with the Dutch and the Germans, concentrate on work of the latter type. This opposition which Hegel sets up is not a strict contrast, since it is not purely stylistic, but involves the subject-matter as well: although as a generalization it is inaccurate, however, it still commands broad assent.[54] Its significance in the *Aesthetics* is that Dutch art is placed on the same level as the classical tradition and contrasted with it by means of a comparative method. On four occasions, the two traditions are explicitly compared and contrasted,[55] and the honours are usually divided equally. Unlike Wölfflin, with whom the comparative method is associated, Hegel does not try to avoid evaluation, and he is not content to show that the Dutch use of colour differs from the Italian, he says it is better ($\ddot{A}$ III. 36, 69-70);[56] he does not simply note the differences between the Christ-child in Raphael and the van Eycks, he asserts the superiority of the former ($\ddot{A}$ III. 49, 125).

It is not surprising that Raphael becomes a central figure in Italian art, uniting human warmth and religiosity. Hegel concentrates on him to a very large extent—Leonardo is mentioned only three times, Titian twice, Michelangelo only once—partly because he painted the Virgin and child, the central motif of Christian art, with such frequency, and partly because of his status at the time. Before the Sistine Madonna arrived in Dresden in 1753-4, German taste had been for French and Dutch schools. Winckelmann began the process of establishing Raphael's reputation in Germany, and by the turn of the century he was admired by all from Wackenroder to Goethe, and as much in Jena as in Weimar.[57] Unfortunately, most of Hegel's remarks are very general, but he mentions the Sistine Madonna twice, once to praise the Christ-child, and once to comment on its pyramid construction, and he devotes some time to arguing for the unity of Raphael's last work, the *Transfiguration*, now in the Vatican (*Ä* III. 96). This work seems to fall into two halves, the lower part being completed by Raphael's pupils, and the unity of the work has been the subject of continual discussion.[58] Rather than try to decide whether Hegel is right about the *Transfiguration*, it may be more instructive to compare the way in which he argues with Heinse and Tieck, for all three agree about the issue itself. Ardinghello thinks the work shows Raphael's art at its most perfect, distilling the quintessence of his religious feelings, and he presents it as an overpowering *tour de force* which silences criticism in its vigour:

Mit einem Wort, es ist, was es sein soll: eine wahre Verherrlichung und Verklärung; die Doppelszene, so vereinigt, füllt den Moment so mächtig, als die Malerei nur leisten kann; und was leere Kritiker tadeln, entzückte gerade den Meister bei der Erfindung und macht den Triumph der Kunst für den Menschen von Gefühl aus.[59]

In a word, it is what it sets out to be: a true glorification and transfiguration; the double scene, united in this way, fills the moment as powerfully as painting can; and what vain critics try to fault was the very thing that gave creative delight to the master and is a triumph of art for the man of feeling.

The monk who tries to explain Raphael's greatness to Tieck's hero Franz Sternbald also picks out this work as the summit of his art, and claims it is a unity because it encompasses a totality of human religious experience, by virtue of which, he adds in this charming anacoluthon, it is 'poetic':

In diesem Bilde ist auf die wundersamste Weise alles vereinigt, was heilig, menschlich und furchtbar ist, die Wonne der Seligen mit dem Jammer der Welt, und Schatten und Licht, Körper und Geist, Glaube, Hoffnung und Verzweiflung bildet auf tiefsinnige, rührende und erhabene Weise die schönste und vollendetste Dichtung.[60]

This picture unites in the most wondrous way all that is sacred, human, and terrible, the rapture of the saints with the sorrows of the world, and dark and light, body and spirit, faith, hope, and despair are all shown in a profound, moving, and sublime way as the most lovely and perfect poetry.

Hegel, as one would expect, explains the unity by means of an appeal to meaning:

Denn einerseits ist Christi sinnliche Verklärung eben die wirkliche Erhöhung desselben über den Boden und die *Entfernung* von den Jüngern, welche deshalb auch als Trennung und Entfernung selbst sichtbar werden muß; andererseits ist die Hoheit Christi am meisten hier in einem wirklichen einzelnen Falle dadurch verklärt, daß die Jünger den Besessenen ohne Hilfe des Herrn nicht zu heilen vermögen. Hier ist also diese gedoppelte Handlung durchaus motiviert und der Zusammenhang äußerlich und innerlich dadurch hergestellt, daß ein Jünger auf Christus, den Entfernten, ausdrücklich hinzeigt und damit die wahre Bestimmung des Sohnes Gottes andeutet, zugleich auf Erden zu sein, auf daß das Wort wahr werde: 'Wenn zwei versammelt sind in meinem Namen, bin ich mitten inter ihnen.' (*Ä* III. 96.)

For on the one hand, Christ's physical transfiguration involves his actually rising above the earth and *departing* from the disciples, and this must therefore become visible as a physical separation; and on the other hand, the fact that the disciples are unable to heal the possessed child without the help of their Lord shows the transfiguration of Christ's majesty in an actual individual case. The use of the double motif is thus fully motivated, and the external and internal connection is made explicit by having one disciple point towards the departing Christ, and so indicate the true vocation of the Son of God, which is to be on earth as well as in heaven, so that the word be fulfilled: 'For where two or three are gathered together in my name, there am I in the midst of them.'

The three approaches stand in marked contrast to one another. Heinse's Ardinghello does not argue for the unity at all, he just asserts, as if it were obvious, that it is there: the 'double scene' is 'united in this way'. We learn nothing more about how. Ardinghello emphatically states a moral position to support his judgement—anyone who disagrees is feeble, and lacks the right feelings, so is not worth arguing with. Tieck's monk has an argument about the significance of the various elements, claiming that they form a totality. But if someone were to ask why they are 'profound', 'moving' and 'sublime', he would have to say that this is evident to him, and someone to whom it is not evident is just insensitive. Hegel on the other hand has a two-part argument, linking an appeal to the inner meaning of what is shown, with the purely visual feature of the pointing disciple, crowning the argument with a biblical quotation. (The lower scene is based on the story of a boy possessed by the Devil, and follows on the narration of the transfiguration in Matthew 17.) Hegel is relying on the aesthetic principle that elements of a work of art are justified if they can be shown to be significant, so if someone were to disagree with him, he could say that they had not understood the picture, and explain it once again. He would not have to denounce a critic on ethical grounds (that is, tell him he is an inadequate human being, as Ardinghello would), because he does not make any reference to himself or his feelings—he simply talks about the picture.

The details of Hegel's comments on Raphael clearly show the difference between locating him as the centre of Italian art, and saying that he was the greatest Italian artist. He is the middle because his style balances all the possible elements of painting—it realizes a totality. If one moves away from the centre, there are losses, but also gains. Hegel says, for example, that he is surpassed by earlier masters in depth and intensity of expression, and surpassed by Titian and the Dutch in the use of colour ($\ddot{A}$ III. 36).

Titian is admitted into the company of northern painters both as a colourist and portraitist ($\ddot{A}$ III. 104, 123). Hegel's remarks about colour are odd, for he admires the realism and subtlety of the Dutch colourists, but seems not to realize how different Titian's use of colour was, and puts them all together. Titian uses colour to structure a composition, and is not unique in this. Hegel rather arbitrarily exempts Correggio 'and a few others' from his strictures on the Italians ($\ddot{A}$ III. 70), but again is probably thinking of his use of chiaroscuro (cf. p. 123). Titian and Dürer are Hegel's examples of great portrait painters ($\ddot{A}$ III. 104), and as he demands a degree of idealization from portraits, it is strange that Raphael is not mentioned along with them. Hegel's understanding of the idealizing involved is curious. He contrasts Titian and Dürer with artists who just copy features accurately. In the one case, he says, the result is almost more like the sitter than he is himself; in the other, the result is true to life, but lifeless ($\ddot{A}$ III. 103–4), as in the case of Balthasar Denner, known as 'Poren-Denner' because of the detailed realism of his work ($\ddot{A}$ I. 127; $\ddot{A}$ III. 63).[61] The reason for the difference is then attributed to the inclusion or avoidance of the 'merely natural', so that a portrait always flatters by selecting those elements of a sitter which reveal his soul, and leaving out the natural ones ($\ddot{A}$ III. 105). This argument would deprive Cromwell of his wart. A feature which has expressive significance cannot fail to be a natural feature of a face, and if a portrait is to be a likeness, it must contain all the natural features, whether they are significant or not. Hegel is confusing the portrait with the sitter—all the sitter's natural features are portrayed, so the painting does not leave any out, it just alters the expression, and adds significance of its own.

The portrait forms one possible telos of painting, for it attempts to reveal the soul of a human individual, rather than embody a principle in a sculpted god ($\ddot{A}$ III. 103). Raphael may hold the central position in painting, but the concern with the realistic representation of the particular is another principle of art which is the province of the Dutch, as exemplified by the van Eyck brothers. They are the most painterly of painters, and Hegel shows boundless admiration for their technical skill, saying that it is almost impossible for anyone to paint better than they did ($\ddot{A}$ III. 125). He knew their work from his trip to Holland, and the Ghent altar piece was in the Solly collection in Berlin. It is this sort of mimetic art which finds a necessary place for ugliness and dissonance, particularly in scenes of the Passion ($\ddot{A}$ II. 105, 139, 153, and $\ddot{A}$ III. 101), but what matters in these scenes, he adds predictably, is not the physical suffering involved, but the spiritual suffering conveyed through it ($\ddot{A}$ II. 162-3 and $\ddot{A}$ III. 58-9, 126-7). Dissonance cannot be allowed to win the day, but must be integrated into a larger context so that it appears to be significant. Hegel criticizes the van Eycks' vulnerable Christ-child on similar grounds—Christ is divine, and the Divine is not ugly ($\ddot{A}$ 111. 49, 125). The portrayal of Christ as purely human is not something Hegel would be prepared to accept, because such a portrayal would be a distortion of Truth. However, his rejection of some of the dissonance found in medieval art is ethical, and grounded in the responses of modern consciousness. 'We' find some of the self-imposed sufferings of medieval saints repellent and barbaric, rather than edifying ($\ddot{A}$ II. 164-5). We no longer share the values of the Middle Ages, and it therefore can appear to be an alien world. As Truth changes, the judgement of art changes with it.

It is the embodiment of shared values and a shared ethos which is the basis for Hegel's celebration of Dutch genre painting. He sings the praises of seventeenth-century Dutch art because it invests the trivial with significance through the act of representation itself, and shows its relation to ethical substance, its importance in a particular way of life. Hegel dwells at length and with obvious personal enthusiasm on the skill with which these artists convey the various textures of materials, their powers of illusion, their ability to fix on the canvas a fleeting moment, and the way in which objects are shown as an end in themselves (see $\ddot{A}$ I. 214-16, 222-5; $\ddot{A}$ II. 225-9; $\ddot{A}$ III. 61-7, 127-31). His ability to appreciate this is rooted in the view he takes of painting which persuades him to see the illusionistic representation of any aspect of reality as an inevitable and legitimate end for an artist; and in his view of the romantic art-form, which, because of the nature of Christianity, leads with similar inevitability to the transformation of the everyday through art, simply through being made the object of art. In Dutch genre painting, art is fulfilling itself by realizing one of its ends, and is so approaching one of its limits—it is aiming at its own end. However, it has not yet reached the edge of its realm, as it still reflects social substance. Hegel is able to argue that these painters were fulfilling a role in their society similar to that played by Phidias, Homer, or Sophocles in theirs, and he does so by interpreting the delight shown in everyday life and the objects of the household as the self-reflection of the bourgeois community. The Dutch, having freed themselves from Spain, established religious and political autonomy, and enjoyed their freedom as a nation of tradesmen, merchants, and shopkeepers ($\ddot{A}$ III. 128-9). Their art thus appears as the affirmation of a newly found identity, and a celebration of their own values and way of life. It therefore embodies Truth, and Hegel recognizes this accordingly, with a firm rebuke for contemporary upholders of the classical ideal:

Sehen wir die holländischen Meister mit diesen Augen an, so werden wir nicht mehr meinen, die Malerei hätte sich solcher Gegenstände enthalten und nur die alten Götter, Mythen und Fabeln oder Madonnenbilder, Kreuzigungen, Martern, Päpste, Heilige und Heiliginnen darstellen sollen. Das, was zu jedem Kunstwerk gehört, gehört auch zur Malerei: die Anschauung, was überhaupt am Menschen, am menschlichen Geist und Charakter, was der *Mensch* und was *dieser* Mensch ist. ($\ddot{A}$ III. 130-1.)

If we look at the Dutch masters in this way, we will soon give up the idea that painting ought not to deal with such subjects, and just portray the ancient gods, myths and fables, or Madonnas, crucifixions, martyrs, popes, and saints. What is part of every work of art has its place in painting too: the expression of what is human, the human mind and character, of what *mankind* is, and what *this* man is.

The Italians occupy the centre of the world of painting, and their achievement is unique, in fact 'a pinnacle of art, such as can only once be reached by a people in the course of historical development' ($\ddot{A}$ III. 123). But the Dutch, on the edge of the art world, have also achieved something historically unique, which has value for us because it had value for them, and it takes a theory such as Hegel's to be able to account for the value of two such different forms of art.[62] But in painting Hegel does not leave it at a simple duality; at the end of the section on sculpture, it is Venetian painting which is compared to Greek sculpture as 'a living need which had to be satisfied' ($\ddot{A}$ II. 429). With at least

PLATE I

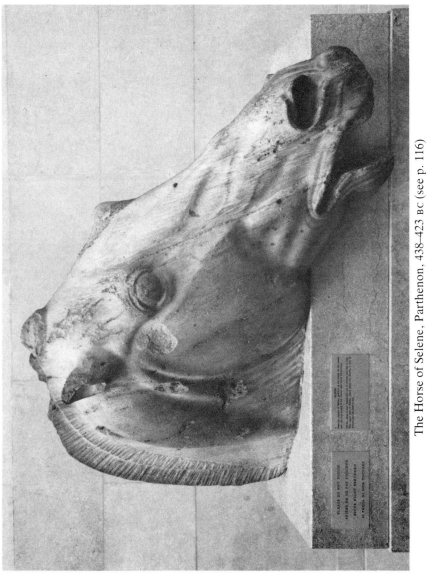

The Horse of Selene, Parthenon, 438–423 BC (see p. 116)

British Museum, London

PLATE II

Carl Ferdinand Sohn, Rinaldo und Armida (see p. 124)
Kunstmuseum, Düsseldorf

Plates II and III reproduce two paintings of the Düsseldorf School which Hegel saw in Berlin in 1828, and singled out for criticism.

PLATE III

Wilhelm von Schadow, Mignon (see p. 125)
Museum der Bildenden Künste, Leipzig

three different empirical high-points to painting mentioned, the section on painting ends with systematic theory gaining the upper hand over Hegel's desire to construct linear historical progressions. The Dutch show the possibilities of modern art, realizing a modern principle, but genre painting such as they produced was no longer possible in Hegel's time, as his review of some examples from contemporary exhibitions shows.[63] The centre of Hegel's theory is the relationship between Beauty and Truth, not dogmatic classicism.

Music

Music is the art with which Hegel, by his own admission ($\ddot{A}$ III. 137), was least familiar. He was an enthusiastic frequenter of the concert hall and opera house,[64] but the few judgements about individual composers and works in the lectures are subjective and not very revealing. (He remarks, for example, that the instrumentation of Mozart symphonies reminds him of a dialogue, 'ein dramatisches Konzertieren' ($\ddot{A}$ III. 176); or that in his experience, Rossini's tunes grow on you (p. 210).) In Hegel's day, Bach was just being discovered through the efforts of Zelter and Mendelssohn, and Hegel describes him as a musician of impressive genius, whom he considers to be 'truly Protestant', 'solid', and 'scholarly', but he adds no details ($\ddot{A}$ III. 211). Handel is also mentioned, in particular for his use of iambic rhythms in the *Messiah*, something which makes his work popular with Germans ($\ddot{A}$ III. 171). It is regrettable that Hegel does not elaborate on this, and he shows no awareness of its importance–the fact that German, unlike Latin, is a strongly stressed language was a significant factor in the development of vocal music from Schütz onwards.[65]

The treatment of music is peculiar in that there is no sustained attempt to locate the ideal. At only one point does Hegel suggest what he conceives to be the 'middle' or 'idealische Musik', and names Palestrina, Durante, Lotti, Pergolesi, Gluck, Haydn, and Mozart, all of whom are said to avoid extremes, and to express the heights and depths of emotion but always return to a point of balance and resolution ($\ddot{A}$ III. 198). This is an odd selection, placing four late-eighteenth-century composers alongside two contemporaries of Bach, Durante and Lotti, and adding Palestrina, whose style has nothing remotely to do with any of the others. It is not easy to argue that there is a centre to the world of music, because the centrality of any style depends upon the system it uses. Classicism may form the centre of the system of tonality relying on the tension between tonic and dominant,[66] but it is not clear where this leaves Bach or Palestrina, let alone medieval composers. Hegel may have been well advised to avoid the subject.

Hegel's main concern in this section is with the content of music. The account is elaborated with passages on the means of musical expression such as rhythm, harmony, or melody, but they only gain interest in relation to the *Philosophy of Nature*, which they illustrate, and can be passed over here. The subject of the content of music can then be divided into three aspects: the placing of music as the art of inner subjectivity; the problem of the relationship between content and form; and, as a solution to that problem, the relationship between words and music.

The content of music is first of all determined as inner subjectivity, the same as painting, with the difference that music is non-spatial. Hegel attempts to construct a transition from painting to music in two ways: he interprets the virtuosic use of colour as an aspiration towards the state of music, in that painting thereby seems to eliminate its own materiality (*Ä* III. 81, 133); and he motivates the transition from materiality to sound by appealing to the *Philosophy of Nature*, in which sound is understood as the double negation of materiality, produced when a body vibrates (see *Ä* III. 133–4 and *Enz.* §§ 299–302). Music seems to eliminate its own objectivity whilst becoming objective, expressing interiority in a sensuous form, but 'remaining *subjective* in its objectivity' (*Ä* III. 133). Because it eliminates all externality by being purely temporal, music is thus the most interior of the arts, and it seems that the goal of the mind's self-exploration must have been reached. It has not, because music is so abstract, losing all the determinateness of sculpture and painting, and returning to the level of architecture (*Ä* III. 139).

Whatever the difficulties Hegel's understanding of music brings with it for his system, it is certainly preferable to the familiar doctrine, tenacious even after the appearance of the *Aesthetics*, that music represents feelings.[67] It need not express any determinate feelings at all, nor need it necessarily arouse any. However, it does have the power to arouse emotions with greater directness than the other arts, and this is understandable on the basis of Hegel's model, because it is direct expression of subjectivity. It is the only purely temporal art, and the immediate self-awareness of a subject is likewise temporal, which is why Kant calls time the form of inner sense.[68] The subject is aware of other objects as existing in space, but his self-awareness is direct and non-spatial, so the purely temporal art of music is a reflection of subjectivity itself:

Indem nun der musikalische Ausdruck das Innere selbst . . . zu seinem Gehalt . . . hat, so dringt sie mit ihren Bewegungen unmittelbar in den inneren Sitz aller Bewegungen der Seele ein. (*Ä* III. 154.)

Because musical expression has interiority itself as its content . . . its own movements penetrate directly into the inner seat of all the movements of the soul.

It is perhaps worth noting how close this assessment comes to that of Hegel's arch-enemy and rival Schopenhauer, for whom music was a direct objectification of the will.[69]

There the similarity to Schopenhauer ends, for Hegel proceeds to explain that the determination of the content of music as subjectivity is only formal, and that it has a more determinate content than that (*Ä* III. 136). A little later, we learn the following:

Der Musiker . . . abstrahiert zwar auch nicht von allem und jedem Inhalt, sondern findet denselben in einem Text, den er in Musik setzt, oder kleidet sich unabhängiger schon irgendeine Stimmung in die Form eines musikalischen Themas, das er dann weiter ausgestaltet; die eigentliche Region seiner Komposition aber bleibt die formellere Innerlichkeit, das reine Tönen . . . (*Ä* III. 141).

However, the musician does not abstract completely from all content whatsoever, but finds it in a text which he sets to music, or, working more independently, clothes some mood in a musical theme which he then elaborates; but as a composer, his true realm remains the more abstract interiority of pure sound . . .

It seems, however, that the composer might have spared himself the trouble of developing the theme:

In einem musikalischen Thema ist die Bedeutung, die es ausdrücken soll, bereits erschöpft; wird es nun wiederholt oder auch zu weiteren Gegensätzen und Vermittlungen fortgeführt, so erweisen sich diese Wiederholungen, Ausweichungen, Durchbildungen durch andere Tonarten usf. für das Verständnis leicht als überflüssig und gehören mehr nur der rein musikalischen Ausarbeitung und dem Sicheinleben in das mannigfaltige Element harmonischer Unterschiede an, die weder durch den Inhalt selbst gefordert sind, noch von ihm getragen bleiben . . . (*Ä* III. 142).

In a musical theme, the meaning it is to express is already exhausted; if it is repeated, or goes on to further oppositions and interpolations, then these repeats, developments, modulations into other keys, etc., often prove to be superfluous for the understanding, and belong rather to the purely musical development and the immersion in the disparate element of harmonic differences, which are neither required by the content, nor supported by it . . .

Hegel then concedes that the development of a theme can sometimes throw light on its 'content', but qualifies this immediately by adding that it still tends to dissipate its effect. The tendency to do just this, he says, is most pronounced in modern music, which is separate from 'a content which is already clear for itself', so that the only object of interest in the music is 'what is purely musical' (*sic, Ä* III. 145), a matter which concerns only connoisseurs and specialists. Hegel's judgement of music which consists of sequences, modulations, runs, developments, and other merely musical things is drastic:

Dann bleibt . . . die Musik leer, bedeutungslos und ist, da ihr die eine Hauptseite aller Kunst, der / geistige Inhalt und Ausdruck abgeht, noch nicht eigentlich zur Kunst zu rechnen. (*Ä* III. 148–9.)

But then the music remains empty and meaningless, and indeed, as it lacks one of the primary aspects of all art, spiritual content and expression, it should not really be counted as art.

Music's formal content, inner subjectivity, is just the medium in which certain determinate contents–'Geistiges'–should be expressed (*Ä* III. 157). There can be no doubt that Hegel's evaluation of music is very low: Orpheus, he observes, was able to enchant animals with his playing, but men cannot be subdued by anything so primitive, as they are only interested in 'the determinate Idea' (ibid. 158). Music is damned to triviality because its content is so indeterminate.

It is probably fair to say that Hegel's strange view, so peculiarly at variance with the fundamental principles of the *Aesthetics*, represents a total misunderstanding of the nature of music, by demanding a 'content' or 'meaning' which is not there.[70] Sound in itself is not enough for Hegel, which is why he regards instrumental music as more or less trivial. He is only prepared to admit music into the arts if it expresses something determinate, i.e. if it is possible to say what it is expressing, and this is why he thinks, contrary to most evidence, that composers take a text or a 'mood' as their starting-point and dress it up in a theme. The content of music must be clear, and furthermore, clear independently of the music—it is just clothed in a melody. In reading these passages, one has the impression that Hegel was a naïve musical layman who liked a good tune, and thought that those aspects of composition into which all the greatest composers have channelled most of their effort are really superfluous. At no other point in these lectures, which are so extraordinary in their erudition and breadth of sympathy, does one feel, as one does here, that Hegel is talking about things he does not really understand.

There are some works of music, perhaps more than is generally credited today in an age used to the idea of 'absolute music', which are representational, and use sets of semi-mimetic conventions to convey determinate contents.[71] However, it is theoretically disastrous for Hegel to push such music into the position of the norm, for it is distinguished precisely by its non-musical aspects. What ought to occupy the centre is music which achieves musical effects by musical means, but on Hegel's account, music is hardly art at all when it is just itself. It is not necessary to look far in order to illustrate the point: the first movement of Beethoven's Fifth Symphony, one of the most famous and popular ever written, ought, according to Hegel's theory, to be the object of purely specialist interest. Its first four notes can hardly be called a tune or a melody, but they are a musical idea, and the rest of the movement consists in nothing but the development of those four notes and the second theme. The effects of the music are a function of how Beethoven works out this thematic material, and it is not necessary to have a technical understanding of what he does in order to be affected by the results. These results, the 'oppositions and interpolations'; the 'repeats, developments, modulations into other keys, etc.', are enjoyed by millions of people as the substance of the work, whether or not they think it represents the march of Fate, or anything else. Nor did Beethoven think up the theme as a suitable expression of a fateful mood he was in—he worked it out. Hegel cannot account for anything like such 'musical thinking'. Musical form is not its own content, but must be linked to another content in order to have any significance, a content which can be formulated in language.[72]

The roots of Hegel's problems are the underlying theory of determinacy and his logocentrism. A language-orientated notion of significance forces Hegel to sacrifice the principle of the identity of form and content in art, because he cannot see what content music could have. The altar on which the sacrifice is made is that of the theory of determinacy. In the case of painting, Hegel was able to describe the determinate feelings expressed in a picture of a Madonna and child, but in the case of music no such thing is possible.[73] Hegel's solution is to shift the centre away from music towards a combination of music and words, so that he can have the interiority of music and the determinateness of language, and so satisfy the two demands of spirit.

The result of this bad theory is a good, if unsystematic, set of observations about the relationship between words and music. Its position is a direct consequence of the need for interiority and determinateness:

> Wenn uns der Gesang die Empfindung z.B. der Trauer, der Klage über einen Verlust erweckt, so fragt es sich deshalb sogleich: was ist verlorengegangen? . . . Das Nähere des Inhalts ist nun eben das, was der Text angibt. ($\ddot{A}$ III. 200.)

> When song awakens a feeling in us, e.g. of sorrow, of lament over a loss, the question immediately arises: what has been lost? . . . It is these further details of the content which the text provides.

The central role given to vocal music is pre-empted by the loose account of musical instruments, which concludes that the human voice is the most complete instrument because it combines the qualities of wind and string instruments, by consisting of a column of air vibrating vocal chords ($\ddot{A}$ III. 175). Despite this, Hegel organizes his material to disguise the fact that vocal music is the only sort of music his theory can understand.

The main theme of the section on vocal music is the balance between music and text:

> Überhaupt ist innerhalb dieser Verbindung von Musik und Poesie das Übergewicht der einen Kunst nachteilig für die andere ($\ddot{A}$ III. 147).

> In general when music and poetry come together, any preponderance of one art is at the expense of the other.

Given this principle, Hegel goes into some detail about the sort of text which is suitable for use as a song or as an opera libretto:

> Poetische Ausarbeitungen tiefer Gedanken geben ebensowenig einen guten musikalischen Text ab als Schilderungen äußerer Naturgegenstände oder beschreibende Poesie überhaupt. Lieder, Opernarien, Texte von Oratorien usf. können daher, was die *nähere* poetische Ausführung angeht, mager und von einer gewissen Mittelmäßigkeit sein; der Dichter muß sich, wenn der Musiker *freien* Spielraum behalten soll, nicht als Dichter bewundern lassen wollen. ($\ddot{A}$ III. 147.)

> Den großartigen Musikwerken liegt . . . ein vortrefflicher Text zugrunde, den sich die Komponisten mit wahrhaftem Ernst ausgewählt haben. Denn keinem Künstler darf der Stoff, den er behandelt, gleichgültig bleiben . . . Mit in sich selbst Plattem, Trivialem, Kahlem und Absurdem läßt sich nichts musikalisch Tüchtiges und Tiefes herauskünsteln. ($\ddot{A}$ III. 205.)

Weighty thoughts cast into poetic form are just as unsuitable in a musical text as would be portrayals of external natural objects or any descriptive verse. Songs, opera arias, oratorio texts, and so on can therefore be weak and rather mediocre as far as the *details* of their poetic execution are concerned; if the composer is to have *free* scope, the poet should not seek to be admired as a poet.

Impressive musical works are based on a first-rate text, the choice of which is a serious business for the composer. For no artist can be indifferent to the material he is working with . . . No solid or substantial music can result from material which is in itself insipid, trivial, banal, or absurd.

Texts should thus avoid triviality and absurdity, but need not be of the highest poetic quality. Simplicity is an advantage, and there should be unity of mood ($\ddot{A}$ III. 201). This is because Hegel divides up the effects of music and text, but unites their aim: the text is to make concrete for the intellect what the music is expressing, and the music is to make the sense of the words palpable to inner feeling:

der Text steht im Dienste der Musik und hat keine weitere Gültigkeit, als dem Bewußtsein eine nähere Vorstellung von dem zu verschaffen, was sich der Künstler zum bestimmten Gegenstande seines Werkes auserwählt hat ($\ddot{A}$ III. 192).

Die Kunst besteht . . . darin, sich mit dem Sinn der ausgesprochenen Worte, der Situation, Handlung usf. zu erfüllen und aus dieser inneren Beseelung heraus sodann einen seelenvollen Ausdruck zu finden und musikalisch auszubilden ($\ddot{A}$ III. 196).

the purpose of the text is to serve the music, and should simply provide a closer idea of what the artist has chosen as the determinate object of his work.

The art . . . is to absorb the sense of the spoken words, the situation, action, etc., and once imbued with it, to find an effective expression for it which is then musically developed.

The sort of texts he finds best are provided by what Hegel calls:

eine Poesie, im Lyrischen wahr, höchst einfach, mit wenigen Worten die Situation und Empfindung andeutend; im Dramatischen ohne allzu verzweigte Verwicklung klar und lebendig, das Einzelne nicht ausarbeitend, überhaupt mehr bemüht, Umrisse zu geben als dichterisch vollständig ausgeprägte Werke ($\ddot{A}$ III. 207).

poetry which, when lyrical, is genuine, extremely simple, and uses few words to point to the situation and feeling involved; and, when dramatic, is clear and lively, without too many complicated entanglements, content to leave things in outline, rather than going into detail and producing fully developed poetic works.

The Latin mass is an ideal text from this point of view, with the advantage that its content is universal, substantial, and well known, and Hegel also finds praise for *The Magic Flute* and for Metastasio and Marmontel in general (*Ä* III. 207–8). Schiller's verse, on the other hand, serves as an example of poetry which is too involved and abstract to be set to music (p. 206).

There is nothing very profound about this, but it makes good sense and is in general confirmed by practice. It has often been observed that many of the finest operas and art-songs have mediocre texts, and Hegel explains why the paradox in this is only apparent. If the texts were complete literary works of art in their own right, they would leave nothing for the music to do, so being mediocre may not necessarily make a text unsuitable. What is decisive is how concrete it is. Maler Müller's mill-wheel prompts a piano motif from Schubert which makes both literary and musical sense; what could any composer do with the much finer poetry of, say, Novalis's *Hymnen an die Nacht*? The poem is complex, the imagery abstract, and the argument involved, so it is no wonder that it has found no takers amongst composers, despite the musical qualities of the writing. The Romantic poets most popular with composers have not been those whose verse is noted for being musical itself, such as Arnim or Brentano (though their doctored folk-song collection *Des Knaben Wunderhorn* has), but those like Eichendorff or Rückert, whose poetry is more of the type Hegel describes. Neither is a bad poet, but not all of the verse they have contributed to very fine songs has been of outstanding quality. Those few great songs by Wolf, for example, which use poems by Mörike and Goethe which are of very considerable literary value in their own right, still do not go against Hegel's general principles. They all have a clear structure or argument, use concrete imagery, and 'indicate a situation or feeling in a few words' as Hegel puts it.

To look at Hegel's case from the other side, one could consider Schubert's attempts to set Schiller. He wrote forty-two Schiller settings (eight poems were set more than once), nearly all of them before 1818 and none at all after 1823. Richard Capell explains the failure of most of them by appealing to the nature of the texts: 'His subjects are abstractions: there is no seizing and fixing a particular moment's vividness.'[74] The sixteen-year-old Schubert's attempt to set *Der Taucher* was doomed from the first, and Schubert's lack of experience manifests itself more in the choice of text than in a lack of musical skill. There is nothing to be gained from adding music to this long ballad, and singer and pianist ramble impotently through the text.[75] Schubert meets with success when he selects verse along the lines Hegel indicates. For example, he judiciously chose just one stanza of *Die Götter Griechenlands*, and produced 'Schöne Welt, wo bist du?', in which the mood is captured by one simple thematic motif (which he used variously in the A minor Quartet and the Octet).[75] Another success of similar concentration, but with dramatic rather than lyrical features, is the 'Gruppe aus dem Tartarus'.

This section redeems Hegel's account of music as a whole. As a layman without any deep knowledge of singing or composition, he is led to ask the right questions by his system of the arts, and reaches sound conclusions on the basis of common sense. He is guided by an awareness of what distinguishes the various arts, and of what each can or can not do. However, one always feels that Hegel was not at home with music, and the whole thrust of his argument subjugates it to the art which in itself combines complete interiority and complete determinateness, and thus forms the true goal of Spirit's journey into the interior—the art of literature.

4

LITERATURE: THE REALM OF GOLD

The Determination of Literature

The true goal of Spirit's self-exploration is the El Dorado of literature, which forms a synthesis of the other arts in that it combines the principle of subjectivity first apparent in painting with full determinateness ($\ddot{A}$ III. 224). This makes literature the highest of the arts, and places it, in contrast to sculpture, on the edge of the world of art, for instead of forming some sensuous material, it works through the organ of 'poetic imagination' ('poetische Vorstellung' or 'Phantasie'), reducing its material to a mere sign—the word ($\ddot{A}$ III. 229-30, 235). Using a language of signs is characteristic of thought rather than art, so the limits marking off a literary use of language from any other are blurred. The first parts of Hegel's account of literature are accordingly devoted to saying in what ways it might be distinguished from non-literature, or, as he puts it, what distinguishes 'Poesie' from 'Prosa'.

The first striking thing about these pages is Hegel's peculiar insistence that literature is a verbal art, not a written one (for example $\ddot{A}$ III. 226-8, or, most strongly of all, p. 320). This is something he never explains, and it is at odds with his belief that the sound of words is relatively unimportant, and that a literary work can be equally well heard or read (p. 229). It may be that he is thinking of the ancient bardic singer as the model of a poet, or he may have the performance of plays in mind—be that as it may, there is no reason to accept his opinion. Hegel's devaluation of the word to a mere sign is typical of his concern with meaning as what is essential, an emphasis on content which culminates in the observation that poetry can be translated without significant loss of value ($\ddot{A}$ III. 229-30). He seems to be working with an instrumental conception of language, so that certain 'spiritual forms' which constitute poetry are then just formulated and communicated in words, a view which has been strongly attacked, and is generally regarded today as unacceptable.[1] Support for Hegel's seemingly philistine statements comes from an unexpected quarter: his attitude to translation is shared by Goethe:

Ich ehre den Rhythmus wie den Reim, wodurch Poesie erst zur Poesie wird, aber das eigentlich tief und gründlich Wirksame, das wahrhaft Ausbildende und Fördernde ist dasjenige was vom Dichter übrig bleibt, wenn er in Prose übersetzt wird.[2]

I have respect for rhythm as for rhyme, for they are what make poetry poetry, but what has a really substantial effect, what educates and improves, is what is left of a poet when he is translated into prose.

It seems hard to believe that any poet, let alone Goethe, should say such a thing, for it is surely impossible to translate lyric poetry from one language to another, or into prose. However, there then comes to mind the example of Goethe's own *Iphigenia* which exists in prose and verse forms, and this provides a clue as to what Goethe and Hegel are really saying. Both are saying that nothing essential is lost through such an alteration of form, and one must bear in mind that the words 'Poesie' and 'Dichtung' cover works of literary prose as well as poetry, in the narrower sense of that English word. If one begins to look for other examples, one begins to see that there are relatively few works which utterly defy translation, most of them being lyric poems. Is it really not possible for a German to understand the essentials of Shakespeare from the Schlegel–Tieck translation, for example? Might one not even extend that claim to George's and Rilke's translations of French poetry?

There are empirical reasons for being charitable to Hegel on this point, but there are theoretical reasons for believing that he is just being consistent. He calls the sound of words 'an external accidental' (*Ä* III. 229), and recalling the categories of Essence he uses to talk about art, we can see that he has to. The sound of language, as opposed to its meaning, is part of its appearance to the senses, so it must be 'external', and as such it is an accident of the substance of the work, part of the soul's body. However, although it must be regarded as 'Schein', rather than Essence, the sound is still a factor to be considered, 'for art cannot allow any of its external aspects to be left completely to chance' (ibid.). So even the sound of its language is relevant to the qualities of a literary work of art.

In practice Hegel does treat literature as the linguistic art, which, because of its medium, is universal and represented equally in all three art-forms (*Ä* III. 232-3). The very universality of language makes it impossible to delimit literature precisely, except by appealing to the general distinction between art and non-art ($\ddot{A}$ III. 237-8). Hegel gives examples of writing which cannot be said to be clearly literary or non-literary ($\ddot{A}$ III. 250), and a comparison between literature and rhetoric shows that any distinction between them cannot be based on differing features, as most of the empirical features of literary works are shared by any example of rhetoric (or, in the modern world, advertising slogans, jingles, and propaganda) ($\ddot{A}$ III. 261-6). Hegel tries to work out the difference between the artistic and non-artistic uses of language in terms of commitment, and because language is the medium of art and the medium in which we make cognitive knowledge-claims, the difference comes down to the difference between Beauty and Truth.

Intuitively, it seems quite reasonable to try to explain literature as special, deviant, or non-serious use of language, in which the normal, serious use of it in discursive prose is suspended. We normally use language to make knowledge-claims, and occasionally use it artistically to do something else which is special. So it appears to most of us, most of the time, and it therefore comes as something of a shock when Hegel reverses this relationship:

Die Poesie ist älter als das kunstreich ausgebildete prosaische Sprechen. Sie ist das ursprüngliche Vorstellen des Wahren, ein Wissen, welches die Allgemeinheit noch nicht von seiner lebendigen Existenz im einzelnen trennt . . . ($\ddot{A}$ III. 240).

Poetry is older than artistically developed prosaic speech. It is the original way of picturing truth, a form of knowledge which does not yet separate the universal from its living existence . . .

By saying 'älter', Hegel makes it clear that he believes poetry came before prose historically, but as usual, the historical claim, whether or not it be true,[3] goes along with a theoretical one. The 'noch nicht' implies that something more is being done in the use of prose than in the use of poetry, and we learn that, paradoxically poetry, not discursive prose, is 'theoretical':

Dieses Auffassen, Gestalten und Aussprechen bleibt in der Poesie rein *theoretisch*. Nicht die Sache und deren praktische Existenz, sondern das Bilden und Reden ist der Zweck der Poesie. Sie hat begonnen, als der Mensch es unternahm, *sich* auszusprechen; das Gesprochene ist ihr nur deswegen da, um ausgesprochen zu sein. ($\ddot{A}$ III. 241.)

In poetry, this activity of understanding, forming and uttering remains purely *theoretical*. The aim of poetry is not the thing before it and its practical existence, but forming and speaking *per se*. Poetry began when man first started to express *himself*; the sole purpose of such utterances is to be uttered.

The word 'theoretisch' as Hegel uses it normally means 'contemplative', and so it does here. Literature is purely theoretical because it is just self-expression, which arises from a desire to say what things are, but is not committed to that. The prosaic mind, on the other hand, is committed to objectivity, and distinguishes its own thoughts and feelings from an independent reality. In literature, one is committed to showing something about the way things are experienced, the way they appear to be; in prose, one is committed to saying something about the way things are. In the former case, one is committed to the Ideal of Beauty, and in the latter case to the Idea of Truth.

Hegel illustrates this by contrasting literary and historical writing. Both artist and historian organize material so as to produce some sort of coherence, but whereas the artist is only committed to imbuing his material with significance, the historian must not only produce a coherent story, but offer explanation of the given material, which means that he is not just expressing himself, but writing about something else (see *Ä* III. 257–61). Literature may use historical material, but it is free to change it, because it has no commitment to it (p. 267). Works of literature likewise contain a host of references to the world, but it is not essential to their being art that they contain any, nor that they make any knowledge-claims.[4] They are felt to be true if the beliefs they express coincide with beliefs held by many other people, and the experience they articulate is common to others, that is, they are true if they reflect Absolute Spirit.[5]

There may therefore be grounds for distinguishing artistic from discursive prose. However, most everyday uses of language do not consist of cognitive judgements, but of demands, requests, exhortations, promises, threats, and a large number of other non-cognitive speech acts. They fall outside Absolute Spirit, and therefore outside art, to the extent that they fall within the sphere of Objective Spirit, the realm of practical reason; in other words, to the extent to which they are involved with action, the realization of a practical end. This is true of most of our non-cognitive linguistic habits, including, to some extent, the telling of jokes. If jokes are just used to make people laugh, they are not art, and Hegel elaborates this by explaining that pure humour is one of art's limits, because it is purely negative, and art must affirm something (*Ä* III. 572–3). Even the most negative literature (Beckett comes to mind) affirms that, for example, the world is a dreadful place or that man is a useless passion, and thereby it becomes self-reflection—the same is not true of a joke. A joke does not claim anything or necessarily show anything, it just makes fun of something. Graffiti often have this characteristic, but some of the best lie on the borderline of art. Hegel mentions an ancient inscription on a monument to the Spartans at Thermopylae, as reported by Herodotus, which runs:

> Four thousand here from Pelops' land
> Against three million once did stand.[6]

This is a bare statement of fact, Hegel says, but it becomes poetic if one reads it as an intentionally formed mode of expression ($\ddot{A}$ III. 241). The effect might be compared to that of modern graffiti which can be read as jokes, and which are undoubtedly humorous, but could also be read as poetry—for example: 'Life is a sexually transmitted disease.' This could be made quite serious in an appropriate context—there is nothing inherently funny in the idea that life is a disease. The point is that if this graffito is a joke, it is not affirming anything, but if it is a line of poetry, it is. We need not be worried by our uncertainty, for 'art' is, on Hegel's account, not a class or set of objects with an empirically determinate number of members so that any object x either is or is not a member of that class; it is a category, in terms of which things can be understood. In the case of literature, Hegel constructs three further categories of explanation which he calls 'genres' (Gattungen). They appear prima facie to be what is normally understood as genres, but on closer examination, it becomes unclear what their theoretical status is, and what they are about.

The Theory of Genres

Hegel introduces the genres as the determinations of literary form, and says that they are grounded in the concept of artistic representation ($\ddot{A}$ III. 321). He describes them as follows:

the *epic* shows 'the form of external reality' developed in an action, which becomes 'eine *Begebenheit* . . . in welcher die Sache frei für sich fortgeht und der Dichter zurücktritt'—'an *event* . . . in which the action proceeds freely of its own accord, and the poet retires into the background' ($\ddot{A}$ III. 321). The result of this is the representation of 'das

Objektive selbst in seiner Objektivität'—'what is objective in its objectivity' (p. 322);

the *lyric*, in contrast to this, shows 'die innere Welt . . . das Sich-*aussprechen* des Subjekts'—'the subjective, inner world . . . the self-*articulation* of the subject', and does not involve any action (ibid.);

the *drama* unites the principles of the epic and the lyric, because in it we see 'ebensosehr eine objektive Entfaltung als auch deren Ursprung aus dem Inneren von Individuen . . . so daß sich das *Objektive* somit als dem *Subjekte* angehörig darstellt'—'both the objective unfolding of the action, and its origins in the inner subjectivity of individuals . . . so that the *objective* is shown as related to the *subjective*' (p. 323).

The grounds for this division are the differences in what is represented (that is in content): in the epic it is objectivity, in the lyric it is subjectivity, and in the drama it is somehow both, or one through the other. That is not all, however, for the lyric is distinguished from the other two by its lack of action. Furthermore, it becomes clear from Hegel's discussion of Homer that the word 'objective' designates *how* something is shown, as well as a content. So the theory of genres is another case of theoretical heterogeneity—there are several things going on at once.

Taking first of all the objectivity/subjectivity opposition, which Hegel regards as the fundamental grounds for the division, drama poses a problem. Hegel ought to argue that it has a distinctive object, neither objectivity nor subjectivity, but a fusion of both. However, when he comes to explain the drama in full, he departs from the framework used for lyric and epic, and argues that the drama is distinct not because of the nature of its object, but because of the nature of its action. The reason why he suggests it is a synthesis of the the other two genres is that it shows:

eine . . . ebensosehr aus dem Inneren des sich durchführenden Charakters entspringende als in ihrem Resultat aus der substantiellen Natur der Zwecke, Individuen und Kollisionen entschiedene Handlung (*Ä* III. 474).

an action which has its origins in the subjectivity of the character concerned with realizing his own ends, but whose result is equally decided by the substantial nature of the ends, individuals, and collisions.

The synthesis of objectivity and subjectivity is achieved with respect to action, in that a dramatic character acts in accord with an inner motivation which is also an objective power. But that does not serve to synthesize epic and lyrical contents: at most, it mixes them. The genres are thus distinguished by at least two things: the object of their discourse, and the nature of their action. Furthermore, when expounding the Concept of the epic, Hegel introduces a wealth of other factors (such as aiming at totality, involving non-teleological action), in order to distinguish it from other narrative literature. This in itself suggests that in making this initial distinction between epic and lyric writing, Hegel has in fact distinguished narrative from lyric, and if this is so, one would expect their synthesis to be, not the drama, but the prose poem.

This is not the place to work out a theory of prose poetry, but it is worth entertaining the possibility of understanding it in this way in order to see what a synthesis of objectivity and subjectivity could be. Hegel, of course, never mentions prose poetry, as it is a form of writing which came to maturity in the late nineteenth century.[7] Nobody quite knows what it is, but there is a general consensus that whatever it is, Rimbaud's *Illuminations* contains some (whereas there is more room for doubt in the case of, for example, Baudelaire's *Petits Poèmes en Prose*). Here is a text entitled 'Marine' from *Illuminations*:

> Les chars d'argent et de cuivre—
> Les proues d'acier et d'argent—
> Battent l'écume,—
> Soulèvent les souches des ronces.
> Les courants de la lande,
> Et les ornières immenses du reflux,
> Filent circulairement vers l'est,
> Vers les piliers de la forêt,—
> Vers les fûts de la jetée,
> Dont l'angle est heurté par des tourbillons de lumière.

This appears to be a description of a marine landscape, existing in its own right independently of the writer, but this reading is quickly dislocated, and the reader realizes that it is simultaneously a description of a plough at work in a field. Both aspects of the text are maintained, nothing suggests that one is more real than the other, neither is used as a metaphor or simile; a plough in a field is seen as a ship on the sea. The text appears to be a description of objectivity, of a reality independent of the writer, but because two realities are juxtaposed, it must also be a way of seeing, something subjective which only has reality in the mind of the poet. The relationship between lyric subjectivity and reality is unstable, so that objectivity and subjectivity are fused in what might be called a vision. 'Marine' cannot be understood as a lyric, nor as narrative. It is something new of its own, irreducible to either.

One might thus say that Hegel has, in fact or by implication, accounted for three modes of literary writing distinguished according to their object: the narrative (which could be in verse or prose), the lyric, and the prose poem (though he did not know it). Lyric and narrative are distinguished by their object, so that the former attempts to express how subjectivity is experienced, and the latter attempts to show how objective reality appears to be.[8] Narrative is about something other than the writer, no matter how personal the statements made may be, and the lyric is about a first-person singular. These two 'modes' of writing are not genres, but the *Aesthetics* does contain a more specific theory which is an account of two genres, the epic and the drama, more specifically, epic and tragedy.[9] They are distinguished by the nature of their action, and the lyric differs from them in having no action at all. In discussing epic and drama, Hegel is trying to explain what marks out two bodies of texts which are relatively few in number (not, for example, two styles), and the models he uses are derived from the *Logic*.[10]

Hegel interprets both epic and drama as a representation of ethical principles. In the case of the epic, the principles are indifferent to one another, but clash, and the model for this conflict is the *Logic of Being*. In the case of drama, the principles are related, but oppose each other, and the model for this conflict is the *Logic of Essence*. An epic shows a society coming to understand its own determinacy through conflict with another, and the drama shows a society coming to understand the internal differences of its own ethical substance by seeing the principles on which it is based enter into conflict.

In the epic, a nation reaches awareness of its identity by clashing with another nation, so that the relationship between the warring powers can be understood from the paradigm of Something/Other. The action must be between alien powers, for an internal conflict would be dramatic (*Ä* III. 351), and it must involve the whole nation so that through the conflict it can gain self-awareness, the knowledge that it is determinate: it is *this* nation, rather than *that* one. Hegel organizes the features he attributes to the epic around the nature of its action. Its characteristics are as follows:

It acts as a '*Volksbuch*', the first book of a nation, produced at a time before national life was fully organized, and forming a basis for ethical life. The principles governing ethical life must already have evolved, but the epic brings them to awareness (*Ä* III. 331-4, 339-47).

It aims at showing the life of the nation in its *totality*, so that its identity may not be distorted (p. 330).

In order that this be done, it is organized around a *unified action*, and events are made *concrete* and enacted by *individuals* (*Ä* I. 266-83, *Ä* III. 330, 348-53). The action is an event (Begebenheit), that is, the meeting of an aim and external circumstances, in which the latter receive as much attention as the former (p. 355).

The action is merely the means by which the nation refers to a power other than itself in order to become conscious of its determinacy. Therefore, the epic is *non-teleological*; the action is not directed towards a conclusion, the interest is in the progress of events, so the epic is slow and detailed (*Ä* III. 330-1, 362-4, 378-9). Chance events are shown, and the attainment of the goal can be held up (pp. 384-5).

As it aims to show the details of national life, the tendency of the epic is to *externalize* and *objectify* (*Ä* III. 343-5).

The human protagonists are *heroic*, meaning that:
   they are a totality in themselves (*Ä* I. 308, *Ä* III. 359);
   they are developed in all respects, not identified with a single pathos (*Ä* III. 360);
   they cannot be judged morally, as morality is being established; they simply assert themselves (pp. 360-1);
   they avoid lyrical outbursts (p. 380).

In the drama, a nation represents its ethical substance by showing the principles of it, which are related like the relata of an Essence relation, embodied in individuals who are in conflict. Each of the characters identifies with one of the principles as a 'pathos', and ignores the rights of the other, declaring it to be inessential. Both are rightly convinced of the justness and importance of their own principle, but both incur guilt by not recognizing the other, for each is constituted through its relation to the other. Consequently, as each succeeds in eliminating the other, each undermines itself. Once one is removed, it becomes apparent that it is essential to the other, so that the result is the downfall of both and the affirmation of their relationship. The destruction of one when it alienates itself from the other makes it clear that their relationship is fundamental, and constitutes ethical substance. As a result of

the basic structure of its action, the drama shows the following characteristics:

It is given unity by its action, and the main interest is in the conflict
and its resolution so that, in contrast with the epic, there is *forward
momentum* towards the catastrophe ($\ddot{A}$ III. 475, 480, 482–6, 488).

Both the action and the characters are determinate and limited, so the
aim is *concentration* rather than totality ($\ddot{A}$ III. 479).

The action is carried out by characters who are not just asserting their
own will, but are *bearers of ends greater than themselves*, who so identify with these ends that they accept full responsibility for the consequences of the acts they motivate ($\ddot{A}$ III. 477–9).

Much is communicated through the speech of the protagonists which
can take the form of lyrical monologue, epic choral interjections, or
dialogue, which is the most dramatic of the forms ($\ddot{A}$ III. 475, 477–9).

Within this general framework, Hegel draws two further sets of distinctions, those between tragic and comic drama, and between classical
and modern. In tragedy, the principles involved are substantial, and
resolution is reached when the individuals bearing them succumb, and
objective ethical substance is affirmed ($\ddot{A}$ III. 521–6). In comedy, the
powers with which the individual identifies are insubstantial, and the
character is not destroyed by the failure of his end, but survives to stand
above the conflict. The resolution is the affirmation of subjectivity
which is able in this way to gain insight into the triviality of the conflict,
and laugh at it ($\ddot{A}$ II. 527–31). The main difference between classical
(Greek) and modern drama is that in the former the conflict is ethical
and objective, being grounded in social reality, whereas in the latter it is
moral and usually internal, being grounded in the values of an individual
subject ($\ddot{A}$ III. 534–8).

This characterization of the distinctive features of the epic and the
drama contains much that is familiar from some of Hegel's contemporaries.[11] For example, his references to the 'Hemmungen' retarding
action in the epic (p. 384) are reminiscent of the essay by Goethe and
Schiller called *Über Epische und Dramatische Dichtung*. It dates from
1797, but was only published in 1827, so Hegel may well have worked
out his theory before he could have known it.[12] More interesting still is
the fact that Hölderlin quite independently reached an almost identical
conception of tragedy as the conflict of subject and object, produced
by the self-diremption of the Absolute (which in Hegelian terms would

be ethical substance).[13] Hegel's concerns are typical of the late eighteenth century.

However, Hegel's model of tragedy contains a problem. According to the model, both of the conflicting principles are moments of ethical substance, and they are equally justified and equally guilty. But if both are in unity within ethical substance, it is unclear how the conflict can arise in the first place. Hegel does not explain this, for good reasons: given his model, a conflict could only begin if one side were to overreach itself and infringe the rights of the other, but if he admits that, the guilt is no longer equal. There must be an original, unprovoked, and reprehensible act, so that the scales of justice are weighted against the first transgressor. The test case for Hegel is the presentation of Creon in *Antigone*, the prime example he gives of tragic conflict, and there are good reasons to believe that the text is against him.

That is a problem immanent to the theory. If one steps outside it, it is hard to evaluate the case Hegel presents for having given the determination of tragedy and epic, but his own text provides evidence that his claims must be severely qualified. He faces up to the immense variety amongst works generally regarded as 'epic', but then gives the following answer:

Diese Schwierigkeit findet jedoch ihre Erledigung darin, daß aus / den vielen epischen Bibeln *eine* kann herausgehoben werden, in welcher wir den Beleg für das erhalten, was sich als den wahrhaften Grundcharakter des eigentlichen Epos feststellen läßt. Dies sind die *Homerischen* Gesänge. (*Ä* III. 338–9.)

However, this difficulty can be obviated by pointing out that of the many epic Bibles, there is *one* above all others which documents what has been worked out as the fundamental character of a true epic. By this I refer to the *Homeric* poems.

This is a blatant reversal of principle and instance, and of itself puts an end to any philosophical or theoretical claims Hegel might make. His model is an extrapolation from one instance, designed to explain Homer, and the only justification for this is that Homer is a model. What appears to be a reconstructive aesthetic theory is in fact literary criticism—what appears to be a universal theory of the epic is an empirical characterization of two texts, the *Iliad* and the *Odyssey* (indeed, it fits the former rather better than the latter). Hegel is brazen because most of his contemporaries would have accepted that 'epic' and 'Homeric' are almost synonymous. In like manner, Hegel more or less identifies tragedy with the *Antigone*, which is a more personal choice. The importance he gives to Homer and Sophocles is due in the main to the philosophical interest he finds in them, an interest not altogether commensurate with their literary features.[14] The value of Hegel's models cannot be decided theoretically, but only on the grounds of the explanation they offer of specific texts, so it is to his critical practice that we must now turn.

The Epic

The most striking thing about Hegel's discussion of epic literature is that he is almost exclusively concerned with the ethos embodied in the text, rather than its style. To be an epic is to have an epic content, regardless of how it is treated. Certain features of Homer's style are mentioned: the use of epithets such as 'rose-fingered dawn', and the adjectival topoi such as 'swift-footed Achilles' (*Ä* III. 277-8), and Hegel refers to the simplicity of the language, describing its movement as 'glatt und ruhig' (*Ä* III. 286-8). However, even in these cases, Hegel is concerned to find cultural reasons for such features, and show how they are linked with the epic ethos. Homer's tendency to externalize and objectivize (*Ä* III. 336, 343-4), and his avoidance of the lyric tone even when characters are expressing themselves (pp. 380-2) are seen as a consequence of the 'Weltanschauung' of the Greeks. In other cases, when the style is almost the opposite of Homeric, epic content is found, and that is what matters to Hegel. Thus the Spanish poems about El Cid, which Hegel knew in Herder's translation, are picked out as the very model of medieval epic poetry (*Ä* III. 405). However, they form a ballad, which is at another stylistic pole from Homer. The following stanza is typical:

> Und so führt der unverzagte
> Cid zehntausend wackre Männer
> Durch die Alpen hin ins Feld.
> Ihm entgegen zog Graf Raimond
> Von Savoyn mit vielen Rossen;
> Doch der Cid, er schlug den Grafen,
> Macht' ihn selber zum Gefangnen,
> Und nur gegen seiner Tochter
> Geiselschaft gab er ihn los.[15]

The lack of epithets, the concentration and economy of the narration, the speed at which events occur, the total absence of any description of battle—all this is the very opposite of Homeric epic style. What interests

Hegel, and leads him to classify the *Cid* as an epic, is that it shows the heroic ethos, in which heroes owe allegiance to a lord or king but remain autonomous and free to serve him or not, as they will. Hegel regards the relationship between the Cid and his king as being the same as that between Achilles and Agamemnon (see *Ä* I. 244-5; *Ä* II. 193: *Ä* III. 342), and he is right in this (see sections 18, 31, and 43 of the poem in which it is made explicit).

However, it appears that embodiment of the heroic ethos is not enough for Hegel; an epic must also show a certain level of consciousness, and be 'naïve' in Schiller's sense. The heroic ethos is found too in *Paradise Lost*, when, in Book II, Satan and his associates debate on their next course of action. Moreover, Milton's style is in many ways Homeric, particularly in his use of epithets and similes. Despite this, Hegel says that *Paradise Lost* is too dramatic and lyrical to be a true epic, and condemns it because it is too self-conscious and subjective—it is not naïve enough, but has the veneer of modernity (*Ä* III. 370, 375, 413). Milton is damned in illustrious company, for Virgil too is condemned as artificial, self-conscious, and decadent (*Ä* III. 306, 368-70, 384). Hegel never actually gives any reasons for these judgements, which are too general to be interesting, and as they are in conflict with the criteria he sets up, one has the impression that he is rationalizing a personal dislike. The impression is strengthened by the attitude he takes to Dante, for the *Divine Comedy* does not involve an epic conflict at all. Hegel nevertheless tries to find one, making specious reference to the original war in heaven (*Ä* III. 349-50), which *does* form a major part of the action in *Paradise Lost*. Although the *Divine Comedy* fulfils Hegel's criteria less well than Milton's work, it is chosen as one of the finest examples of Christian epic literature, and the reason is partly Hegel's own taste, and partly because he thinks it embodies the complete 'Weltanschauung' of medieval Catholicism (*Ä* III. 406). This is unjustified, as it ignores the humanist and classical aspects of the poem, but it shows that Hegel's main concern is the extent to which the ethical principles of a society are embodied in the work of literature. From the point of view of its action, *Paradise Lost* has every claim to being epic, in Hegel's sense, and the *Divine Comedy* has none.[16] Hegel's dismissal of Milton may also be prompted by the central role given to Satan, for he says, in one of his more dogmatic assertions, that the Devil is aesthetically 'unusable' because he is 'nothing but the embodiment of deceit, and therefore an utterly prosaic character' (*Ä* I. 288-9).

The central theme of Hegel's discussion of the epic is really what might be called the conditions of the possibility of epic poetry, put in cultural terms. This is a question which also interested Marx, who posed it in a similar way, opposing the world of Homer and the modern world of political economy, and asking:

ist Achilles möglich mit Pulver und Blei? Oder überhaupt die Iliade mit der Druckerpresse, und gar Druckmaschine? Hört das Singen und Sagen und die Muse mit dem Preßbengel nicht notwendig auf, also verschwinden nicht notwendige Bedingungen der epischen Poesie?[17]

is Achilles possible with powder and shot? Or indeed the Iliad alongside the printing-press, and the printing-machine? Are not the singers and soothsayers and the muse bound to fall silent with the advent of the press-handle; in other words, do not necessary conditions of epic poetry disappear?

Having observed that Vulcan, Jupiter, and Hermes cannot stand up to competition from Roberts and Co., the lightning-conductor, and the Crédit Mobilier, Marx goes on to wonder why Greek art and their epics are still enjoyed, and indeed 'in certain respects are still held up as a norm and as unattainable models'.[18] His answer is the fascination exerted by the unattainability of the cultural forms which they represent:

Der Reiz ihrer Kunst für uns steht nicht im Widerspruch zu der unentwickelten Gesellschaftsstufe, worauf sie wuchs. Ist vielmehr ihr Resultat und hängt vielmehr unzertrennlich damit zusammen, daß die unreifen gesellschaftlichen Bedingungen, unter denen sie entstand, und allein entstehen konnte, nie wiederkehren können.[19]

The appeal their art has for us is not in conflict with the undeveloped state of society which gave birth to it. On the contrary, it is the result of it, and is inextricably bound up with the fact that the immature social conditions under which, and only under which, their art was able to flourish, can never return.

Marx has fully accepted Hegelian premisses: the literary form of the epic is only possible under certain cultural and social conditions, and they are historical—once they have passed, they can never return.

Hegel's discussion of the Homeric poems accordingly focuses attention on the difference between the world they show and the modern one, and at the heart of the difference is the conception of the Divine, and the role played in Homer by the gods. The result of what Hegel says is always that Greek mythology is rational, and peculiarly suited to art. He regards the gods as the embodiment of 'substantial powers' as individuals ($\ddot{A}$ I. 290), and never tires of mentioning Herodotus'

remark that Homer and Hesiod gave the Greeks their gods (for instance
Ä II. 34, 76; *Ä* III. 335). The gods, whilst behaving like human characters and interacting with them, are distinguished from men by their
immortality. Consequently, they are never existentially threatened,
never totally committed to a cause in the way that (tragic) human
characters are, and have an air of cheerful serenity which Hegel is at
pains to stress, as he regards it to be characteristic of art as such (see
Ä I. 208-10, 290-1).[20] The role of the gods in human affairs is explained
so as to make it rational in terms of modern psychology. Hegel's general
thesis is that 'the gods seem to accomplish things alien to men, but in
fact only act out the substance of men's inner mind' (*Ä* I. 296), and he
illustrates it with the example of Achilles being restrained by Hera from
drawing his sword against Agamemnon (in Book I of the *Iliad*). Because
the Greeks thought about psychology as they did, Achilles' own inner
hesitation is externalized and embodied in the objective action of a god,
Hegel says, and he thus derives one of the most striking features of
Homeric style[21] from the self-understanding of the Greeks. He gives
further examples: Achilles' invulnerability is interpreted as a way of
externalizing the inner quality of courage (*Ä* I. 294, *Ä* II. 102): the need
to render the abstract more concrete also extends to nature, and Homer
thus expresses the fact that the heat contributed to the outbreak of
plague amongst the Argive forces by saying that Apollo was angry with
them and shot them with darts, which are really the rays of the sun
(*Ä* II. 71-2; more examples can be found throughout the lectures. See
Ä II. 77-81, 102-4 and *Ä* III. 336-7, 366-9). Everything in Homer is
given physical presence—just as Phidias' gods betray their lack of interiority through their blindness, so Homer eliminates interiority by
externalizing it. His heroes are sculptural figures, three-dimensional
and unchanging.

This produces a problem, for if we find Greek sculpture cold, we
should surely find Homer cold too because of the same lack of inward-
ness. Marx explained the attraction of Homer as a peculiar form of
nostalgia; Hegel explains it by appealing to the identity of Beauty and
Truth:

So hat z.B. Homer heimisch von seiner Welt gesprochen, und wo
anderen heimisch ist, sind wir auch einheimisch, denn da schauen wir
die Wahrheit an, den Geist, der in seiner Welt lebt und *sich* darin hat,
und uns wird wohl und heiter zumute, weil der Dichter selbst mit
ganzem Sinne und Geist dabei ist. (*Ä* III. 335-6.)

Homer spoke of a world familiar to him, and where others feel at home, we can feel at home too, for we can then see the Truth, the Spirit which lives in that world and recognizes itself in it, and we feel happy and at ease because the poet himself has his heart and soul in his work.

The *Iliad* is not our Truth, but we can enjoy it because it was Homer's Truth, and we can sense that it was. He has given expression to a particular way of experiencing the world, and as experience cannot be refuted, but can only change, it is something to which we can still attach value. Hegel stresses how alien Greek ethics and self-understanding are by contrasting them with Christianity: death had no affirmative meaning for the Greeks, as is shown by Achilles' complaint to Odysseus that he would rather be a slave in the world above than stay in Hades (*Ä* II. 135; see *Odyssey*, Book XI); Achilles' honour attaches to possessions and actions, not to his person, as would be the case for a medieval knight (*Ä* II. 176); love hardly figures in the poems, and when it does, it is largely carnal (*Ä* II. 183-4); there is a delight in physical objects for their own sake, an interest we can only recover through art (*Ä* II. 343-4). But the heroic ethos is not merely alien, it is also one which Hegel admires: Homer's heroes are at home in the world, and feel free in nature and the human surroundings they have created for themselves (*Ä* I. 338-9), and in their relationship to each other (*Ä* 244-5); such value is attached to the individual, that the details of every personal combat are an important part of the narrative (*Ä* II. 103);[22] the Greeks suffer fewer losses than the Trojans because they help each other in battle (see *Iliad* XVII), not, so Hegel believes, as a result of military drill and discipline, as would be the case today, but because of their ethical values (*Ä* III. 342-3). Hegel also admires Homer for showing the full range of his heroes' characters:

Achill liebt seine Mutter, die Thetis, er weint um die Briseis, da sie ihm entrissen ist . . . Dabei ist er der treuste Freund des Patroklos und Antilochos, zugleich der blühendste, feurigste Jüngling, schnellfüßig, tapfer, aber voll Ehrfurcht vor dem Alter . . . Ebenso zeigt sich aber Achill auch als reizbar, aufbrausend, rachsüchtig und voll Grausamkeit gegen den Feind . . . dennoch erweicht er sich, als der alte Priamos zu ihm ins Zelt kommt . . . Bei Achill kann man sagen: Das ist ein Mensch! (*Ä* I. 308.)

Achilles loves his mother, Thetis, he cries over Briseis when she is taken away from him . . . At the same time, he is the most loyal friend Patroclos and Antilochos have, and also the rising star of his generation, full of vigour, swift-footed and brave, but full of veneration for his elders . . . But equally, Achilles shows himself to be irritable, hot-headed and vindictive, treating his enemy with cruelty . . . even so, he relents

when old Priam comes to him in his tent . . . One can truly say of
Achilles: There goes a real man!.

One might wonder whether Achilles cries over Briseis, or over the
fact that Agamemnon has insulted him by taking her, a reading which
fits Hegel's general view of him rather better than his own (see *Iliad*
I). Be that as it may, Hegel goes on to ask the awkward question as to
how it is, given Achilles' admirable heroic qualities, that he is capable
of such cruelty to Hector, dragging his corpse round the walls of Troy.
His answer is that Achilles is thereby being true to himself, and showing that he is a complete human being:

Für die Vernünftigkeit des in sich Totalen und dadurch Lebendigen
aber ist diese Inkonsequenz gerade das Konsequente und Rechte. Denn
der Mensch ist dies: den Widerspruch des Vielen nicht nur in sich zu
tragen, sondern zu ertragen und darin sich selbst gleich und treu zu
bleiben. (*Ä* I. 311.)

For the rationality of something which is a living whole, this apparent
inconsistency is in fact both consistent and appropriate. For being
human means not simply having within oneself many contradictory
aspects, but living through the contradictions whilst retaining one's
identity and remaining true to oneself.

Hegel dismisses those who seek to pass moral judgements on Achilles
with the words: 'Achilles *is* who he *is*, and as far as the epic is concerned, that is an end of the matter' (*Ä* III. 360). This is to insist that
the aesthetic assessment of the *Iliad* be distinguished from the moral
judgement of Achilles, and to suggest that the latter is fatuous anyway.
However, Hegel himself is not morally neutral, as has been seen, but
thinks Achilles is admirable, and in fact shows what it is to be human.
He provides Achilles with a moral justification: it is quite acceptable
to indulge in slaughter if you are a bit of a young hothead, and you can
be forgiven for desecrating the bodies of your enemies if in so doing you
are just showing that you are a complete man. The Greeks would have
been horrified by what Achilles does to Hector, and in one of the very
rare 'authorial comments' on the action, his decision to kill a dozen
high-born Trojan captives to add to Patroclos' funeral pyre is described
as an evil thing (Book XXIII). Hegel may be right that being human has
nothing to do with being humane, but he ought not to use moral arguments if his case is really that moral judgements are inappropriate.

   More seriously, these comments point to some features of Homer
which undermine Hegel's belief that 'cruelty, wickedness, meanness,

and atrocity' are all alien to classical art ($\ddot{A}$ II. 105). The heroic ethos of the epic poems is in fact hard, savage, and cruel to quite the same extent as anything in the Middle Ages, which Hegel elsewhere finds too barbarous for the modern sensibility ($\ddot{A}$ II. 164-5). Characters in Homer who are presented as perfectly admirable behave with unrepentant brutality,[23] something which it can be hard to recognize, as many of us would like to feel that admirable men cannot be brutal as well. Hegel recognizes this whilst excusing it, but cannot obscure the fact that it invalidates his view of Greek culture.

Throughout this section one is kept aware of Hegel's theoretical concerns. The systematic nature of art is put in the foreground: the *Iliad* and *Odyssey* are unified totalities ($\ddot{A}$ I. 284 and $\ddot{A}$ III. 248, 358, 377, 388-9), constructed around one individual, giving them the concreteness he demands from art ($\ddot{A}$ III. 337-8), a reason which he adduces for believing that they were written by one poet. Hegel looks for and finds determinateness, both in the descriptions of nature ($\ddot{A}$ I. 328), and in the portrayal of human protagonists, who themselves form microcosms of epic art, total individuals who remain unchanged from beginning to end ($\ddot{A}$ I. 308 and $\ddot{A}$ II. 359). But most interesting of all is the way in which the features of these two texts are integrated into Hegel's view of the development of subjectivity. The Greeks are radically incapable of being subjective and interior, it seems, so that even when Hector is taking leave of his wife Andromache, he expresses himself in an objective, externalized, epic manner ($\ddot{A}$ III. 382). The *Iliad* shows the first stage of the exploration of man's soul, the 'triumph of the Occident over the Orient' ($\ddot{A}$ III. 353), but as the journey into the interior progresses, knowledge is expanded by the Christian ethos, embodied above all in Dante.

Hegel places Dante in parallel with Homer in several respects: he created a living poetic language for his nation ($\ddot{A}$ III. 286); the *Divine Comedy*, like the Homeric poems, is based on a unified action which makes possible the representation of a total world-view ($\ddot{A}$ III. 249); and it too is slow-moving, devoting much time to individual episodes and details ($\ddot{A}$ III. 384). But Dante did not give Christians their God, as Homer gave the Greeks their gods, and his work shows that the self-understanding of subjectivity has changed, for the progression towards the interior has moved on:

Denn in der Christlichen Welt ist das Subjekt nicht als bloße Akzidenz der Gottheit zu fassen, sondern als unendlicher Zweck in sich selbst, so daß hier der allgemeine Zweck, die göttliche Gerechtigkeit im

Verdammen und Seligsprechen, zugleich als die immanente Sache, das ewige Interesse und Sein des Einzelnen selber erscheinen kann. (*Ä* III. 249.)

For in the Christian world, the subject is not just an accidental of divine substance, but an infinite end in itself, so that here the universal end, divine justice in damnation and redemption, can at the same time be shown as immanent to the eternal interest and being of the individual himself.

The anchor of Hegel's reading of Dante is the new fusion of objectivity and subjectivity in the Divine judgement of human individuals. He is aware of the problems attaching to this. As he says, Dante's claim borders on presumption, in that he passes the Church's judgement on many contemporaries whom he portrays in Damnation (*Ä* II. 185), 214-15). Hegel justifies the enterprise with reference to the work's structure: as it is built around the poet's own journey, on which he is reporting, he has the right to add his own comments, and an inescapable element of subjectivity is present (*Ä* III. 358). (With odd exceptions such as Canto XII of the *Inferno*, Dante does usually add comments.) Hegel no doubt finds subjectivity acceptable in Dante, but not in Milton, because Dante is able to repeat in a new way the Greek achievement—Achilles does not develop, he is who he is, and as such shows universal features; in a similar way, the souls in the *Divine Comedy* are fixed eternally in one state by Divine judgement, and are not fully individualized, but represent specific sins or virtues which are themselves universal:

'Io eterno duro' steht über den Pforten der Hölle—sie sind, was sie sind, ohne Reue und Verlangen, sprechen nicht von ihren Qualen—diese gehen uns und sie gleichsam nichts an, denn sie dauern ewig—sondern sie sind nur ihrer Gesinnung und Taten eingedenk, fest sich selber gleich in denselben Interessen . . . (*Ä* III. 114).

'Io eterno duro' stands above the gates of Hell—they are what they are, without remorse and without aspirations, and do not mention their sufferings—it is as if these can be of no concern either to them or to ourselves, for they go on eternally. Their thoughts revolve exclusively around their own beliefs and deeds, fixed as they are with their old interests, the same as they always were . . .

It may not be true to say that the souls in Hell are 'without remorse and without aspirations', but they are without hope, and they do show great concern with talking to Dante, either to explain their own case or to get news from him. And the final fate of the characters is as Auerbach has observed in a study inspired by Hegel, the fixing of their earthly nature for all eternity.[24] Auerbach has called the following passage from the *Aesthetics* one of the finest ever written on Dante:[25]

Statt einer besonderen Begebenheit hat es das ewige Handeln, den absoluten Endzweck, die göttliche Liebe in ihrem unvergänglichen Geschehen und ihrem unabänderlichen Kreisen zum Gegenstande, die Hölle, das Fegefeuer, den Himmel zu seinem Lokal und senkt nun die lebendige Welt menschlichen Handelns und Leidens und näher der individuellen Taten und Schicksale in dies wechsellose Dasein hinein . . .
. . . wie die Individuen in ihrem Treiben und Leiden, ihren Absichten und ihrem Vollbringen waren, so sind sie hier für immer, als eherne Bilder versteinert, hingestellt. In dieser Weise umfaßt das Gedicht die Totalität objektivsten Lebens . . .
Wie die Homerischen Helden für *unsere* Erinnerungen durch die Muse dauernd sind, so haben diese Charaktere ihren Zustand für *sich*, für ihre Individualität hervorgebracht und sind nicht in unserer Vorstellung, sondern an *sich selber* ewig. Die Verewiging durch die Mnemosyne des Dichters gilt hier als das eigene Urteil Gottes . . . (*Ä* III. 406–7).

Its object is not a particular event, but eternal action, the constant workings and immutable circles of divine love, and it is set in Hell, Purgatory, and Heaven. Into this changeless existence it plunges the living world of human activity and suffering, and more especially of individual deeds and destinies . . .
. . . the individuals are found here as they were, with their concerns and troubles, their goals and achievements, petrified for ever as brazen images. In this way the poem encompasses the totality of objective life . . .
Whereas the muse allows the Homeric heroes to endure in *our* memories, so these characters have produced their condition for *themselves*, for their individuality, and are eternal not in our minds but *in themselves*. Being fixed for eternity by the mnemonic art of the poet is equated with the judgement of God . . .

The power of Dante's vision of eternity comes from its earthly realism. The souls show the same concerns as they always did on earth,[26] and are condemned to be as they always were, so that each is 'known in his innermost being' (*Ä* III. 407). They are, as it were, finally turned into themselves by eternity, aware of what they are through memory and unable to change, each with a punishment designed to fit the crime, and each still maintaining individual characteristics. Hegel mentions the example of Ugolino (*Ä* I. 336) who died of hunger in prison together with his sons, and is found by Dante gnawing on the skull of Archbishop Ruggieri who betrayed him (*Inferno*, Canto XXXIII).[27] In contrast to the Greek heroes, who do not reflect about themselves and the rights and wrongs of their actions, the souls in Dante know themselves finally for what they are—consciousness has moved on.

Hegel's critique of Klopstock's *Messias* combines reflection on artistic merit and on the ethos represented, and links its artistic failings with the problems of the project as a whole. Klopstock condemns himself to disaster by trying to take seriously a world view which belongs to the past, and mixing it with alien contemporary material:

einerseits Gottvater, die Geschichte Christi, Erzväter, Engel usf., auf der anderen Seite die deutsche Bildung des achtzehnten Jahrhunderts und die Begriffe der Wolffischen Metaphysik. Und dies Gedoppelte erkennt sich in jeder Zeile. (*Ä* III. 370.)

on the one hand there are God the Father, the story of Christ, patriarchs, angels etc., and on the other hand eighteenth-century German culture and the concepts of Wolffian metaphysics. And one is aware of this duality in every line.

Klopstock has not understood his historical position, and constructs a world of angels and devils which in his own day was theologically questionable, and demands that this exercise of his own imagination be taken seriously at face value. Hegel derives his aesthetic faults from this basic mistake, for as a result of it:

das Bestreben sichtlich wird, durch eine geschraubte Rhetorik der Erhabenheit seinem Gegenstande auch für den Leser dieselbe Anerkennung der begeisternden Würde und Heiligkeit zu verschaffen, zu welcher der Dichter selbst sich heraufgehoben hatte (*Ä* III. 413–14).

one can see the effort being made to create in the reader, by means of a strained use of the rhetorical sublime, the same recognition of inspiring dignity and sanctity to which the poet managed to raise himself.

Examples of what Hegel is referring to are easy to find. Satan's speech in Book II consists to a large extent of a desperate accumulation of exclamations, and wholly inappropriate rhetorical questions. But Hegel picks on another detail, the character of Abbadona, the penitent devil. Having listened to Satan's discourse, Abbadona realizes what a mess he is in, and tries to save his neck by launching into a verbal attack on Satan so that the wrath of the Almighty should spare him (*Messias*, Book II). Hegel sees through this inept piece of writing:

Wäre Abbadona ein Mensch, so würde die Hinwendung zu Gott gerechtfertigt erscheinen, bei dem Bösen für sich aber, das nicht ein einzelnes

menschliches Böses ist, bleibt sie eine nur gefühlvolle moralische
Trivialität. (*Ä* III. 371.)

Had Abbadona been a man, his turning to God would have been justified, but as he embodies evil as such, not an isolated piece of human
evil, his act can only be a piece of sentimental moral triviality.

By making Abbadona repentant for the most cowardly of reasons,
Klopstock shows that he has not understood the heroic ethos or the
sublime style which alone could save his poem from sentimentality. The
fallen angels could achieve heroic stature and sublimity by accepting
their lot, as do Dante's souls, abandoning hope, and being what they are.
As it is, Abbadona's self-interested penitence is as far from the sublime
as one can get—moral triviality.

Hegel's rejection of Klopstock raises the question of whether a
modern epic is possible at all. As modern society is complex and heterogeneous, it is not clear on what ethical principles it is based, or even if it
is based on any at all that are accepted by all its citizens, rather than
just a particular group. Similarly, to act as if one were the embodiment
of an ethical principle and to assert one's will without reflection is not
heroic, but ridiculous. The actions of the citizens of the modern state
are controlled by laws, but even if a modern Achilles were to escape
arrest, the results of his actions would be unpredictable because of the
complexity of social life. No individual has the power to influence
events which Achilles enjoyed, so the modern epic hero is acting in a
way inappropriate to social reality, as does Don Quixote (*Ä* I. 257). The
closest the twentieth century has come to Achilles is Superman, a figure
of fantasy, but even he, the embodiment of an American ethical ideal, is
constrained by the need to consult with those who have social and political authority (such as the Chief of Police or the President). The self-
understanding of modern civil society cannot be articulated in epics, nor
in comic books, but is so complex and problematic that is is the object
of investigation by sociologists, psychologist, and historians—'fine art
has been overtaken by thought and reflection', the poetry of imagination
being replaced by the prose of thought. The attempt to articulate the
total self-understanding of society can still be made, but in the modern
state[28] it will be necessarily particular and subjective. It will be the
author's view, with no guarantee that it be shared by anyone else. This
modern literary form, the partial, subjective epic which gives a particular, limited view of society, is the realist novel which Hegel sees beginning with Cervantes (*Ä* II. 217–18), but which he does not fully theorize.[29]

The conclusion of Hegel's reflections on the matter is to agree with Marx that there can be no serious epic of modern life. Epic writing must abandon seriousness, and/or representation of social reality, and Hegel finds an example of this in Goethe's *Reinecke Fuchs*. On the basis of Hegel's criteria, there are two features of the poem which one could call epic: the relationship between the King (the lion) and his vassals, and the static view of character which is shown. The King, like Agamemnon, is *primus inter pares*, his vassals autonomous: 'Reinecke and the others too carry on as they like' (*Ä* I. 246). Hegel says that in the Middle Ages, barons and knights did in fact behave like the animals in *Reinecke Fuchs*, each being a man of honour, and doing just as he liked, in a way that is no longer possible in an organized state (*Ä* II. 193). Each animal remains true to his own nature, and that nature does not alter, any more than Achilles or Ugolino alters. The whole story-line is founded on the ever-disappointed expectation that Reinecke will change his ways and reform, which would amount to his ceasing to be a fox. Every animal has a fixed nature, and behaves predictably, so that Braune the bear can be trapped through his desire for honey, and Hinze the tom-cat through his urge to catch mice. Epic characters cannot change because they embody ethical powers, but if they are just human individuals, as they are in the novel, they are free to develop. Indeed, one type of novel which became particularly popular in Germany, the 'Bildungsroman', thematizes the development of its hero who is educated, and changed, by his experience.

Reinecke Fuchs avoids the ridiculous because it does not portray social reality, and the animal world it does show cannot be taken seriously at face value. If social reality is to be shown, it must be treated ironically, and Hegel illustrates this in an interesting pendant to the idyll, in which he contrasts Voß's *Luise* with Goethe's Homeric *tour de force*, *Hermann und Dorothea*. In *Luise*, the family outing is a piece of banally philistine self-deception, for simply by having coffee and sugar on the table, we are reminded that the idyll is in fact set in the world of imports and exports, balance of payments deficits, colonialism, and the like—the world of political economy, in which communal autonomy is a lost dream. Goethe not only shows a village society which is more autonomous (it drinks its own wine), but, more importantly, it is set in the context of the French revolution rumbling in the background. The idyll is not escapist because it is threatened, and thus shown to be limited. To put it in Lukácsian terms, Goethe shows that his awareness goes beyond that of his characters by showing that the idyll is part of a greater, and less idyllic, whole (see *Ä* I. 250-1, 339-40 and *Ä* III. 414-15).

The pleasure a modern public takes in epic poetry will on the whole, despite *Reinecke Fuchs* and *Hermann und Dorothea*, be retrospective. The great epics are documents of past cultures, 'which one must accept as individuals, with the right to be the way they were', so that our reading of them will be educative and mind-broadening, something to which, Hegel notes, the Germans have only recently become susceptible, and for which they should be grateful (*Ä* III. 373). For the future, Hegel speculates that there is only one context in which alien and indifferent national principles could clash in an epic conflict. As far as future epics are concerned, he says:

so möchten diese nur den Sieg dereinstiger amerikanischer lebendiger Vernünftigkeit über die Einkerkerung in ein ins Unendliche fortgehendes Messen und Partikularisieren darzustellen haben (*Ä* III. 353).

they could only deal with the victory of the future vigorous rationality of America over incarceration is measuring and particularizing which goes on *ad infinitum*.

A future epic conflict would be a war between Europe and America. There can be no more European epics:

Denn in Europa ist jetzt jedes Volk von dem anderen beschränkt und darf von sich aus keinen Krieg mit einer anderen europäischen Nation anfangen; will man jetzt über Europa hinausschicken, so kann es nur nach Amerika sein. (Ibid.)

For in Europe now, every nation is limited by the other, and cannot start a war with another European nation on its own; if one seeks to go beyond Europe, it can only be to America.

Proclaimed from the stage of world history, these words are full of dramatic irony. But in a way Hegel is right about Europe. He has seen that the future will be an age of alliances, and appears to have seen, as many others did not, that such is the dependence of the European nations on each other, that a war between them would not be epic, but a tragedy.

The Drama

The dramatic conflict of tragedy consists, like epic action, in a conflict of ethical powers, but in a tragedy they are not indifferent, but related, and ultimately support each other. One of the first to express doubts about the universal applicability of Hegel's model was Goethe in a conversation with Eckermann, and Eckermann is probably right to add that it was designed to fit just one play, Sophocles' *Antigone*.[30] Hegel's reading of this work has been very influential, and discussion of it has tended to centre on the portrayal of Creon, who, if Hegel is correct, should have as much right on his side as Antigone.[31]

Hegel's exposition of his view is spread, repetitively, throughout the *Aesthetics*. The central issue is that of guilt and justification. According to the model, Antigone is acting out of love for a brother, a love not based upon subjective passion, but upon her responsibility for, and self-imposed identity with, the objective law of the family (*Ä* II. 184; see *Antigone*, ll. 905–13). This law is one ethical principle of Greek society, and she accepts it as her 'pathos'. Creon must embody the law of the state, so that in defying him, Antigone incurs guilt by failing to acknowledge the validity of that law, just as Creon incurs guilt for transgressing the law of the family. In his detailed discussion and critique of Hegel's reading, Brian Vickers has condensed it into a diagram which clearly shows the sets of antitheses Hegel discovers in the play.[32] One should add that Hegel twice calls *Antigone* one of the finest works of art of all time (*Ä* II. 60 and *Ä* III. 550), the reason being, by implication, its systematicity ('Everything in this tragedy is consistent . . .' (*Ä* II. 60)).

Character	Creon	Antigone
Sex	Male	Female
Social allegiance	State	Family
Social roles	Ruler; father; husband	Citizen; daughter; sister
Ethical loyalty	Political law	Family, unwritten law
Sphere	Upper world	Nether gods
Nature	Reality; light	Unreality; darkness
Movement	Upwards	Downwards
Action	Subdue by force	Evade by craft
View of the other	Subjective self-sufficiency	Arbitrary human violence
Human result	Destruction	Destruction
'Absolute' result	Re-establishment of the harmony of the 'ethical substance'	

It is not necessary or desirable here to try to show that there are other possible readings of the play besides Hegel's. What matters is whether his is itself a possible reading of the text, and whether his model is coherent. The decisive factor is the understanding of Creon, about which Hegel is most clear in the section on Greek religion in the *Philosophy of Religion*: 'Kreon ist nicht ein Tyrann, sondern ebenso eine sittliche Macht. Kreon hat nicht Unrecht'–'Creon is not a tyrant, but also an ethical power. Creon is not wrong.'[33] There are several reasons for challenging this.

Creon claims to be upholding the law of the state, and goes so far as to say that Antigone is breaking the bounds of *established* law (*Antigone*, l. 481). However, there is no law, written or unwritten, stipulating that one of the brothers be left unburied in such circumstances. Creon does not put into action an established law of the state, but *issues a decree*, as Antigone always insists.[34]

This decree is freely decided upon by Creon, and its content could have been otherwise. It is therefore irremediably subjective, a fact which Creon admits, and which is confirmed by the chorus (ll. 211-15). He does not consult with anyone, but calls a meeting of the council to tell them what he has decided.

Furthermore, the decree is so controversial that it is actively opposed. Creon does not attempt to get a consensus of opinion or seek advice, but mutters darkly about personal enemies (ll. 290 ff.), which suggests that he sees the issue as a personal one. What makes the decree controversial, and is crucial in Hegel's model, is that in making it Creon transgresses the established laws of the family, and offends the nether powers. His is the original guilty act which is needed to start the tragedy, and to which Antigone merely reacts. Creon could, for example, have had Polyneices buried outside the city in order to make a distinction between him and Eteocles, and would thus have fulfilled what he takes to be the needs of the state without overreaching himself and offending the gods. As Goethe mentioned to Eckermann, Creon's decision actually harms the city, for it is infected with pollution in retribution for not burying Polyneices. There are unnatural happenings and sacrifices fail, and the old prophet Teiresias blames it directly on Creon's decision (ll. 1,015 ff.).

This constitutes a case against Hegel based on Sophocles' text, and on the immanent structural weakness of his model which cannot account for the origin of any tragic conflict without an original, unprovoked, and unjustified act which singles out the first transgressor as the guilty party. However, going beyond the text, Hegel creates further difficulties for himself in the version of the myth he chooses to relate. He says that Oedipus' sons had agreed to reign for alternate years until Eteocles broke the arrangement ($\ddot{A}$ I. 271), which would mean that it would have been more just of Creon to leave *his* body unburied.[35] The relative rights and wrongs of the brothers' claims to power do not figure in *Antigone*. Creon simply argues that as Polyneices attacked Thebes and Eteocles defended it, Polyneices is a traitor, which questionably assumes that Eteocles was defending the city rather than his own power. The possession of power is enough to justify him in Creon's eyes.

It is, I think, the fact that Sophocles is drawing on a myth which is the clue to the convincingness of Hegel's interpretation. Although he makes constant reference to Sophocles, what he says makes better sense as a reading of the mythological material used rather than of the play itself. Hegel reads the play through the spectacles of his own *Phenomenology*, where the myth is manipulated in order to help him expound his view of Greek ethical life. It might be more profitable to see Hegel as another myth-maker, rather than as a reader of Sophocles. Hegel's version of the myth is of interest in its own right, and itself provides material which could interest a dramatist, intrigued by the idea that, as it were, 'some say that Creon was not a tyrant at all . . .'.

What Hegel's model of tragic conflict does point to very clearly is that Greek drama is set in a determinate ethical framework, and poses questions of right and wrong which are problematic, and cannot be avoided. In a modern novel, the subject-matter of which could be seen to raise moral issues, any moral judgements passed will depend on the personal values of the reader, because the ethical framework is indeterminate and the characters to some extent opaque. Emma Bovary, for example, can be made out to be evil, abject, pathetic, or admirable according to the values of the critic, which suggests that it is not only possible, but necessary to read *Madame Bovary* without trying to subject the characters to moral judgement. It is difficult to do the same in the case of the *Oresteia*, for the moral questions are thematized, with each character arguing his or her case, aware of what is being done and why, and of the need for justification. In Greek tragedy, there are not just characters, but issues—as Hegel puts it, the characters identify with something universal greater than themselves ($\ddot{A}$ II. 189). There are sections of Aeschylus and Sophocles to which an audience listens as if it were a jury.

Hegel devotes quite a lot of attention to Aeschylus' *Oresteia* trilogy.

His attitude to Agamemnon parallels his defence of Creon: he has to sacrifice Iphigenia because of the interests of the state (*Ä* III. 544). And once again, this simplifies the text and ignores the choice Agamemnon made, which could have been different, a choice which Hegel accepts and Aeschylus problematizes. Agamemnon is put under pressure from his men to carry out the sacrifice, but he is not compelled to do so. Calchas warns of pollution (*Agamemnon*, ll. 126-55), the cause is presented as questionable (ll. 445-55), the sacrifice is a brutal act of violence (ll. 227-48), and Agamemnon's values are questioned by the contrast of the promiscuous Helen (for instance l. 62) with the innocent maiden Iphigenia (ll. 208-9, 244-7).[36] In the same way, by reducing Clytemnestra's motivation for murdering Agamemnon to her identity with the interests of the family and therefore the revenge of her daughter is grossly to over-simplify (*Ä* III. 544). Clytemnestra has private passions too: she usurps Agamemnon's position and power, replaces him permanently with her lover Aegisthus, and revenges herself on her husband for his having taken Cassandra as his mistress. Hegel does not show that none of this is relevant, and if any of it is, his reading is weakened; it naïvely accepts the arguments Clytemnestra uses to justify herself (ll. 1,414-20) as a full and genuine account of her motivation.

The one case in which Hegel's formal, simplified model of a conflict between ethical powers does work convincingly is that of the final play of the trilogy, *The Eumenides*. The ancient powers of nature, in the form of the Eumenides, are pursuing Orestes for the murder of his mother (the subject of the second play, *The Libation Bearers*), and are confronted and opposed by Apollo, whom Hegel believes to embody the younger powers, the rising principle of self-consciousness. The Eumenides, he says, are justified in their hounding of Orestes, but he then qualifies this:

Das Recht jedoch, das sie gegen Orest geltend machen, is nur das Recht der Familie, insofern dieselbe im Blute wurzelt . . . Apollo stellt der natürlichen, schon sinnlich im Blute begründeten und empfundenen Sittlichkeit das Recht des in seinem tieferen Rechte verletzten Ehegatten und Fürsten entgegen. (*Ä* II. 59.)

But the right they put forward against Orestes is only the right of the family, to the extent that it is a blood relationship . . . Apollo opposes this natural ethical value, which draws its legitimacy from the senses and the feelings of the blood, with the right of the spouse and prince whose injured right is more profound.

The difference, he adds, may appear to be superficial, as both the blood relationship between mother and son and the freely chosen relationship between man and wife are principles of the family. However, the blood relationship is merely natural, whereas the relationship between man and wife is a product of 'the free ethical life of the self-conscious will' (ibid.), and is therefore 'higher'. The conflict is between nature and Spirit:

> Der Begriff und das Wissen von der Substantialität des ehelichen Lebens ist etwas Späteres und Tieferes als der natürliche Zusammenhalt von Sohn und Mutter und macht den Beginn des Staats als der Realisation des freien, vernünftigen Wollens aus. (Ibid.)

> The concept and knowledge of the substantiality of conjugal life is something later and deeper than the natural bond between mother and son, and signals the beginnings of the state as the realization of free rational volition.

Hegel's explanation does seem to account accurately for the issues at stake, but by integrating the play into the nature/Spirit opposition, Hegel obscures the fact that it is presented more as a power struggle between the old gods and the Olympians. The issue is decided at the end in a court scene. The parties go before Athene, and she summons the Areopagus, the jury of which casts an equal number of votes for Apollo and the Eumenides. Athene has the casting vote, and of course, as she herself is a product of parthenogenesis, being without a mother, and is also an Olympian, she votes for Apollo and Orestes.[37] For Hegel, this is not the victory of self-interest, but of reason, a further step away from nature down into the depths of subjectivity. (As he himself mentions, the Pythia, Apollo's priestess, recounts the god's genealogy in her opening speech, and shows him to be four stages removed from the forces of nature in Gea, mother-earth ($\ddot{A}$ II. 61).) A human court passes judgement on the relative value of the gods ($\ddot{A}$ II. 68), and by making this court the Areopagus in Athens, Aeschylus gives mythological significance to a familiar national institution ($\ddot{A}$ I. 355). Athenian justice also brings about a final resolution to the conflicts in the House of Atreus by allotting both causes a place in society ($\ddot{A}$ III. 532, 550). Athene indeed tells the Eumenides that they have not been defeated (l. 795) or dishonoured (l. 824), and asks them to stay in Athens (l. 869) with the assurance that no family will prosper without paying them due respect (l. 895), and Hegel notices that in return, the Eumenides are to protect Athens from natural disaster, which neatly confirms his identification of them with nature ($\ddot{A}$ II. 68). Tragedy comes to an end when the rights of both powers are recognized. It is interesting to note how Hegel's main argument about *The Eumenides* reverses one he uses in *Antigone*: Antigone, he stresses, acts out of duty, her *natural* love for a brother, an 'objective relation' (objektives Verhältnis) (*Ä* II. 184), which ensures the justice of her cause. Her cause would be far weaker if she were to act out of subjective passion. Now we learn that subjective relations are superior to objective, natural ones, and this is part of the reason for Hegel's sympathetic reading of Creon. Antigone's allegiances are pure, but primitive; Creon has history on his side.

The Eumenides links up the 'Antigone' model of drama—a conflict of ethical powers—with another type Hegel identifies with the Oedipus plays, which illustrates the opposition of nature and culture. (Hegel does not comment on the fact that it synthesizes the two in this way, though he might well have presented it as the ultimate realization of Greek drama for that reason.) The Oedipal conflict has nothing to do with incest, but with consciousness:

Hier handelt es sich um das Recht des wachen Bewußtseins, um die Berechtigung dessen, was der Mensch mit selbstbewußtem Wollen vollbringt, dem gegenüber, was er unbewußt und willenlos nach der Bestimmung der Götter wirklich getan hat. (*Ä* III. 545.)

The issue here is the right of conscious awareness, the justification of what a man achieves as a result of self-conscious will, as opposed to what he actually does unconsciously and without volition as determined by the gods.

What interests Hegel, is that despite being unaware of what he was doing as he did it, Oedipus punishes himself for his actions, and is banished as a guilty man. Hegel comments:

Das Recht unseres heutigen, tieferen Bewußtseins würde darin bestehen, diese Verbrechen, da sie weder im eigenen Wissen noch im eigenen Wollen gelegen haben, auch nicht als die Taten des eigenen Selbst anzuerkennen; der plastische Grieche aber steht ein für das, was er als Individuum vollbracht hat, und zerscheidet nicht in die formelle Subjektivität des Selbstbewußtseins und in das, was die objektive Sache ist. (Ibid.)

The view of our modern, deeper consciousness would be that as they lay outside both the knowledge and the will of the agent, these crimes should not be recognized as the deeds of his own self; but the integral Greek answers for everything which he as an individual does, and draws no distinction between the formal subjectivity of self-consciousness and the objective state of affairs.

The Greek identifies with what he does, the modern with what he knows he has done, and thus has a narrower conception of responsibility. Oedipus is 'plastisch' (see 'Sculpture', chapter 3 above), which is admirable, but it also means that he is not as deep as we are. Moderns like us know more about the interior than the Greeks did, but we are also fragmented —there is gain and loss (see *Ä* I. 246-7, 279). A modern Oedipus would feel guilt on discovering what he had done, but his conscience would be punishment enough, and he would not inflict physical wounds on himself as further punishment. Nor would his guilt be passed on to his offspring. A modern can be guilty of murder or manslaughter, and can avoid punishment by pleading diminished responsibility, but the ancient is responsible for everything he does, so that although his fellow men can show understanding for his situation, the offended gods demand retribution, and pollute his city with plague until it is exacted.

Here as in the case of *Antigone*, Hegel is interpreting a myth, not a play. *Oedipus the King* consists in Oedipus' discovery of who he is and what he has done, and Hegel does not discuss this action at all. He could have made all the comments he does if Sophocles had never dealt with the material. Hegel's concern as usual is with 'the pre-existing national conditions' which are peculiar to the works under discussion, and which he says are responsible for keeping Greek tragedy off the modern stage (*Ä* III. 507). Some of the things the Greeks put on stage are too strong for us: Philoctetes' screams and groans and his stinking wound, for example, or the human sacrifices in the Iphigenia plays of Euripides (ibid.). Ironically, Hegel uses the phrase 'die Barbarei des Menschenopfers'—'the barbarism of human sacrifice', 'barbarian' being the name the Greeks gave to foreigners. Can these plays be the products of the same nation which produced Laocoön refusing to shout with pain, and kept ugliness and dissonance out of art? Hegel has once more burst the framework of his cultural hermeneutics and admitted the presence of aspects of Greek culture with which he cannot deal. The Greeks too were un-Greek barbarians. Hegel need not have been worried by our being too sensitive to stomach what Sophocles or Aeschylus offer us. In generations succeeding his own, some of 'us' have become less squeamish about the sort of sex and violence with which Attic tragedy is largely concerned.

In general, Hegel's theory of tragedy is an interpretation of myths used in some plays by Aeschylus and Sophocles, and only works properly in the case of *The Eumenides*. Hegel writes mainly about tragedy, and mainly about those two playwrights—Euripides is dismissed as a decadent seeker after effect who tries to be 'moving'

($\ddot{A}$ III. 546, 562). Comedy is given more summary treatment, and the prime example cited is Aristophanes, of whom Hegel has a very high opinion, saying that you have to read him to know just how good people can feel ($\ddot{A}$ III. 553). He is a great comic poet because he only ridicules what is in itself insubstantial: those who abuse power or act against the interests of the state ($\ddot{A}$ II. 117-20; $\ddot{A}$ III. 503-4, 530, 552-5, 569). In other words, the message behind the bawdy mockery is really pious, and the playwright who heaps ridicule on Athenian politicians is really a pillar of society. Aristophanes is a good playwright if his attacks are just, his plays are good if what they say is right. Even in comedy, Beauty is Truth.

With the demise of the polis and the loss of a generally accepted mythology, the intimate relationship between drama and contemporary social reality is lost, and ancient tragedy is replaced by a new form of drama which Hegel regards as Shakespearian. The use of mythology is replaced by the use of historical material,[38] and the interest shifts from a conflict between ethical powers embodied in individuals to a conflict between characters or within one character (see $\ddot{A}$ I. 248-52, 357-8 and $\ddot{A}$ III. 500, 561, 564). The characters embody moral, rather than ethical principles, which are universal rather than socially specific, and Shakespeare accordingly has a more universal appeal than the Greek tragedians ($\ddot{A}$ III. 498-9).[39] Examples Hegel gives of characters with an overriding passion are Othello, whose pathos is jealousy ($\ddot{A}$ I. 277; $\ddot{A}$ II. 200; $\ddot{A}$ III. 561), and Macbeth, who is driven by political ambition (Herrschsucht; $\ddot{A}$ II. 200-3, 210; $\ddot{A}$ III. 561).

It is *Hamlet* which Hegel chooses above all others for comparison with ancient drama, for he sees Hamlet himself as the paradigm of the 'modern' hero, whose conflicts are internal. Hegel describes the action in classical terms, saying: 'Hamlet's mother insults the manes of the dead man by promptly marrying his murderer' ($\ddot{A}$ I. 279), and draws a parallel with the *Oresteia*. Hamlet is encouraged by the ghost of his father as Orestes is by Apollo, with the difference that what in Aeschylus is 'an ethical claim' becomes in Shakespeare 'nothing but a villainous crime', so that Hamlet, unlike Orestes, runs no danger of transgressing another ethical law in taking revenge ($\ddot{A}$ III. 559). The issue is not like a jury case, but is concerned instead with Hamlet's own character:

Die eigentliche Kollision dreht sich . . . um den subjektiven Charakter Hamlets, dessen edle Seele für diese Art energischer Tätigkeit nicht geschaffen ist und, voll Ekel an der Welt und am Leben, zwischen Entschluß, Proben und Anstalten zur Ausführung umhergetrieben, durch das eigene Zaudern und die äußere Verwicklung der Umstände zugrunde geht. (Ibid.)

The real collision revolves around . . . Hamlet's subjective character, for his noble soul is not made for this sort of energetic activity, and, full of disgust with the world and with life, pulled this way and that between decisions, trials, and preparations for action, he is ruined by his own temporizing and the entanglements of external circumstances.

Hamlet is the tragedy of the melancholic, a 'beautiful, noble soul' (*Ä* II. 207), which cannot act:

er . . . verharrt in der Untätigkeit einer schönen, innerlichen Seele, die sich nicht wirklich machen, in die gegenwärtigen Verhältnisse sich nicht hineinlegen kann. Er wartet ab, sucht in der schönen Rechtlichkeit seines Gemüts nach objektiver Gewißheit, kommt aber, selbst nachdem er sie erlangt hat, zu keinem festen Entschluß, sondern läßt sich durch äußere Umstände leiten . . . handelt übereilt, wo er hätte besonnen prüfen müssen, während er, wo er der rechten Tatkraft bedurfte, in sich versunken bleibt, bis sich ohne seine Handlung in diesem breiten Verlauf der Umstände und Zufälle das Schicksal des Ganzen wie seiner eigenen stets wieder in sich zurückgezogenen Innerlichkeit entwickelt hat. (*Ä* II. 208).

he . . . remains caught in the inactivity of a beautiful, inward soul, which cannot realise itself, cannot participate in the actual world around it. He waits to see, searches in his fine and honest soul for objective certainty, but even when he has found it, he can make no firm decision, but is led on by external circumstances . . . acts precipitately when he should have checked things carefully, whilst remaining buried in introspection when he should have acted with vigour, until, without his ever doing anything, the fate of all, including that of his own retiring, introspective soul, has been decided by the broad course of chance events and circumstances.

The problems are in Hamlet's personality from the first. He has nameless wishes which can never be fulfilled, and is marked from his first speech by a sympathy with death:

Äußerlich genommen, erscheint der Tod Hamlets zufällig durch den Kampf mit Laertes und die Verwechslung der Degen herbeigeleitet. Doch im Hintergrunde von Hamlets Gemüt liegt von Anfang an der Tod. Die Sandbank der Endlichkeit genügt ihm nicht; bei solcher Trauer und Weichheit, bei diesem Gram, diesem Ekel an / allen Zuständen des Lebens fühlen wir von Hause aus, er sei in dieser greulhaften Umgebung ein verlorener Mann, den der innere Überdruß fast schon verzehrt hat, ehe noch der Tod von außen an ihn herantritt. (*Ä* III. 566–7.)

Looked at externally, Hamlet's death seems to have been brought about accidentally by the duel with Laertes and the exchange of daggers. But death is in the background of Hamlet's mind from the very beginning. The sands of finitude cannot satisfy him; with his melancholy and gentle nature, the sadness and distaste all life's circumstances awaken in him, we feel that in this frightful environment he is already a lost man, almost consumed by inner weariness before death comes upon him from without.

This view of Hamlet has become so familiar today that it sounds almost banal. It should therefore be remembered that Hegel was writing at a time when it was commonplace to criticize Shakespeare for Hamlet's inactivity, and complain that the play never gets off the ground because of it (see *Ä* I. 300). Hegel is one of the first to espouse a view of the play which has since become dominant, and he shows remarkable critical imagination.[40] He takes his cue from Goethe, who, he says, has the insight that *Hamlet* is about 'a great deed being consigned to a soul which is not equal to it' (*Ä* I. 300). The passage he quotes was indeed written by Goethe, but the view is that of Serlo, a character in *Wilhelm Meisters Lehrjahre*, who is contradicting Wilhelm's opinion that Hamlet is 'not by nature melancholic or reflective'.[41] Hegel is articulating something coming to be felt by numerous commentators at the beginning of the nineteenth century, but it was still novel, and what enables him to see Hamlet in the way he does is his awareness of historical difference and his willingness to find different principles in different ages. As a result, he does not criticize Shakespeare for being unclassical, but looks for what distinguishes his plays from any others, and so tries to understand *Hamlet* on its own terms.

The material of Greek drama is myth, which Shakespeare replaces with history. Goethe and Schiller, however, try in their early plays to show dramatic conflict against the background of contemporary social reality, and the only way in which this is possible is to show a conflict between characters who take heroic responsibility upon themselves by moving outside the established laws which make heroism impossible, and those established laws themselves. The heroic individual fights the prosaic reality of society. Figures like Karl Moor, Major Ferdinand, or Marquis Posa do not represent particular ethical principles, but universal moral principles: human rights (*Ä* I. 255-6; *Ä* III. 557-8). Even though our modern form of political organization may enjoy our assent, art remains a formal need (though not a need of Spirit), and is inimical to the complex world of political economy (*Ä* I. 255). So in moving from fifth-century Athens to eighteenth-century Germany, we have moved from one pole to another, from a state in which social substance provided the material of drama to a state in which social substance renders drama impossible. The hero is now an outsider, and the view of society expressed is subjective. It is this subjectivity which Hegel criticizes in Schiller—in words one could place in the mouth of any middle-aged conservative today, he calls 'all the going on about nature, human rights, and reforming the world' in Schiller's early plays the 'gush of subjective enthusiasm' (*Ä* III. 558). Schiller improves when he overcomes the undisciplined excesses of youth and restores the principles of ancient tragedy to the modern drama (*Ä* III. 559), an enterprise one would expect Hegel, given his historical principles, to view with scepticism. In general, whilst he seems to understand why Goethe and Schiller wrote their first plays in the way they did, using direct everyday language of 'unadorned coarseness and power' (*Ä* III. 491), Hegel finds the results over-rhetorical and boring, largely because they are too dissonant for his taste (ibid. 494). The danger is that the fight against prosaic circumstances will itself be prosaic. Such is the tenor of his adverse remarks about Goethe's *Götz von Berlichingen*. He quotes its opening and the first of the scenes entitled 'Saal' in Act III. All this is, he says, 'easy to visualize, and understandable given the nature of the situation and the characters', but he nevertheless condemns both scenes as 'utterly trivial and intrinsically prosaic' because they show only 'quite ordinary appearances and objectivity' (*Ä* 351). Hegel seems to object to the portrayal of ordinary low life in the theatre, but yet he praises Goethe's choice of subject, saying that choosing the collision between the medieval heroic ethos and a modern legal framework as his first theme showed Goethe's sureness of sense (*Ä* I. 257). He also accepts the representation of reality in Homer and in genre painting, so why not in Goethe? The reason seems to be at least in part, that it is tiresome in the theatre but more acceptable in a text or a painting, which is why Hegel thinks *Götz* did not run for very long on stage. It enjoyed more success when read, when the frequent scene changes are less disturbing (*Ä* I. 351). He might have added, but did not, that the play's representation of the details of everyday life give it an epic character, which might explain why it is better read than staged.

Although Hegel praises Schiller's mature plays for their energy and effectiveness on stage (*Ä* III. 494), it is Goethe's classicism which lies closest to his heart, and the example of it he mentions most frequently is *Iphigenia*. In *Tasso*, the resolution is subjective (*Ä* III. 533), but in

Iphigenia the transformation which takes place at the end leads Hegel
to declare it to be the finest example he knows of the use of a classical
framework with a modern content (*Ä* I. 356). Goethe alters some
aspects of Euripides' original in order to tone it down for the needs of
a modern audience (*Ä* III. 507), but the most significant difference
betweeen Euripides and Goethe is that Goethe brings about a resolution
through a change in the attitudes of the human protagonists rather than
through the actions of the gods (*Ä* I. 297-9). Iphigenia refuses to trick
Thoas, and openly tells him that Orestes and Pylades are about to
escape. By trusting in his good nature, she avoids a potentially disastrous
fight between the Greeks and the Taurians, and instead of allowing her
brother to decide the issue in single combat with Thoas, 'she manages,
in a gentle human way, to coax permission to return to her own people
out of him' (*Ä* I. 298). Even after he has agreed to this, she insists further that he let them go with his blessing, not with resentment. Iphigenia
places power in the hands of a potential enemy, and as a result he does
of his own accord (though under pressure from her), what she wants
of him. If it were a Greek drama, Hegel would see the conflict as that
between Thoas representing the laws of the state (that foreigners be
sacrificed) and Iphigenia and Orestes representing the law of the family.
In Goethe's play he sees the triumph, through Iphigenia, of Christian
subjectivity, the truth she finds within herself, 'in des Menschen Brust'
(*Ä* I. 297), over the limited, particular interests of the men in the play,
the triumph of the universal over the particular, of modern morality
over classical ethics.

In *Iphigenia*, then, Hegel's interest is as usual directed by his theoretical concerns and his cultural hermeneutics. However, it is *Faust*
which offers him the closest parallel with philosophy. He calls it 'the
absolute philosophical tragedy', showing 'the tragic attempt to mediate
subjective knowledge and striving with the Absolute' (*Ä* III. 557).
Unfortunately, he does not elaborate on this, and in another passage,
there is a note of critical dissent, containing direct criticism of the
imaginative freedom Goethe allowed himself in *Faust*:

man mag die großen Kabiren, die Korybanten, die Darstellungen der
Zeugungskraft usf. herausputzen, soviel man will, so gehören dergleichen
Anschauungen nach allen Zügen—von der alten Baubo, die Goethe auf
dem Blocksberg auf einem Mutterschwein voranreiten läßt, nicht zu
sprechen—mehr oder weniger noch der Dämmerung des Bewußtseins
an (*Ä* II. 63-4).

no matter how much one tries to dress up the great Cabiri, corybantes, symbols of fertility, etc., all these sorts of things—not to mention old Baubo who Goethe has leading the ride over the Blocksberg on a sow— still more or less belong to the twilight of consciousness.

The second part of *Faust* was published in full form only after Hegel's death, but one can surmise from these words that the 'klassische Walpurgisnacht' at least would not have met with his approval. 'Kabiren' are referred to by the sirens and others (*Faust II*, ll. 8074, 8178, 8216-18), and one of Goethe's plans (of 6 February 1830) includes a role for corybantes too. Both belong to the more primitive side of symbolic art, but are found in Goethe's most philosophical work. Perhaps the lack of detailed comment on *Faust* was a diplomatic omission on Hegel's part.

Measured by his own theoretical claims, Hegel's account of drama is disappointing. What appears to be theory is on the whole empirical description, and works in very few cases. But Hegel's more substantial insight is that drama has its roots in our self-understanding, and that the forms of drama alter as self-understanding alters. The clear ethical concerns of the classical character go along with a different form of self-understanding and a different form of drama from those of Hamlet, the paradigm of the Romantic 'schöne Seele'.[42] But both can be called tragic characters because they are free to make decisions and act upon them. However, when society regulates and constrains the behaviour of its members through positive laws, and also by virtue of its sheer complexity, heroism turns to bathos, and the individual who acts as if he were autonomous looks ridiculous. If a modern Achilles had had twelve captives killed at Patroclos' funeral, he would have been condemned by a court of inquiry; epic heroes cannot be heroic if they have to worry about being convicted of war crimes. And if, along with social complexity and legal regulation, we have a society which understands the human subject to be influenced by upbringing and environment, unconscious drives, and the message encoded in its DNA, the scope for heroic action, whether epic or tragic, is small indeed. In such a society, art has been overtaken by thought, and those ancient forms of Beauty, found wanting by the demands of Truth, will be abandoned.

The Lyric

Hegel does not have a theory of the lyric in the way that he has a theory of epic and drama. He explains this himself by observing that as lyric poetry is distinguished by being subjective and particular, there are very few general things to be said (*Ä* III. 442–3). There are not even particular cultural or historical circumstances under which the lyric thrives—it is spread equally over all three art-forms.[43] So instead of trying to determine the Concept of the lyric, Hegel is content with listing characteristics which distinguish lyric from epic poetry. The unity of a lyric poem is not constituted by any action, but by its mood or subject-matter (*Ä* III. 421), so that epic material (like an event) can be treated lyrically by focusing on the reaction of the subject to the event (*Ä* III. 422–7, 443–4). Its content is subjectivity, but what it expresses about subjectivity should not be just subjective, but contain something of universal interest, in order to be more than the 'Lirum-larum' of song (*Ä* III. 429). From a formal point of view, it shows concentration (in contrast to epic expansiveness; ibid. 444–7), and with its musical tendencies, the temporal element gains in importance (pp. 447–50).

In ordering the subject, Hegel ignores the art-forms and has recourse to the *Logic of Concept* with the schema of universal, particular, and individual (*Ä* III. 419–20). The subject-matter of the lyric is thus considered according to the degree of universality or subjectivity it shows, and its forms are ordered according to the same criterion, so that they range from the 'hymnos' or dithyramb to the 'Lied' (*Ä* III. 450–60). The short section on the historical development of the lyric is abruptly broken off in order to consider a matter in which Hegel was far more interested, the issue of national poetry in contemporary Germany (*Ä* III. 470). His right to do so is defended by implication earlier, when he says that it is only possible to understand properly the lyrics of one's own nation (*Ä* III. 432). The discussion which follows is confined to Klopstock, but if one draws together what Hegel has to say about German poetry of his day, one finds three clear levels: Klopstock's glorious failure, Schiller's noble but limited success, and the crowning triumph of Goethe.

Despite his assertion that many of Klopstock's poems, which he describes as being 'of thorough, if austere workmanship', are classics (*Ä* III. 471), what Hegel actually praises is his attitude, his boldness and enthusiasm. He admires Klopstock rather than his poetry, and has respect for what he tried to do rather than what he actually did, which inspires few compliments, and not a little sarcasm. Thus amongst

Klopstock's early odes, many of which are said to be 'utterly prosaic'
(*Ä* III. 471), he singles out the poem *Selmar und Selma*:

> Weine du nicht, o die ich innig liebe,
> Daß ein trauriger Tag von dir mich scheidet!
> Wenn nun wieder Hesperus dir dort lächelt,
> Komm ich Glücklicher wieder!
>
> Aber in dunkler Nacht ersteigst du Felsen,
> Schwebst in täuschender dunkler Nacht auf Wassern!
> Teilt ich nur mit dir die Gefahr, zu sterben,
> Würd ich Glückliche weinen?

Hegel's comment on it is of the sort usually reserved for the Romantics:

ein trübseliger, langweiliger Wettstreit zwischen Liebenden, der sich
nicht ohne viel Weinen, Wehmut, leere Sehnsucht und unnütze melan-
cholische Empfindung um den müßigen, leblosen Gedanken dreht, ob
Selmar oder Selma zuerst sterben werde (p. 471).

a dreary, tedious competition between lovers, which, not without a lot
of tears, mournfulness, empty longing, and pointless feelings of melancholy, revolves around the dull, tiresome question of whether Selmar
or Selma will die first.

This is the sort of contempt Hegel expresses for a form of sentimentality
which stands at the opposite pole from Greek plasticity, being characterized by indeterminateness: it is gloomy rather than bright, involves
yearning rather than enjoyment of what is actual, and melancholic feeling rather than thought.[44] However one may regard Hegel's moral
position in this, *Selmar und Selma* is hardly an appropriate object for
such polemics. It is concentrated and clear, the yearning is not 'empty'
but has a definite object, and there is no emotional self-indulgence on
the part of the lovers, but an attempt to offer comfort to each other.
To call it a competition over who can die first is nothing short of cheap
ridicule, which does no justice to its formal qualities, the parallels of
day and night and the balancing of the final line of each stanza. The
form is of medieval pedigree: Klopstock has produced a 'Klage' in the
form of a 'Wechsel', so that the parted lovers sing to each other in
alternate stanzas, and built it around the motif of the 'Tagelied', in
which the coming of day forces the lovers' separation.[45]

In general, Hegel has little time for the more private side of Klopstock, for the very reason that it is private. Poems like *An Fanny* or

An Cïdli are not universal enough for his liking; he calls them 'domestic affairs, about cousins and aunts' (*Ä* III. 428–9). He also has some hard things to say about Klopstock's high-toned rhetoric (*Ä* III. 454, 455), as he did in the case of *Messias* (see 'The Epic', chapter 4 above), but is generous in his judgement of the patriotic verse (in which the tone often degenerates into the sort of strident bombast he is talking about) because his main interest is in the subject-matter. However, Hegel's sympathy extends only to what Klopstock was trying to do, not the results. In order to write national poetry of universal interest to the community, Klopstock needed a mythology, and so made the bold but doomed attempt to breathe new life into the old Germanic gods. In the modern age, Hegel says, these figures are 'totally untrue and hollow', and to treat them seriously is to succumb to 'a sort of foolish hypocrisy' (*Ä* III. 472), from which one might gauge what his reaction to Wagner's *Ring* would have been. Klopstock is more successful, he thinks, when he deals with figures from German history, such as Hermann, or with great contemporary political events, as he does in *Die Etats Généraux*, which is quoted at some length (*Ä* III. 472–3). Klopstock is fated to failure by his historical position, and Hegel gives him most credit for simply asserting himself and the dignity of poetry and the German language (p. 472). He is seen as performing a necessary service to German letters, but the man who actually succeeded in drawing together art and social morality, and thus in writing national poetry, was Schiller (*Ä* III. 474).

What distinguishes Schiller in Hegel's estimation is that he is concerned with issues and principles, but manages to treat them in a poetic way (*Ä* III. 424, 430, 460–1). As the interest of his work lies as much in what he says as in how he says it, Hegel tends to refer to him as if he were another philosopher (see *Ä* III. 437–8), a potential discussion partner who often provides a good formulation of something Hegel wants to say. For example, he quotes *Das Ideal und das Leben* to illustrate the nature of the Ideal (*Ä* I. 207) and defends Schiller's dictum 'Ernst ist das Leben, heiter ist die Kunst'–'Life is serious, art is cheerful' (*Ä* I. 208; it is the last line of the prologue to *Wallenstein* of 1798). In the former case, Schiller uses the image of the shades in the phrase 'der Schönheit stillem Schattenlande', and Hegel draws out its implications: Beauty is mediated by thought so as to be removed from natural existence into an autonomous world of its own. Schiller had the gift of putting such things in a pithy, concrete way, a gift Hegel himself did not completely lack—one thinks of the image of the thousand-eyed Argus in the *Aesthetics*, or the more famous one of the owl of Minerva in the *Philosophy of Right*. Purely literary comments on Schiller are comparatively rare: Hegel mentions the chorus lines in *Die Kraniche des Ibykus*, saying (oddly) that they are lyrical rather than epic or dramatic (*Ä* III. 420), and comments on how the stages of bell-casting are used to structure *Das Lied von der Glocke* (*Ä* III. 426). As if to confirm that Schiller's poetic talent enabled him to express his own ideas better than he could himself, Hegel quotes lines 398–409 of this poem as an expression of his general view of Schiller's poetry (*Ä* III. 461).

The centre of lyric poetry is occupied by Goethe, whom Hegel revered both as an artist and as a man. He is a national figure because of his specifically poetic gifts:

besonders sind Goethes Lieder das Vortrefflichste, Tiefste und Wirkungs-vollste, was wir Deutsche aus neuerer Zeit besitzen, weil sie ganz ihm und seinem Volke angehören und, wie sie auf heimischem Boden erwachsen sind, dem Grundton unseres Geistes nun auch vollständig entsprechen (*Ä* III. 474).

Goethe's songs in particular are the finest, most profound, and most effective things we Germans have from recent years, because they belong completely to him and his people and, being a product of native soil, are in complete harmony with the key-note of our Spirit.

Goethe is a national poet not because of his themes, nor through any conscious desire on his part to transcend the personal, but simply because the fruits of his labours were grown on native soil. This is enough because he is a natural poet: 'everything he experienced became a lyrical effusion' (*Ä* III. 442; see also p. 425). This 'naturalness' is the unreflected naïvety of his production which makes of him a unique anomaly, a modern Greek (see 'Sculpture', chapter 3 above). Goethe is modern because of his subjectivity, depth of feeling, and interiority, and Greek in his manner of production, and the way in which these two features combine is well illustrated by Hegel's comments on *Die Leiden des jungen Werthers*. It was, we are told, a sort of occasional poem, a spontaneous expression in artistic form of Goethe's own pain, 'the confusion and torment of his own heart' (*Ä* I. 266). The content of the work comes from 'Herz' and 'Brust', deep in the interior as it was penetrated through the romantic art-form, but this subjectivity is put into an objective form and made universally accessible without the conscious reflection typical of modern artists. Goethe is the complete artist, the synthesis of the classical and the romantic: his content is modern (for it is his 'Humanus' whose self-exploration is the substance of modern art), and the form of his production is Greek (for he possesses the instinctual intelligence, the 'großer Sinn', which made the Greeks a nation of artists). And yet, though *Werther* shows these qualities in Goethe, Hegel does not find them in the eponymous hero, and for all his tendency to regard the work as autobiographical, he does not equate Werther with his creator. Werther, he says, is:

ein durchweg krankhafter Charakter, ohne Kraft, sich über den Eigensinn seiner Liebe erheben zu können. Was ihn interessant macht, ist die Leidenschaft und Schönheit der Empfindung . . . (*Ä* I. 313).

a thoroughly sick character, without the strength to rise above the wilfulness of his love. What makes him interesting is his passion and fineness of feeling . . .

He is a romantic, in fact a Romantic, who has lost touch with the objectivity of classicism, and is lost in the pure, indeterminate interiority of 'Empfindsamkeit'.

The way in which Goethe synthesizes romantic content and classical form is the leitmotiv running through all of Hegel's remarks about his poetry. Thus Goethe's ballads are said to be distinguished 'by the deeper feeling running as a lyrical strain through the graphic clarity of the whole' (*Ä* III. 424), and 'his first songs' are praised above all his other lyric productions because they are 'the most sincere and unstudied' (*Ä* I. 368). The synthesis Goethe achieves is thus a double one: 'anschauliche Klarheit'–'graphic clarity' is married to 'innigere Seele'–'a deeper soul', and the 'Innigkeit' is also 'unabsichtlich'–'unstudied'. Goethe is Hellenic both in the classical clarity of his form and the spontaneity of his creative psychology. It is this 'naturalness' which is the ultimate proof of Goethe's poetic gift:

In den späteren Tagen eines durchweg reflektierten Bewußtseins, das jener in sich zurückgedrängten Naivität fernsteht, sind solche Darstellungen von höchster Schwierigkeit und geben den Beweis eines ursprünglich poetischen Geistes. (*Ä* II. 206–7.)

In a late age of full reflective consciousness, which is so far away from this withdrawn naïvety, it is extremely difficult to write in this way, and such works bear witness to a mind which is fundamentally poetic.

Accordingly, the ultimate test of a poet's Hellenic qualities is his ability to write folk-songs, those most un-classical examples of poetry. Goethe did not need classicism to be classical, and did not need to imitate the Greeks, for he was one of them anyway.

Hegel tends to see Goethe in his role as the Olympian patriarch of German letters, and chooses examples which support this, leaving out the ones which would put it in a wider context. He never mentions *An den Mond*, for example, which is obscure and has anything but 'graphic clarity'. The lack of clarity and irrationalism which is sometimes found in Goethe is accepted in only one case, that of *Die Braut von Korinth*, where it is found in a classical framework. Hegel discusses this ballad in the same context as Schiller's *Die Götter Griechenlands*, interpreting it as a criticism of the 'false asceticism' attaching to a certain form of Christianity by opposing it to the healthy Greek attitude to love and marriage (*Ä* II. 116). The poem tells how a young man from Athens visits the lately Christianized family of his bride to be, and how the wraith of the girl, who was sent to an early grave, comes to him in the night. The girl's mother discovers them making love, and the ghostly daughter announces that her lover too will now die, and demands that the ancient funeral rites be enacted so that they might join the old gods. Hegel's reading of the poem is characteristic of him, but he adds:

Es ist mit großer Kunst dem Ganzen ein schauderhafter Ton gegeben, vornehmlich darin, daß es ungewiß bleibt, ob es sich um ein wirkliches Mädchen oder um eine Tote, eine Lebendige oder ein Gespenst handelt ... (*Ä* II. 116).

With consummate artistry the poem has been lent an air of horror, principally because it is kept uncertain whether it is a real girl or a dead one, a living person or a ghost ...

For once the supernatural is not explained as a projection of a character's mental state, but is accepted as inexplicable, and the element of indeterminacy as to whether the girl is alive or dead is singled out for praise. Hegel normally has no time for the uncanny, the indeterminate, or the inexplicable, but he accepts it here. In the case of *Der Erlkönig*, which he mentions twice, the subject of the irrational is avoided. It is given as an example of how Goethe does not explicitly express the deeper feelings of his characters, but indicates them through reference to external objects (*Ä* I. 374, *Ä* II. 458). What Hegel does not point out is that the reader is left in doubt as to what the external objects are, as the poem consists in the conflicting interpretations of reality given by father and child: the one sees bands of mist in the willows and hears the wind in the trees, and the other sees the Erlking with his daughters and hears his voice inviting him to come and play and then threatening violence. Rationality and clarity are played off against irrationality and obscurity—in the end, the child is dead, so perhaps it had understood more than its father could explain. The poem is another example of Goethe's interest in the twilight areas of consciousness of which Hegel is usually dismissive (see the discussion of *Faust* above). What interests Hegel about *Der Erlkönig* is the way in which the romantic content, which is essentially interior, is obliquely conveyed through something external, i.e. the symbolic mode of representation which is necessary in the romantic art-form.

Hegel's own taste in the matter of poetry shows a clear dislike of vigour, and a liking of refinement which approaches the bloodless and the anodyne. Just as Goethe's early drama is censured, so are some of his early poems, such as *Willkommen und Abschied*, despite the praise found for 'seine ersten Lieder'. Hegel is respectful and discriminatory, but his praise is faint:

In '*Willkommen und Abschied*' z.B. ist die Sprache, die Schilderung zwar schön, die Empfindung innig, aber sonst die Situation ganz gewöhnlich, der Ausgang trivial, und die Phantasie und ihre Freiheit hat nichts weiter hinzugetan. (*Ä* II. 242.)

In *Willkommen und Abschied* for example, the use of language and the portrayal of the scene are effective and the sentiment is genuine, but apart from that the situation is banal and the ending trite, and imaginative freedom has added nothing.

This is a peculiar set of criticisms. To say that the 'Situation' is quite ordinary is to suggest that night-time gallops to secret trysts with lovers happen every day, which was as untrue in the 1770s as it is today. But the word 'Situation' also covers the more general background to a work of art (see *Ä* I. 260-1), so it may be that Hegel is objecting to the treatment of romance in a contemporary middle-class context. The reference to the trivial ending is also unclear: the action ends with the lovers' parting—how else could a meeting end?—but the poem ends with a direct exclamation from the poet:

> Und doch, welch Glück, geliebt zu werden!
> Und lieben, Götter, welch ein Glück!

Hegel usually uses the term 'trivial' to indicate that mind has not sufficiently subjugated matter, so perhaps he means to say that such directness is too unmediated for art. This is a value-judgement, and there is no reason to accept it, but when he finally claims that the poem shows no evidence of imagination, Hegel is clearly wrong. In the first stanza alone an oak tree is seen as a giant towering up in a cloak of mist, and the interstices of the bushes are transformed into a hundred black eyes. Whether or not we find such images striking, they are images, and as such are the work of the imagination. Hegel is not willing to see this because the whole poem is too involved with reality. He is looking for evidence that direct experience has been completely left behind, absorbed into a poem in the way that reality is absorbed into the categories of thought in the *Logic*: 'aufgehoben'. Thus in the poem he calls 'Ich hab mein Sach auf nichts gestellt', which is entitled *Vanitas! Vanitatum Vanitas!*, he finds what he wants. Different realms of experience are all worked through at some length, and, he adds, 'selbst methodisch'—'even showing method', until they are annulled, raised up, and preserved in 'freie sorglose Heiterkeit'—'carefree cheerfulness' (*Ä* III. 430). This cheerfulness is what counts for Hegel, and he ignores the fact that it is conveyed through the refrain of 'Juchhe!', as direct and uncultivated as anything he condemns in *Des Knaben Wunderhorn* (*Ä* I. 374-5).

Hegel himself draws attention to the failings of *Willkommen und Abschied* by contrasting it with *Wiederfinden*, a completely different sort of poem from the *West-östlicher Divan*. It makes little literary sense to make such a comparison, but Hegel is not interested in that. *Wiederfinden* exemplifies the sort of poetry he most admires and which he finds above all in the *Divan*. It is in this collection that he sees reality finally overcome, and the chains shackling the poet to sense-experience and emotion broken at last:

Überhaupt haben wir in den ähnlichen Produktionen dieser Art keine subjektive Sehnsucht, kein Verliebtsein, keine Begierde vor uns, sondern ein reines Gefallen an den Gegenständen, ein unerschöpfliches Sich-Ergehen der Phantasie, ein harmloses Spielen . . und dabei eine Innigkeit und Frohheit des sich in sich selber bewegenden Gemütes, welche durch die Heiterkeit des Gestaltens die Seele hoch über alle peinliche Verflechtung in die Beschränkung der Wirklichkeit hinausheben. (*Ä* II. 242.)

In works such as these we find none of the subjective yearnings of being in love, no lust, but pure pleasure in objects, an inexhaustible promenade of the imagination, harmless play . . . all accompanied by the heart-felt enjoyment of a mind moving in its own element, lifted above painful involvement in the constraints of reality by the joy of creation.

Hegel sees Goethe's achievement as consisting in freeing himself from his 'gloomier early poems' in order to reach the 'untroubled cheerfulness' in which all reality is negated and mind enjoys itself alone

(*Ä* I. 477). Hegel is deluding himself about Goethe—the *Trilogie der Leidenschaft* was to follow the *Divan*, and it is full of 'the subjective yearnings of being in love.' Negating the otherness of the physical world did not come as easily to Goethe as it did to Hegel, who writes here in the best tradition of the ascetic ideals of Platonism and Christianity. His identity with Goethe was to a large extent imagined, but it would have been neat, giving embodiment in two personalities to the identity of Beauty and Truth, which is what Hegel would have liked. One should not forget their difference, which in immanent Hegelian terms lies precisely in art's commitment to the experience of the senses and the medium of the senses. The speculative heart of Hegel's theory rests, like all his thought, on the identity of identity and non-identity: Beauty and Truth are identical and different. Within this framework, it is of course possible to stress one or the other at various times, according to one's judgement and one's wishes. And with that possibility one has detected the cancer cell of ideology within the heart of theory.

CONCLUSION

In an essay published some six years after Hegel's death, one of his lesser-known pupils, Heinrich Theodor Rötscher, concluded that as a result of the preceding decades of intensive theoretical activity in Germany two attitudes to art common in the eighteenth century had disappeared: nobody any longer demanded that art have a moral effect and be edifying or instructive; and nobody demanded that it imitate nature.[1] The positive result was that art was regarded as autonomous, and works of art were judged by criteria immanent to themselves. Rötscher assigns the main role in bringing about this change to Hegel, because he tried to understand every work of art as a realization of the Concept of art as individual.[2] In picking out this feature of the *Aesthetics* as crucial, Rötscher has not taken Hegel's own critical practice as paradigmatic, but indicated the importance of his purely philosophical achievements, the way in which Hegel understands the universal, particular, and individual in the *Logic of Concept*, and draws on it in his philosophy of art. Hegel made it possible to understand each work of art as a rational system of its own, so that the critic can finally get to grips with what is unique and irreducible about art. It is the speculative method in aesthetics which allows the concreteness of art to be understood.[3]

Rötscher's forgotten essay is highly significant for a number of reasons. It shows us how a contemporary viewed the changes brought about by idealist aesthetics, and the revolution in critical practice he thought it had made possible. It also shows us that a man familiar with Hegel's thought as a whole places his main emphasis on the consequences of understanding art as an instance of the category 'Idea', and hence as a system. Rötscher is drawing on the *Logic* as much as the *Aesthetics*, and recognizes the importance of aspects of the theory which have since become buried under the rubble of 'Hegelianism', of the 'World Spirit' and the 'Spirit of the Age'. As a result, Rötscher's notion of literary criticism is surprisingly modern. He sees a literary work of art as a set of relations, and the role of the critic as that of discovering new ways in which the various elements combine and thus of expanding the possible readings of a text.[4] Understood in such a way, Hegel's *Aesthetics* can be seen to have grounded criticism, not as a science with rules governing experimental procedures, but as a rational hermeneutic exercise.[5]

Rötscher brings us to the limits of Hegel's theory by addressing himself to the question of hermeneutics. A philosophy of art implies a hermeneutic theory, but does not itself provide one. In sketching one himself, Rötscher goes beyond Hegel whilst still operating within the framework he offers, and the sort of critical practice he outlines differs from the sort which Hegel himself provides. This prompts a final reflection upon the relationship between the two parts of this study, between Hegel's principles and his illustration of them, and at the same time a reflection upon the limits of this reading of Hegel and of Hegel's philosophy of art.

Throughout this study, there has been an attempt to assess as well as describe, and to engage in Hegel's own theoretical project, taking his text as a starting-point. This has resulted in a peculiar sort of ventriloquism, similar to a kind in which Hegel himself sometimes engages, in which it is not clear whether I am the dummy Hegel is talking through, or Hegel is the dummy I am talking through. This act is designed to make the issues, and the theory (not the text), as comprehensible and as coherent as possible given the distance separating the early nineteenth from the late twentieth century. Part Two is more often to do with the opinions of an individual than with issues, so there is less ventriloquism. Part One might have concluded with reflections of the sort provided by Rötscher, but in fact what follows is to a large extent concerned with a metaphysical belief about the development of man's self-understanding, and with using art to show that it involves an increase in interiority. One must therefore ask how, in Hegel's text, instances relate to principles.

The first fundamental point is that principles have a measure of independence over instances because no principles imply any instances; they can only be used to justify them. One could preserve or modify a general Hegelian theory, and use it to justify quite different judgements by interpreting the instances differently. All that is implied by the general theory is that art is systematic and historical, and that thesis can be exemplified in any number of different ways. If we are motivated by an interest in Hegel's project, we need not be over-concerned with his own instantiation of his theory. But one of the striking things about his empirical observations, and this is the second fundamental point, is that they are only insightful when backed up by strong theory. When he abandons it, or when it is itself a mess, he rarely has anything of interest to say about actual artistic developments. The material in Part Two does in any case contain much that is of theoretical interest. The section on architecture shows a breakdown of the triadic historical schema, and has implications for Hegel's semiotics; the account of Greek sculpture shows an absurd attempt to equate Beauty with intellect and to avoid the issue of the erotic in art; his views on painting show a firm rejection of contemporary classicism, which makes it clear what a difference there is between having classicism as a theoretical ideal (as he does) and embracing it as an empirical ideal (as Winckelmann did); his rejection of instrumental music as trivial reveals a logocentrism deep in his thought; and his whole treatment of literature shows an overriding concern with the social and cultural background to art which dominates his interest in the features of literary texts. In addition, some of those details have been found to be of interest in their own right, most notably perhaps the assessment of Dutch genre painting and the Gothic cathedral, and his brilliant analysis of the differences between ancient and modern narrative and drama. If such judgements and analyses can still be found to be interesting, they cannot simply be matters of personal taste, but must be based upon some evidence which makes it possible for them to be accessible to those whose taste does not coincide with Hegel's own.

The question of taste appears to play no role in Hegel's theory comparable to that of the 'sensus communis' in Kant's *Critique of Judgement*, but it is partially accounted for. Hegel regards personal taste as purely subjective, and, he adds, it is a blessing that it is so:

Denn unter den Menschen z.B. ist es der Fall, daß, wenn auch nicht jeder Ehemann seine Frau, doch wenigstens jeder Bräutigam seine Braut —und zwar etwa sogar ausschließlich—schön findet, und daß der subjektive Geschmack für diese Schönheit keine feste Regel hat, kann man ein Glück für beide Teile nennen. (*Ä* I. 68.)[6]

For amongst human beings one observes that even though not every husband finds his wife beautiful, at least every bridegroom thinks his bride is, often to the exclusion of all others. And it is fortunate for both parties that it is so, and that subjective taste has no fixed rule for beauty.

If every man were to fall in love with the same woman, human society would not last long. This clearly suggests that the same applies to art, and that everyone will have their own favourites for purely subjective reasons. Hegel does not develop this line of thought, but instead raises the issue, not of individual taste, but of communal taste, 'the taste of nations' (ibid.), which he says is of the greatest variety. At a number of points in the text, some of which have been noted, he gives examples of how national taste differs, and grounds these differences in the different ethical norms and values involved.[7] If we draw this together, it seems that Hegel excludes the question of personal taste from his considerations and reflects upon the differences in norms of taste within the framework of art's role as Absolute Spirit, distinguishing those ethical norms from the question of aesthetic quality. In other words, to take an example already considered (see 'Sculpture', chapter 3 above), we must admit the high quality of Greek sculpture even though we may not like it very much. The art-critic is concerned to understand the nature of the object before him, and to judge it, regardless of his own taste. The extent to which the critic succeeds in talking about the object, rather than his taste, will be the extent to which his discourse is rational, and therefore of interest to others. This is the implication of Hegel's theory which Rötscher takes up.

Now if Hegel has grounded this way of talking about art, he has grounded only a particular way of talking about it, a way which is not very common.[8] The justification for this discourse is itself provided by a theory which reconstructs the intuitions of a particular speech community within a particular tradition—Hegel himself, and the educated, intellectual, middle-class students who attended his lectures in Berlin in the 1820s, and constitute the 'we' who evaluate art according to how successfully it integrates form and content. Hegel's selection of those intuitions is not arbitrary, for it draws on continuous themes in aesthetics since Plato. But it is manipulative, it does select, and it is based on a European view of art up to 1830. What of the Negro sculptures which inspired the cubists? What of Japanese water-colours? What of our century, or the next? Hegel himself has given a firm answer to such questions:

Was das Individuum betrifft, so ist ohnehin jedes ein *Sohn seiner Zeit*; so ist auch die Philosophie *ihre Zeit in Gedanken erfaßt*. Es ist ebenso töricht zu wähnen, irgendeine Philosophie gehe über ihre gegenwärtige Welt hinaus, als, ein Individuum überspringe seine Zeit, springe über Rhodus hinaus. Geht seine Theorie in der Tat drüber hinaus, baut es sich eine Welt, *wie sie sein soll*, so existiert sie wohl, aber nur in seinem Meinen—einem weichen Elemente, dem sich alles Beliebige einbilden läßt.[9]

As far as the individual is concerned, each is in any case a *son of his time*; in the same way, philosophy is *its time comprehended in thought*. It is as foolish to imagine some philosophy going beyond its world as to imagine an individual skipping over his age, jumping across Rhodes. If his theory does indeed go beyond it and constructs a world *as it ought to be*, that world does exist, but only in his own mind—a malleable medium, capable of imagining all sorts of things.

This well-known passage serves as a reminder not to look for predictions or prescriptions in the *Aesthetics*, and to bear in mind that the lectures were held a century and a half ago. Hegel's first-person plural will in many ways be a third-person plural now, so to see ourselves from their vantage-point will be to see ourselves as others see us, those others representing a tradition which they themselves see drawing to an end. It is for that reason that the *Aesthetics* can be of interest today. If modern art is a negation of the tradition, we can begin to understand it by understanding what it is not. If modern art is playing with the limits of traditional art, it is as well to know what the limits are, and legitimate to decide that they have been widened so far that it is meaningless to talk about art any more. It may be that we regard the art-world as big business and nothing more, and therefore attach greater value to the disruption of it than to producing works of art. It may be that we do not accept the values implied by the theory, that we are not interested in coherence, or the identity of form and content, in which case we will not need the theory. It can always be opposed, for whatever reason.

However, simple opposition can be returned in kind, and will just bounce off. What is harder is to undermine the theory from the inside by dislocating the centre, and understanding it from a vantage point which shows it up as limited and particular. One can go some way towards that by reversing the claim of the theory to ground critical practice, and show that it is just the product of a particular form of practice, in other words, to show that it does not offer justification but rationalization, and that the theory is ideology. Hegel himself does use the theory to rationalize beliefs which do not follow from it. However, to dislocate the theory itself is a major task, and may mean dislocating the whole tradition on which it draws. It seems to have thought of everything already, and to suck up all opposition (see 'The System of the Arts', chapter 2 above). If we are condemned to have been understood by Hegel, we can either acquiesce or rebel. The only course of action clearly not in our interests is to ignore him.

NOTES

INTRODUCTION

1. Karl Marx, 'Kritik des Hegelschen Staatsrechts' (1843), in *Marx/ Engels Werke* I, Berlin, 1956, esp. pp. 213–17.
2. *Werke* 10. 405.
3. *WL* II. 504.
4. Hotho's original was published in three volumes in 1835, 1837 and 1838 respectively, and in a second edition in 1842. For further details see: *G. W. F. Hegel–Einleitung in die Ästhetik*, edited by Wolfhart Henckmann, Munich, 1967, and *Die Idee und das Ideal*, edited by Georg Lasson, Hamburg, 1931.

CHAPTER I

1. Th. W. Adorno, *Ästhetische Theorie*, Frankfurt, 1970, p. 502.
2. His other justifications most prominently, and from our point of view most interestingly, concern the truth-content of art (e.g. p. 193).
3. Roger Scruton, *The Aesthetics of Architecture*, London, 1979, p. 292. Sadly, it is hard to disagree, but Scruton's own work is a notable exception to the rule.
4. As can be inferred from *Ä* I. 25–6.
5. Hegel probably has in mind a work by one G. Ph. Chr. Kaiser published in Nuremberg in 1813, called: *Ideen zu einem Systeme der allgemeinen reinen und angewandten Kalliästhetik*. See Henckmann's note in his edition of Hegel's *Introduction*, p. 130.
6. Which is the answer to Friedrich Theodor Vischer, when he accuses Hegel of assuming what he has to prove ('Plan zu einer neuen Gliederung der Ästhetik', in *Kritische Gänge*, Tübingen, 1844, Band I, pp. 345–7). Vischer also regrets that Hegel neglected 'die begeistete Natur, die menschlich sittliche Welt'–'nature when it has been imbued with Spirit, the human ethical world' (p. 357), and gives the examples of a beautiful state and the beautiful poses of soldiers in battle (p. 358). Whatever else one might wish to say about this, the Hegelian view is that they are category errors, the confusion of the aesthetic and the political.
7. *Ä* I. 157–202. Lasson has attacked Hotho for drawing together all Hegel's remarks on the subject, and placing them in an arbitrary position (Vorrede, XII). It hardly matters.
8. This important shift in aesthetic theory is concisely discussed by

Dieter Henrich in 'Kunst und Natur in der Idealistischen Ästhetik', in *Nachahmung und Illusion*, edited by H. R. Jauß, Munich, 1964.

9. The axis of the shift is the revision of the mimesis theory, as in Schelling, to the claim that what art imitates is nature's productive process, which makes the artist an autonomous creator. See his Munich speech of 1807, *Über das Verhältnis der Bildenden Künste zur Natur*, in *Schriften von 1806-13*, Darmstadt, 1976. Some consequences of this idea are shown by Teodora Kuklinková in 'Schöpferische Aktivität als Quelle des Schönen bei Hegel und in der marxistischen Ästhetik', in *Hegel Jahrbuch*, 1975.

10. A view supported by Hans-Georg Gadamer, *Wahrheit und Methode*, fourth edition, Tübingen, 1975, p. 55; and Roger Scruton, *Art and Imagination*, London, 1974, p. 162.

11. C. W. F. Solger, *Vorlesungen über Ästhetik*, edited by K. W. L. Heyse, Leipzig, 1829, p. 1.

12. One of Hegel's first reviewers, Christian Hermann Weisse, whose articles appeared in six instalments between 1 and 7 Sept. 1838 in the *Hallische Jahrbücher für Wissenschaft und Kunst*, edited by the Hegel pupils Arnold Ruge and Theodor Echtermeyer, ascribed most of Hegel's failings to the exclusion of natural beauty. However, his only argument is that 'alle wahren Künstler haben von jeher zur Natur als zu einer erhabenen Göttin aufgeschaut'–'all true artists since time immemorial have regarded Nature as a sublime Goddess' (p. 1708), which is not true, and beside the point anyway. The young Georg Lukács includes an interesting discussion of the theme of art and nature in Hegel, Vischer, and Weisse in his *Heidelberger Ästhetik* (*Werke* 17, Darmstadt and Neuwied, 1974, pp. 192-211).

13. Which is the answer to Adorno, who claims that Hegel completely misunderstands the substance of beauty, again using the devaluation of nature in Hegel to unseat the whole theory: 'Was jedoch Hegel dem Naturschönen als Mangel vorrechnet, das dem festen Begriff sich entziehende, ist die Substanz des Schönen selbst'–'But the very thing Hegel singles out as the failing of natural beauty, the fact that it escapes strict concepts, is the substance of beauty itself' (*Ästhetische Theorie*, p. 114). That remains to be seen. If, as I suspect, 'fester Begriff' means an empirical concept, what Hegel called a 'Vorstellung', Adorno has got Hegel quite wrong.

14. Support for this view of the relationship between art and nature is given, on the basis of different theoretical presuppositions, by Hans Wagner in *Philosophie und Reflexion*, third edition, Munich and Basle, 1980, pp. 267, 290-1.

15. To sum up in terms commonly used in Germany, we could say that Hegel's theory is a 'Werkästhetik', rather than a 'Künstler-' or 'Produktionsästhetik', or, like Kant's, a 'Rezeptionsästhetik'.

16. *Kritik der Urteilskraft* §1 (footnote).

17. The extremely important fact that there are two theories of beauty

in Kant has been pointed out by Charles Taylor. See *Hegel*, Cambridge, 1975, p. 470 (footnote).
18. *Art and Imagination*, p. 3.
19. Ibid. vii.
20. Ibid. 163.
21. Ibid. 139.
22. Ibid. 138. It is apparent at the end that the ideal 'we' grounds all the demands of the book (pp. 242–3).
23. Ibid. 138. The word is a leitmotiv of the book, first entering on p. 47, and present in the final chord on p. 248.
24. They are distinguished from 'us' on p. 245.
25. For a reading of the *Aesthetics* as a sociology of art, done from a basically Marxist point of view, see Thomas W. H. Metscher, 'Hegel und die philosophische Grundlegung der Kunstsoziologie' in *Literaturwissenschaft und Sozialwissenschaften – Grundlagen und Modellanalysen*, Stuttgart, 1971, pp. 13–80. On the problems of theoretical heterogeneity I am indebted to an unpublished paper called 'Hegels Ästhetik' by Reinhold Aschenberg.
26. Reported by Joseph Kosuth in an essay called 'Art after Philosophy, I and II' in *Idea Art*, edited by Gregory Battcock, New York, 1973, p. 78.
27. Cf. Richard Wollheim, *Art and its Objects*, Harmondsworth, 1970, §§ 1–3, 40, 63–4.
28. As does, for example, Käte Hamburger in *Wahrheit und Ästhetische Wahrheit*, Stuttgart, 1979, p. 144.
29. Prime examples are W. E. Kennick ('Does Traditional Aesthetics rest on a Mistake?' in *Collected Papers on Aesthetics*, edited by C. Barrett, Oxford, 1965) and W. B. Gallie ('The Function of Philosophical Aesthetics' in *Aesthetics and Language*, edited by William Elton, Oxford, 1967). Similar views are found in P. F. Strawson's 'Aesthetic Appraisal and Works of Art' in *Oxford Review* No. 3 (Michaelmas 1966).
30. As is implied by Stuart Hampshire in 'Logic and Appreciation' in Elton's collection of essays, esp. pp. 165–6.
31. See Kennick, p. 19.
32. Another essay in the Elton volume by Margaret Macdonald, called 'Some Distinctive Features of Arguments used in Criticism of the Arts' illustrates the vicious circle involved. She says that good judgements are passed by good critics—of course, good critics are the ones who pass good judgements because they have the 'appropriate' qualities (p. 130). In the end we are admonished to think what we think already whatever the critics say, because even the good ones are not infallible. On this account, however, we could never know what would count as a mistake.
33. See Haig Katchadourian, 'Common Names and "Family Resemblances"', in *Wittgenstein*, edited by George Pitcher, London, 1968.
34. See Beryl Lake, 'A Study of the Irrefutability of two Aesthetic

Theories' in Elton's collection. She shows that the theories of art by Croce and Bell are non-empirical, therefore unverifiable, therefore 'caused' (*sic*) by prejudice.

35. Hegel's classicism has been usefully discussed by Helmut Kuhn in 'Die Vollendung der klassischen deutschen Ästhetik durch Hegel' (1931), reprinted in *Schriften zur Kunst*, edited by Wolfhart Henckmann, Munich, 1966. Peter Szondi has remarked that this classicism is a limitation in *Poetik und Geschichtsphilosophie I*, Frankfurt, 1974, pp. 302-7, but later qualifies this (p. 493).

36. F. W. J. Schelling, *Philosophie der Kunst*, reprinted from the 1859 edition edited by Karl Schelling, Darmstadt, 1976, p. 4.

37. Cf. *Kritik der Reinen Vernunft*, A727/B755 ff.

38 It is the perception of this that lies behind Lake's attack on Bell and Croce (see note 34 above). Hegel's Concept of art legislates over instances, but it is not a definition.

39. Grounds for the possibility of such a synthesis have been unwittingly given by Willard Van Orman Quine in his classic essay 'Two dogmas of empiricism' in *From a Logical Point of View*, New York, 1953. Quine argues that the analytic/synthetic distinction is not absolute, but contextual, a difference in degree.

40. See for example Kroner, II, pp. 297-8.

41. 'Logical' in contrast to psychological, or real, or human, and so on, as explained.

42. The account is not very satisfactory, at times (e.g. *Enz.* § § 396-8) degenerating into mere catalogue.

43. A pertinent example is Georg Lukács, who argues for the overriding importance of the socio-historical in Hegel's *Aesthetics* in 'Über die Besonderheit als Kategorie der Ästhetik' in *Werke* 10, Darmstadt and Neuwied, 1969.

44. As for example in the preface to *Zur Kritik der Politischen Ökonomie* of 1859.

45. The Idea of Beauty is to be proven from the presuppositions of science 'der Notwendigkeit nach' (*Ä* I. 43).

46. Cf. Gerd Wolandt, 'Standpunkte der Kunstphilosophie' in *Die Aktualität der Transzendentalphilosophie: Hans Wagner zum 60. Geburtstag*, edited by Wolandt and Schmidt, Bonn, 1977.

47. This is attempted by Hans Wagner, *Philosophie und Reflexion*, p. 279, in a tradition going back to Schiller's *Briefe über die ästhetische Erziehung des Menschen*.

48. A view held, for example, by Hermann Glockner ('Die Ästhetik in Hegels System' in *Hegel Studien*, *Beiheft* 2, Bonn, 1965, esp. pp. 438-9) and Rüdiger Bubner (see his introduction to the Reclam edition of the *Aesthetics*, esp. pp. 22-3). Jack Kaminsky believes that Hegel sees the 'metaphysical speculation' of philosophers providing material for artists, which, if true, would indeed be absurd (*Hegel on Art*, p. 168).

49. Weisse, review, p. 1682.

50. Ibid. 1683.

51. Karl Rosenkranz, 'Hegels Ästhetik' in *Kritische Erläuterungen des Hegelschen Systems*, Königsberg, 1840, p. 186. The review originally appeared in the *Jahrbücher für Wissenschaftliche Kritik* in 1836.

52. Weisse, review, p. 1688. This is a criticism he makes repeatedly, e.g. p. 1696.

53. More detail on what is meant by a logic of 'development' can be found in Wolfgang Krohn, *Die Formale Logik in Hegels 'Wissenschaft der Logik'*, Munich, 1972. For a more sceptical account of *Concept*, and its links to the *Psychology* see Klaus Düsing, 'Hegels Begriff der Subjektivität in der Logik und in der Philosophie des Subjektiven Geistes' in *Hegel Studien, Beiheft* 19, 1979.

54. Cf. *Ä* I. 16. A serious exposition of this more frivolous point of view is given by Charles Batteux, who declares the object of art to be pleasure (*Les Beaux Arts réduits à un même principe*, second edition, 1773, p. 27). Batteux is at the opposite pole from Hegel in every respect—his 'même principe' is the imitation of nature.

55. As expounded in his *Gedanken über die Nachahmung der griechischen Werke in der Malerei und Bildhauerkunst*, 1755.

56. 'Die Erreichung des Eigentümlichen in allen Theilen zum Ganzen ist der Endzweck der Kunst' (*Die Horen*, 7. Stück, 1797, p. 35. Hegel quotes the previous sentence with two trivial errors. It reads 'wie der vorgelegte Gegenstand es verlanget', not 'wie der vorgedachte Gegenstand es erfordert' as given on *Ä* I. 34).

57. Hegel calls Hirt 'one of the greatest real connoisseurs of our time' (p. 33), uses his work on architecture as a source, and was grateful for his efforts on behalf of a public art gallery in Berlin (cf. *Ä* III. 108-9). Hirt was a very learned but conservative scholar, who refused, as late as 1833, to recognize the Elgin marbles as works of fifth-century classicism (A. Rumpf, *Archäologie*, Berlin, 1953, p. 68). Goethe knew him, and admired his erudition, whilst being scornful of his pedantry. See H. B. Nisbet, 'Laocoon in Germany: The Reception of the Group since Winckelmann' in *Oxford German Studies*, 10 (1979), pp. 43-7.

58. The discussion is found in the third volume of Meyer's history, which appeared in Dresden, 1824–36 (see p. 206).

59. The source of this is a description of a painting of Hercules and Abderus from *Philostrats Gemälde*, a work which is partly translation of Philostratus' *Eikones*, and partly original material. The theme is the taming of the mares of Diomedes, who devoured Hercules' friend Abderus whilst he was fighting Diomedes. Goethe notes how we are shown enough to recognize the theme, but are not shown the unnecessary horrors of Abderus' half-eaten body. See Goethe, *Sämtliche Werke*, edited by Ernst Beutler, Zurich, 1950, vol. 13, pp. 834–6.

60. Despite their central importance, these shifts in Hegel's meaning have been virtually ignored in the literature. The one exception to the rule is R. S. Lucas, 'A Problem of Hegel's Aesthetics' in

Renaissance and Modern Studies IV (1960), and 'Hegel und die Abstraktion', *Deutsche Vierteljahresschrift* 38 (1964).

61. 'Scheinen' and its derivatives are hard to translate. 'Illusion' is wrong, 'representation' is badly misleading, 'presentation' and 'showing' make for barely acceptable English, suggesting that the Idea is being handed over as a prize or unveiled by a beauty queen. Knox renders the formula as 'the pure appearance of the Idea to sense' (p. 111), an inelegant paraphrase. 'Reflection' is neater, and more accurately preserves the technical meaning of an Essence-relation, which Hegel also calls 'Reflexion'. The main sense of 'Schein' is conveyed by 'appearance'.

62. Hegel describes the everyday use of categories as 'Abbreviaturen' in the *Logic* (*WL* I. 13).

63. This may be why Gadamer is capable of calling it 'eine idealistische Verführung'—'a tempting Idealist illusion', and continues: 'Sie wird nicht dem eigentlichen Tatbestand gerecht, daß das Werk als Werk und nicht als Übermittler einer Botschaft zu uns spricht'—'It fails to do justice to the fact that the work appeals to us as a work and not as the conveyor of a message' (*Die Aktualität des Schönen*, Stuttgart, 1977, p. 43). This is precisely wrong. It describes a doctrine which Hegel must contest in order to have any justification for a philosophy of art, and which, as we have seen, he explicitly rejects (e.g. *Ä* I. 77).

64. Lukács has recognized the significance of the parallel between Beauty and Truth. Cf. his remarks on 'Selbstorganisation' in the *Heidelberger Ästhetik*, pp. 191–2. Something very similar lies behind Scruton's justification of the rationality of art criticism; see *Art and Imagination*, pp. 98–100, 124, 139–41, 246. Käte Hamburger, in contrast, thinks it is nonsense to talk about art and truth, but she blocks any possible understanding of the issue by summarily rejecting all coherence theories of truth (*Wahrheit und Ästhetische Wahrheit*, p. 18).

65. This is a major thesis of both Scruton's books.

66. R. G. Collingwood, *The Principles of Art*, Oxford, 1938, pp. 333–6.

67. Contrast Hegel's contemplative theory with Adorno, who passes judgement on the beliefs. He defines the truth of art as its embodiment of 'richtiges Bewußtsein'—'correct consciousness' (*Ästhetische Theorie*, p. 285) which seems to mean the cultural pessimism of deracinated bourgeois intellectuals like Adorno (ibid. *passim*).

68. Solger, *Vorlesungen über Ästhetik*, pp. 48–74.

69. Wollheim, *Art and its Objects*, §§14–19. Cf. Scruton, *Art and Imagination*, pp. 126–7.

70. Goodman, *Languages of Art*, London, 1969, pp. 50 and 85.

71. Ibid. 69.

72. Chimpanzees in a research institute in Nevada now paint.

73. Benedetto Croce, *Estetica—Come Scienza dell'Espressione e Linguistica Generale*, sixth (revised) edition, Bari, 1928, ch. 13.

74. Ibid. 3–4.

75. Ibid. 130.
76. *The Principles of Art*, p. 130.
77. Ibid. 131–5 and 139–44.
78. Max Bense has a similar position. He believes that works of art are instruments for the production of 'aesthetic objects', which they make visible (*Aesthetica I*, Stuttgart, 1954, p. 22). As Bense never explains how an account of one of these objects would differ from an account of the work producing it, they seem to be superfluous metaphysical postulates. For further criticism of the 'ideal object' thesis, see Wollheim, op. cit., §§21–4.
79. Gregory Battcock in the introduction to *Idea Art*, p. 1.
80. As is suggested by Goodman, op. cit. 255.
81. Despite his rhetoric about dissonance being the truth over harmony (*Asthetische Theorie*, p. 168), Adorno believes this too, as is apparent from his comments on the sense of Beckett's senselessness (pp. 230–1) and his notion of 'Stimmigkeit' or 'Artikulation' (see pp. 216, 252, 262, 266, 277–8, 280–4).
82. Karl Rosenkranz, *Ästhetik des Häßlichen*, Königsberg, 1953, p. 5.
83. Ibid. 44.
84. *The Aesthetics of Architecture*, p. 241.
85. Ibid. 242.

CHAPTER 2

1. Cf. Hartwig Zander, *Hegels Kunstphilosophie*, Ratingen, 1970, pp. 63–72. Zander criticizes Lasson, Bassenge, and Henckmann for presenting the *Division* as part four of the *Introduction*. The *Division* is introductory, but ought to be made distinct from the rest which has quite a different function, so the solution reached in the Suhrkamp *Werkausgabe* used in the present study seems to be optimal.
2. Lasson claims that the division into two is authentic, but deprives his argument of much of its force by dividing the first section into two again (see Lasson, pp. xii and 123, and compare Zander, pp. 69–72). Lasson appears not to have had any of the later lecture notes, nor Hegel's own manuscript, as Hotho did. I am grateful to Professor Klaus Düsing and Dr. Annemarie Gethmann-Siefert for information about the work being done on this matter at the Hegel-Archiv in Bochum. Hotho's own notes from 1823 should be appearing in the Meiner Verlag, Hamburg, in the near future, with an introduction by Frau Gethmann-Siefert discussing some of the textual problems.
3. Weisse, review, p. 1693.
4. Ibid.
5. See *Ä* I. 107–9, 393–413; also *Enz.* §§455–9.
6. See *Ä* I. 109–11, *Ä* II. 13–126.
7. Hegel uses 'romantic' in roughly the eighteenth-century sense of modern as opposed to classical. It can be more or less equated

with 'Christian' and the intellectual and artistic movement called 'Romanticism' is its most developed stage. It was not clear from the way the word was used in the 1790s whether the sense was systematic or historical. See 'Romantisch–Romantik–Romantiker' by Hans Eichner in *'Romantic' and its Cognates*, Manchester, 1972.

8. See *Ä* I. 111–14, *Ä* II. 127–242.

9. Thus Kaminsky thinks that: 'In Hegel's view, only one who has an awareness of the philosophical advances of Christian over Greek thought can truly appreciate Gothic architecture' (*Hegel on Art*, p. 61).

10. Karelis, p. lxxiv, who adds that the theory therefore 'contravenes the ordinary usage of the term "art" by excluding utterly vision*less* sculpture, painting and music from the category of art altogether'.

11. Christoph Helferich, *Kunst und Subjektivität in Hegels Ästhetik*, Kronberg, 1976, p. 48.

12. '. . . eine inhaltlich durchgeführte Kunstsoziologie': Frank Dietrich Wagner, *Hegels Philosophie der Dichtung*, Bonn, 1974, p. 140.

13. The historical origins of the art-forms are discussed by Szondi, *Poetik und Geschichtsphilosophie I*, pp. 362 ff.; Kuhn, *Die Vollendung der klassischen deutschen Ästhetik durch Hegel*, esp. §§7–9; and Gadamer, 'Hegel und die Heidelberger Romantik' in *Hegels Dialektik*, Tübingen, 1971.

14. Walter Müller-Seidel, for example, calls the demand for the identity of form and content as a measure of artistic quality a 'längst zur nichtssagenden Redensart degradierte[s] Kriterium'–'a criterion which has long since degenerated into an empty turn of phrase', which he thinks must be wrong anyway because Goethe's *Pandora* is a great work of art, and its form is more important than its content (*Probleme der literarischen Wertung*, Stuttgart, 1965, p. 37). See also the discussion following Meyer Schapiro's paper 'On Perfection, Coherence, and Unity of Form and Content' in Part One of the symposium *Art and Philosophy*, edited by Sidney Hook, New York, 1966. A lack of reflection on the status of the terms is common to both.

15. The problem is that although one does not wish to condemn works of art which are modest but successful, there seems to be some relationship between quality and substantiality, and it seems paradoxical that a trivial work should be of aesthetic merit. See John Casey, *The Language of Criticism*, London, 1966, chs. 2 and 9; and John M. Ellis, *The Theory of Literary Criticism: A Logical Analysis*, California, 1974, ch. 4. Compare 'Problems and Solutions', ch. 1.

16. Despite his agreement with this (*Ästhetische Theorie*, pp. 215–22), Adorno believes that Hegel identified content with 'theme' (ibid. 222, 224, 528–9). The criticism has some justification in the case of music (see 'Music', ch. 3).

17. Quoted by James Morris in *Pax Britannica* (1968), Harmondsworth, 1979, p. 345.

18. This applies to symbolic forms such as allegory and metaphor. Peter
Szondi has taken exception to this, arguing that in poetry metaphor
is the principal means of overcoming the difference between meaning
and expression (*Poetik und Geschichtsphilosophie* I, 391–8). As he
notes, Hegel is fully aware of this, but he distinguishes the poetic
use of metaphor from the form itself, which, as a form, does involve a distinction between signifier and signified, and can therefore
be used as an external decoration. Szondi takes the transformation
of metaphor in art to be the norm for metaphorical language.
Hegel's use of 'symbol' is misleading, for it tended to designate the
ideal of art (see Gadamer, *Wahrheit und Methode*, pp. 66–77). He
derived it from Friedrich Creuzer's notion of 'mystical' symbolism;
what Creuzer called 'plastic' symbolism is the eminent mode which
Hegel identifies with the classical Ideal (see Friedrich Creuzer,
Symbolik und Mythologie der alten Völker, besonders der Griechen,
second edition, Leipzig and Darmstadt, 1819, §32).
19. Christian Hermann Weisse, *System der Ästhetik als Wissenschaft
von der Idee der Schönheit*, Leipzig, 1830 (Part I), p. 304.
20. Weisse, review, p. 1682.
21. Helmut Kuhn does not mention it in 1931—he says that it is the
formula of 'Scheinen der Idee' and the art-forms which are the first
things one associates with Hegel ('Hegels Ästhetik als System des
Klassizismus' in *Archiv für Geschichte der Philosophie* XL (1931),
p. 90). Dieter Jähnig may well be correct in supposing that the
recent flow of articles was started by the postscript to Heidegger's
'Der Ursprung des Kunstwerks' which appeared in *Holzwege* in
1949 ('Hegel und die These vom "Verlust der Mitte"' in *Spengler
Studien—Festgabe für Manfred Schröter zum 85. Geburtstag*, edited
by A. M. Koktanek, Munich, 1965, p. 148).
22. Benedetto Croce, *Estetica*, p. 337.
23. Hermann Glockner, 'Die Ästhetik in Hegels System', pp. 438–9.
24. Theodor Litt, *Hegel—Versuch einer kritischen Erneuerung*, Heidelberg, 1953, pp. 93–4.
25. Gerd Wolandt, 'Standpunkte der Kunstphilosophie', pp. 199 and
203.
26. Rüdiger Bubner, 'Über einige Bedingungen gegenwärtiger Ästhetik'
in *Neue Hefte für Philosophie* 5 (1973), pp. 47–8.
27. Athanas Stoikov, 'Hegel et le destin de l'art' in *Hegel Jahrbuch* 8
(1971), pp. 268–72.
28. Christoph Helferich, *Kunst und Subjektivität in Hegels Ästhetik*,
p. 74.
29. Karsten Harries, 'Hegel on the future of art' in *Review of Metaphysics*, Vol. XXVII (1973–4), p. 679.
30. Jörn Rüsen, 'Die Vernunft der Kunst' in Rüsen, *Ästhetik und
Geschichte*, Stuttgart, 1976. (Reprinted from *Philosophisches
Jahrbuch* 80, 1973.)
31. Rüsen, p. 54.
32. Willi Oelmüller, 'Hegels Satz vom Ende der Kunst' in Oelmüller,

Die Unbefriedigte Aufklärung, second edition, Frankfurt, 1979. (Originally in *Philosophisches Jahrbuch* 73 (1965–6), pp. 75–94.)
33. Ibid. 259.
34. Walter Bröcker, 'Hegels Philosophie der Kunstgeschichte', in Bröcker, *Auseinandersetzungen mit Hegel*, Frankfurt, 1965.
35. Hans-Georg Gadamer, *Wahrheit und Methode*, p. 536.
36. Erich Heller, the eponymous essay in *The Artist's Journey into the Interior*, London, 1965.
37. Dieter Henrich, 'Kunst und Kunstphilosophie der Gegenwart', in *Immanente Ästhetik–Ästhetische Reflexion*, edited by Wolfgang Iser, Munich, 1966, pp. 11–32.
38. Albert Hofstadter, 'Die Kunst–Tod und Verklärung' in *Hegel Studien, Beiheft* 11.
39. Jähnig, op. cit.
40. Helmut Kuhn, 'Die Gegenwärtigkeit der Kunst nach Hegels Vorlesungen über Ästhetik' in *Hegel Studien, Beiheft* 11.
41. Jan Patočka, 'Die Lehre von der Vergangenheit der Kunst', in *Beispiele. Festschrift für Eugen Fink zum 60 Geburtstag*, edited by Ludwig Landgrebe, The Hague, 1975, pp. 46–61.
42. Frank Dietrich Wagner, op. cit. 146–56.
43. Reiner Wiehl, 'Über den Handlungsbegriff als Kategorie der Hegelschen Ästhetik' in *Hegel Studien, Beiheft* 11.
44. T. J. Reed, 'Critical Consciousness and Creation: the Concept Kritik from Lessing to Hegel' in *Oxford German Studies*, 3 (1968).
45. Otto Pöggeler, *Hegels Kritik der Romantik*, Bonn, 1956.
46. Werner Koepsel, *Die Rezeption der Hegelschen Ästhetik im 20. Jahrhundert*, Bonn, 1975, p. 87.
47. Ibid. 269 ff. The book reads like an unconscious Adorno parody.
48. John Boardman, *Greek Art*, London, 1973, p. 111.
49. *Ä* II. 237. An unacknowledged reference to the central stanza of Goethe's *Die Geheimnisse*:

Humanus heißt der Heilige, der Weise,
Der beste Mann, den ich mit Augen sah . . .

I am grateful to Professor Siegbert Prawer for drawing this to my attention.
50. Weisse, *System der Ästhetik*, Part I, pp. 303–4.
51. The Concept of Beauty is worked out in §9. The critique of Hegel is part of a general critique of his system, the main theme of which is that both art and religion are reduced to the Idea of Truth. For a more recent fomulation of Weisse's position see Rüdiger Bubner, 'Über einige Bedingungen gegenwärtiger Ästhetik', esp. p. 60. Under the motto 'heteronomy', Bubner criticizes aesthetic theories which determine art by relating it to philosophy.
52. See Hugo Friedrich, *Die Struktur der modernen Lyrik*, Hamburg, 1956, esp. ch. 1.
53. See Pöggeler, op. cit. The violence of some of Hegel's attacks on the Romantics seems to have proceeded from personal animosity

towards the Jena group, particularly Friedrich Schlegel, as he is much kinder towards the Romantics in Heidelberg. The critique, as Pöggeler shows, is at root a moral one.

54. The title given by Ernst Gombrich to the end of the eighteen century in *The Story of Art*, twelfth edition, London, 1972. See esp. pp. 397-8 on the rise of subjectivity and individuality.

55. It may be worth noting that two key terms of modern art-criticism and journalism are of quite recent origin. 'Hackneyed' is first recorded in its present sense in 1749 (*OED* supplement), and 'cliché' dates from 1892.

56. See Bubner, op. cit. 62-3. Bubner regards the recent history of art as an 'Emanzipationsbewegung'–'emancipatory movement' (p. 62) leading to the dissolution of the concept that art is a body of works, and replacing works with events and processes. He assumes that if somebody calls these events art, they are art, and so much the worse for aesthetics. If they are as radically different from all previous examples of art as he believes them to be, it makes little sense to include them in the same concept. Bubner is consistent in recommending a return to Kant (p. 63) as a consequence of his position, for he has replaced the question of what art is with the question of the aesthetic attitude, which can be adopted towards anything.

57. One notable exception to the rule is Georg Lukács's *Theorie des Romans*, written in 1914.

58. This thesis has been associated most notably in modern times with Hans Sedlmayr's semi-polemical work *Verlust der Mitte*, Salzburg, 1948 (ninth edition, 1976). Sedlmayr sees it as the symptom of a general cultural crisis which he attacks from a position of humanist moral conservatism. For some criticism and a comparison with Hegel see Jähnig, op. cit.

59. *Kritik der Urteilskraft*, §53.

60. The development of these efforts up to Hegel's time has been reviewed by Paul Kristeller in 'The Modern System of the Arts' in *Journal of the History of Ideas* 12 (1951), pp. 496-527, and 13 (1952), pp. 17-46. See esp. 13, pp. 37-41.

61. Weisse, review, p. 1695.

62. Rosenkranz, *Hegels Ästhetik*, pp. 202-4.

63. *Hegels Philosophie der Dichtung*, pp. 158-68.

64. Ibid. 166.

65. As for example by Batteux, *Les Beaux Arts réduits à un même principe*, p. 20.

66. Zander suggests that the progression be read as an account of 'subjektive Selbstentfaltung' in all possible contexts from the external to the internal (op. cit. 120).

67. The textual evidence is not sufficient for Hans Herrmann, whose facile view can stand for others too: 'Durch die Erfahrung seines persönlichen Geschmacks geleitet, empirisch, setzt Hegel die klassische Skulptur der Griechen als das klassische Kunstwerk

überhaupt an'–'Led astray by the experience of his personal taste, Hegel empirically sets up the classical sculpture of the Greeks as the classical work of art *per se*' (*Der Gegenwärtigkeitsgedanke in der theoretischen Behandlung des Dramatischen Kunstwerks bei Lessing, A. W. Schlegel und Hegel*, Breslau, 1934, p. 52).

68. The phrase comes from his *Gedanken über die Nachahmung der griechischen Werke in der Malerei und Bildhauerkunst* of 1755.

69. It is with reference to this musical view of art that Jähnig tries to decentralize Hegel's theory, by saying that it is tendentiously 'christlich-platonisch' and ignores the musical nature of art (op. cit. 166–72).

70. See Gillo Dorfles, *Der Kitsch*, translated by Birgid Mayr, Tübingen, 1969 (originally Milan, 1968).

71. See 'Einige Bemerkungen zum Problem des Kitsches' in Dorfles, op. cit. 49.

CHAPTER 3

1. Zander, *Hegels Kunstphilosophie*, p. 193.

2. Pliny, *Natural History* XXXV. 5, 43.

3. For further support for this point of view and a critique of the sculptural view of architecture, see Scruton, *The Aesthetics of Architecture*, pp. 5–10.

4. Possibly because he thinks that what comes third in Hegel is always best, Kaminsky thinks that romantic architecture realizes its Concept. See *Hegel on Art*, p. 58.

5. See F. Gladstone-Bratton, *A History of Egyptian Archaeology*, London, 1967.

6. Egyptian eschatology was rather more complex than Hegel, or anyone else at that time, realized. Whilst they did distinguish the body from the Ba, or soul, the vital force in the body, called the Ka, needed food, and remained attached to the body after death. The Egyptians seem to have regarded the body as essential to any form of life, which is why they went to such lengths to preserve it. The body, the Ba, and the Ka were again distinct from the Akh, the soul after the rites of passage into the next world. See Jacquetta Hawkes, *The First Great Civilisations*, London, 1973, pp. 420–1.

7. Some aspects of Hegel's semiotics are examined by Jacques Derrida in 'Le Puits et la Pyramide' in *Marges de la Philosophie*, Paris, 1972 (originally in *Hegel et la Pensée Moderne*, edited by Jean Hyppolite, Paris, 1971), and I am grateful to Geoff Bennington for pointing out that they also feature in Jean-François Lyotard's *Discours, Figures*, Paris, 1978, pp. 27–52. Unfortunately, neither comments on the deferring of the pyramid's 'signifié' to the Field of Rushes.

8. This is a Greek view, and lest it seem trivially obvious, one might note in passing that it is contradicted by no less than Alberti, who regarded the column as the remnant of a pierced wall, and mainly

decorative. See Rudolf Wittkower, *Architectural Principles in the Age of Humanism*, fourth edition, London, 1973, p. 34.

9. For advice on this and other points, I am indebted to John Boardman.

10. The Greeks found nothing offensive about engaged columns, and they can be found in the Temple of Apollo at Bassae and in the Tholos at Delphi. See John Boardman, *Greek Art*, pp. 126, 138.

11. '. . . Säulen und Mauern zu verbinden, bleibt doch immer ein Widerspruch. Aber wie er das untereinander gearbeitet hat, wie er durch die Gegenwart seiner Werke imponiert und vergessen macht, daß er nur überredet!'—'combining columns and walls must always be a contradiction. But when confronted with the results, you have to say that the way he has worked them in together is so impressive, it makes you forget he is just being persuasive!' (*Italienische Reise*, Erster Teil, Vicenza, den 19 September; *SW* 11, p. 57.)

12. *The Ten Books on Architecture* by Marcus Vitruvius Pollio, a Roman architect whose work exerted immense influence for many centuries; and the *Geschichte der Baukunst bei den Alten*, Berlin, 1821-7, and *Die Baukunst nach den Grundsätzen der Alten*, Berlin, 1809, by Alois Hirt.

13. See Wittkower, op. cit., esp. Part IV.

14. See Vitruvius, *The Ten Books on Architecture*, translated by Morris Hicky Morgan, New York, 1960 pp. 13-14, 72-3.

15. They are the cathedrals of Antwerp and Cologne, and the church of St Sebaldus in Nuremberg (*Ä* II. 339). The remarks concern the number and height of the aisles and the use of number mysticism.

16. Hegel once more shows no awareness of the large body of complex medieval architectural theory relating it to music and mathematics, in this case (unlike Vitruvius) in the context of cosmology and theology. See Otto von Simson, *The Gothic Cathedral*, New York, 1956, ch. 2.

17. This is mentioned with approval by Hans Sedlmayr, *Die Entstehung der Kathedrale*, Zurich, 1950, p. 14.

18. Hegel uses the term 'Gotteshaus' but never says that the cathedral was built as a representation of the Celestial City, though he comes close to it. The first person to claim this was A. N. Didron in 1845 (see von Simson, op. cit. 8), and the evidence is strong, though it is not clear how it should be interpreted. Sedlmayr's view is rejected by von Simson, though he accepts the principle. For a critique of *Die Entstehung der Kathedrale* and further discussion see Martin Gosebruch, *Unmittelbarkeit und Reflexion*, Munich, 1979, pp 9-39.

19. See David Watkin, *The Rise of Architectural History*, London, 1980.

20. Gisela M. A. Richter, *The Sculpture and Sculptors of the Greeks*, New Haven and London, 1970, p. 131.

21. On the Greeks' use of colour see Richter, op. cit. 124-32 and Boardman, *Greek Art*, p. 130. A more general discussion of the widespread use of paint and coloration in sculpture is given by

Howard Hibbard, *Masterpieces of Western Sculpture*, London, 1977, pp. 12–14.

22. How the technical difficulties have been surmounted is discussed by Rudolf Wittkower in *Sculpture*, Harmondsworth, 1979, pp. 184–8.

23. The blank eye has been exploited by Modigliani.

24. See Richter, op. cit. 50–6.

25. Wittkower, *Sculpture*, p. 187.

26. Sir Kenneth Clark, *The Nude*, Harmondsworth, 1960, p. 32.

27. Hegel forms part of a German intellectual tradition offering a moral critique of modernity which stretches from Schiller, through Marx to Marcuse. Its continuity is remarkable.

28. Sir Kenneth Clark, *The Nude*, p. 23.

29. In the *Geschichte der Kunst des Altertums* he mentions various factors, including the commonness of nudity in gymnasiums (Book IV, ch. 4, §27).

30. Ernst Gombrich, 'Hegel und die Kunstgeschichte' in *Neue Rundschau* 88/2 (1977), p. 205. Hegel's visit to see the tomb is mentioned by Rosenkranz in *Hegels Leben*, Berlin, 1844, p. 365.

31. In the first preface to his *Lives*, Vasari uses the image of the arts being born, growing up, becoming old, and dying. See *Lives of the Artists*, translated by George Bull, Harmondsworth, 1965, p. 46. On p. iii of the introduction to his *Geschichte der Baukunst bei den Alten*, Hirt describes art history as the history of the birth, perfection, and decline of art.

32. In passages such as this which reach general conclusions about the relationship between specific physical features and what they express, Hegel has accepted one of the main theses of physiognomy, which Lavater called the 'harmony between moral and physical beauty' (see Johann Caspar Lavater, *Physiognomische Fragmente, zur Beförderung der Menschenkenntniß und Menschenliebe*, Leipzig und Winterthur, 1775). Hegel's own statements about physiognomy are cautious, and he rejected Gall's pseudo-science of phrenology (*Ä* II. 369–70). It is interesting to note that Lavater stresses the importance of the nose (op. cit. 237), and answers the Socrates problem by declaring him to have been full of moral iniquity, especially in his youth (ibid. 68). One should also be clear that Hegel's rationale is his own; Lavater's view of the Greek profile is that the straightness of the nose is irrelevant, the important matter being one of proportion (ibid. 128).

33. Sir Kenneth Clark, *The Nude*, p. 65.

34. Contrast the description of Laocoön in Wilhelm Heinse's *Ardinghello*, which finds aesthetic meaning in the genitals: 'Selbst die Schamteile des Alten richten sich empor von der allgemeinen Anspannung, Hodensack und Glied zusammengezogen . . .'–'Even the old man's genitalia are lifted upwards because of the general tension, his scrotum and penis pulled together . . .' (*Ardinghello*, edited by Max Baeumer, Stuttgart, 1975, p. 240). Heinse was a champion of the unity of the erotic and the aesthetic.

35. See Boardman, *Greek Art*, pp. 118-19, 124.
36. See Nietzsche, *Zur Genealogie der Moral*, III. §6. For an elegant criticism of the notion that there is nothing erotic about the nude see Sir Kenneth Clark, *The Nude*, p. 6.
37. All are listed in an offhand way as examples of excellence in *Ardinghello* (p. 187), which suggests they came most readily to mind at the time (1787).
38. See *The Nude*, pp. 219-21, 386. The reasons for its rise to fame are outlined by H. B. Nisbet in 'Laocoön in Germany: The Reception of the Group since Winckelmann'.
39. Nisbet points out that what he calls Winckelmann's 'visionary approach' (op. cit. 27) encouraged a fateful tendency to read ideas into the work.
40. Hegel also mentions it as a good example of the different handling of old and young figures (*Ä* II. 421).
41. See Richter, *The Sculpture and Sculptors of the Greeks*, pp. 50-1.
42. Because Hegel considers romantic art to embody a more adequate conception of Truth than classical art, Nisbet has understood him to be critical of the Laocoön, and remarks that his view is, ironically, typically Romantic (op. cit. 54). Hegel does hold this view, but it is a moral one; his aesthetic judgement of the Laocoön is that it is manneristic and decadent, but, paradoxically, if it were more ideal it would be even further removed from the ethical ideal of Christian feeling than it is.
43. Cf. *Rechtsphilosophie*, §173, Zus.
44. See also *Ä* III. 50, 57, 85, 86.
45. Rosenkranz, *Hegels Leben*, pp. 350-1.
46. As noted by Knox, *Hegel's Aesthetics*, p. 814.
47. Giorgione is a notorious case who divides scholars today. The work in question has suffered from changes in taste. It is praised by Max von Boehm in 1908 (*Giorgione und Palma Vecchio*, Bielefeld and Leipzig 1908, p. 100) and attacked as kitsch in 1937 by Duncan Philips (*The Leadership of Giorgione*, Washington 1937, p. 170).
48. See Rüdiger Klessmann, *The Berlin Gallery*, London, 1971 pp. 31-2.
49. Ibid. 44.
50. Ibid. 22.
51. Martin Gosebruch, *Unmittelbarkeit und Reflexion*, p. 164.
52. See *Die Düsseldorfer Malerschule*, Mainz, 1979, p. 442. For further details of the critical reaction see *Die Düsseldorfer Malerschule*, edited by Irene Markowitz, Düsseldorf, 1969, pp. 333-4.
53. Cecil Gould, *The Paintings of Correggio*, London, 1976, pp. 93-4.
54. See Erwin Panofsky, *Early Netherlandish Painting*, Harvard, 1966, Vol. I, p. 1. The distinction was common at the time, and is found in Winckelmann.
55. *Ä* III. 36, 49, 55, 125.
56. The Venetians are untypical Italians as far as colour is concerned, and they are placed alongside the Dutch.

57. See Herman Grimm, *Das Leben Raphaels*, Berlin, 1886, pp. 28-40. Wackenroder's *Herzensergießungen eines Kunstliebenden Kloster-bruders* of 1798 was one of the first pieces of Romantic literature to sing his praises.

58. It is discussed by Grimm (op. cit. 473 ff.) and, for example, in Paul Oppé's classic *Raphael* of 1909.

59. Heinse, *Ardinghello*, p. 127.

60. Ludwig Tieck, *Franz Sternbald's Wanderungen* (1798), in *Frühe Erzählungen und Romane*, edited by Marianne Thalmann, Munich, 1964, p. 847.

61. Denner was popular in Hegel's day, but was criticized by Winckelmann (see *Werke* I. 152-3).

62. Winckelmann rejected the Dutch aesthetic. See *Gedanken über die Nachahmung . . .*, §§47, 55.

63. The significance of Dutch painting for Hegel is examined from a Marxist point of view by Ursula Apitzsch and Berthold Hinz in 'Dialektik in Hegels Kunsturteil', *Hegel Jahrbuch*, 1975, pp. 247-60.

64. Rosenkranz, *Hegels Leben*, pp. 347, 365.

65. See Thrasybulos Georgiades, *Musik und Sprache*, Berlin/Heidelberg/New York, 1954, chs. 8 and 9.

66. Something like this is argued by Charles Rosen in *The Classical Style*, London, 1971. See the account of the string quartet, esp. p. 137.

67. One of the best-known writers on music in the nineteenth century still found it necessary to attack it. See Eduard Hanslick, *Vom Musikalisch-Schönen*, Leipzig, 1854.

68. *Kritik der reinen Vernunft*, A33/B49.

69. *Die Welt als Wille und Vorstellung* I, §52.

70. This has been most clearly recognized by Manfred Bukofzer in 'Hegels Musikästhetik', published in the proceedings of the *Deuxième Congrès International d'Esthétique et de la Science de l'Art*, Paris, 1937, Vol. 2, pp. 32-5. There cannot really be any doubt that this reading of Hegel is correct. One of the aphorisms from his Berlin period cites a piece by Carissimi as proof of the 'senselessness' of music. See Rosenkranz, *Hegels Leben*. p. 557.

71. Nikolaus Harnoncourt argues that this applies to most Baroque music in his notes to his recording of Vivaldi's Op. 8 concertos with the Concentus Musicus Wien, Telefunken, 'Das Alte Werk' (1977). Having rejected the notion, common before the late eighteenth century, that music represents specific emotions, Hegel misses the specificity, and follows another tradition of comparing music unfavourably with language, joining such as Kant, Herder, or Moses Mendelssohn in regarding instrumental music as trivial. One must turn to Heinse and Wackenroder for a justification of instrumental composition. See Hugo Goldschmidt, *Die Musikästhetik des 18. Jahrhunderts*, Zürich and Leipzig, 1915.

72. Despite the overwhelming textual evidence, this reading of Hegel is challenged by Adolf Nowak in the most erudite and detailed study

of Hegel's philosophy of music to date, *Hegels Musikästhetik*, Regensburg, 1971. Nowak attributes to Hegel his own view (shared by Bukofzer—see note 70 above) that the content of music can be identified with purely musical processes,and justifies this with reference to the *Logic* rather than the *Aesthetics* (pp. 153–62), i.e. what Hegel ought to have said, rather than what he did say. In the *Logic*, Hegel is concerned with the identity of the *categories* 'form' and 'content', and this does not prevent him from citing music as an instance of a formal art with an abstract content. Hegel's low estimation of instrumental music still causes Nowak embarrassment (see pp. 180–4).

73. Adorno, who has no illusions about Hegel's position, is prepared to challenge this, saying that music does have determinate content, and yet 'spottet doch der Inhaltlichkeit, wie sie Hegel visierte'— 'makes a mockery of the sort of content Hegel had in mind' (*Ästhetische Theorie*, 'Frühe Einleitung', p. 528). The trouble is that for Hegel, 'determinate' seems to mean 'verbal'. Cf. Hanslick, op. cit. 95–104.

74. Richard Capell, *Schubert's Songs*, revised edition, London, 1957, p. 11.

75. This setting is similarly adduced to illustrate the justice of Hegel's views by S. S. Prawer in his introduction to *The Penguin Book of Lieder*, 1964, p. 13. It is significant that it has only been recorded twice, both times by the encyclopaedic Dietrich Fischer-Dieskau: first on HMV with Karl Engel, and then in the second volume of the complete set on Deutsche Grammophon with Gerald Moore.

76. Cf. Capell, op. cit. 158.

CHAPTER 4

1. See Szondi, *Poetik und Geschichtsphilosophie I*. 396–7. He expresses the widespread contemporary view that the material of literature is not imagination, but language (pp. 478–85).

2. *Dichtung und Wahrheit*, Part Three, Book 11 (Goethe, *SW* 10. 540).

3. Ruth Finnegan suggests it is not in *Oral Poetry*, Cambridge, 1977, p. 268.

4. The battle of Borodino in *War and Peace* is the same battle historians write about, a fact which causes immense problems for analytic philosophers who approach a text on the level of the proposition. See John Ellis, *A Theory of Literary Criticism*, ch. 2.

5. The status of a piece of writing may depend on how it is read. See Jonathan Culler, *Structuralist Poetics*, London, 1975, p. 163.

6. Herodotus, *The Histories*, Book VII (de Sélincourt's translation, Harmondsworth, p. 520).

7. This should not be taken to imply that no examples could be found before then. Ulrich Fülleborn has suggested that, for example, Luther's translations of the Psalms should be classified as prose

poems (*Das Deutsche Prosagedicht*, Munich, 1970, p. 34). In Hegel's day, however, the concept of the 'Prosagedicht' was unknown— Fülleborn quotes a passage in Hofmannstal from 1893 as its first occurrence, it being a translation of Baudelaire's 'poème en prose' (ibid. 9).

8. For further explanation of the meaning of 'objectivity' and 'subjectivity' see Käte Hamburger, *Die Logik der Dichtung*, second edition, Stuttgart, 1968, pp. 119–41, 187–8. Hamburger lends implicit and explicit support to the Hegelian model.

9. Few theories of literature use genres today, despite appearances. For example, Emil Staiger's *Grundbegriffe der Poetik*, Zurich, 1946, is really a discussion of styles, which are found together in many of the greatest works.

10. The theory of tragedy thus has deep roots in the system, as is recognized by A. C. Bradley, who rather quaintly remarks that it is bound up with Hegel's 'view of the function of negation in the universe' (*Oxford Lectures on Poetry*, London, 1950, p. 69).

11. See Peter Szondi, *Poetik und Geschichtsphilosophie II*, Frankfurt, 1974.

12. Goethe and Schiller distinguish 'retarding' motifs from 'regressive' ones, only the latter being typically epic. See Goethe, *SW* 14. 367–70.

13. Jürgen Söring has clearly brought out the fact that Hölderlin understands tragic conflict in terms of the Logic of Essence (i.e. the theory, not the text, which did not then exist). See *Die Dialektik der Rechtfertigung*, Frankfurt, 1973, p. 63.

14. *Antigone* plays an important exemplary role in chapter 6 of the *Phenomenology* of 1807.

15. *Der Cid* 17, in Herder, *Sämmtliche Werke*, edited by Berhard Suphan, Berlin (1877–1913), vol. 28, 1884, edited by Curt Redlich, pp. 430–1.

16. Given Hegel's understanding of epic and dramatic action, the final judgement as to whether *Paradise Lost* is epic or dramatic rests on a theological nicety. If Satan and his followers are completely other than God, an alien and independent power, the conflict between them is epic. If, on the other hand, Satan is acting as an instrument in God's design, and is thus an element in the divine scheme of things, the conflict is dramatic. From God's point of view, the whole action is dramatic, and he is the script-writer as well as an actor; from man's point of view, the action is epic, as he has an absolute choice between good and evil.

17. Karl Marx, *Grundrisse der Kritik der Politischen Ökonomie* (1857–8), Berlin, 1974, p. 31.

18. Ibid.

19. Ibid.

20. There is, for example, a lack of tragic seriousness in the treatment of Diomedes' wounding of Aphrodite in Book V of the *Iliad*.

21. See Erich Auerbach, *Mimesis*, Berlin, 1946, ch. 1.

22. András Horn neatly confirms Hegel in disagreeing with his judgement on this point. In discussing Hegel's principle of form/content identity, Horn cites 'manche(r) Zweikampfbeschreibung der "Ilias"'– 'a good number of duels described in the "Iliad"' as an example of pure form without content (*Kunst und Freiheit*, den Haag, 1969, p. 22). By calling 'content' 'der innere Vorgang, um den es eigentlich zu tun ist' (ibid.), he shows that as a modern he wants interiority, as Hegel would expect, but also that he cannot cope with the historical 'otherness' of Homer, as Hegel can.

23. See for example the killing of Adrestus at the beginning of Book VI of the *Iliad*, the murder of Dolon in Book X, or the way that the great Hector discovers Patroclos crawling back to his lines, dazed, wounded, and unarmed, and promptly drives a spear through his abdomen, mocking him as he dies (Book XVI).

24. Erich Auerbach, *Dante als Dichter der Irdischen Welt*, Berlin and Leipzig, 1929, p. 108.

25. *Mimesis*, p. 185.

26. See *Mimesis*, ch. 8.

27. There are many other striking examples of the punishment fitting the crime: the lustful allowed instinct to govern reason, so they are blown about by an eternal storm (Canto V); flatterers are buried in human faeces (Canto XVIII); makers of discord are themselves split open with wounds (Canto XXVIII).

28. An oral-epic verse tradition still flourishes in parts of Yugoslavia, Asia, and Africa where society is still a community and not as complex and regulated by laws as it is in the industrial countries. See Ruth Finnegan, *Oral Poetry*, pp. 247 ff.

29. What a Hegelian theory of the novel could be can be seen from Lukács's *Die Theorie des Romans*, written from 1914 to 1915.

30. Johann Peter Eckermann, *Gespräche mit Goethe*, Part 3, 28 Mar. 1827. They were in fact discussing a book by Hinrichs, but the ideas are all found in Hegel.

31. The reception of Hegel's reading is discussed by Hermann Funke in 'ΚΡΕΩΝ ΑΠΟΛΙΣ', *Antike und Abendland* XII, Heft 1 (1966).

32. Brian Vickers, *Towards Greek Tragedy*, London, 1973, p. 526. See *Ä* I. 287; *Ä* II. 60, 69; *Ä* III. 544, 549–50.

33. *Werke* 17. 133.

34. The distinction is between 'nomos', which is what Creon claims to be obeying, and 'kerygma', which is what Antigone says he has issued. See Vickers, op. cit. 529–30, 532.

35. In *Oedipus at Colonnus* Sophocles uses another version, according to which the brothers had agreed that Creon should take over, but then quarrelled. Ismene reports that Eteocles seized power and banished Polyneices, placing Eteocles clearly in the wrong (ll. 371 ff.).

36. Vickers elaborates the case against Agamemnon by appealing to Aeschylus' imagery (op. cit. 352–7).

37. There is direct comparison between the rights of the gods, but for one argument Apollo uses to undermine the Eumenides' case. He

denies that Orestes is a blood relative of his mother by appealing to the Greek belief that the woman is just an incubator for a man's sperm, so that although Orestes is Agamemnon's son, any woman could have given birth to him (*The Eumenides*, ll. 657–66).

38. This is a difference quoted by Walter Benjamin as distinguishing 'Tragödie' and 'Trauerspiel'. See *Ursprung des deutschen Trauerspiels* (1925), edited by Rolf Tiedemann, Frankfurt, 1978, pp. 44–5.

39. In the *Philosophy of Right*, morality (Moralität) is the sphere of universal interaction between individuals, and ethics (Sittlichkeit) that of social interaction, which is therefore particular.

40. See *Shakespeare: Hamlet* in the *Casebook* series, edited by John Jump, London, 1969, especially the 'Introduction' and Part 1.

41. Their discussion occurs in Book IV, ch. 13. See Goethe, *SW* 7. 263 for the words Hegel quotes.

42. Hegel describes Novalis, for example, in the same terms as Hamlet. See *Werke* 20. 418.

43. *Ä* III. 419, 432. On p. 431 Hegel does suggest that some form of social organization is a necessary background to the lyric, but it amounts to no more than acquiring the sentimental education necessary for writing poetry.

44. Some of Hegel's most virulent polemics are on the subject of the 'Gefühlstheologie' associated with Schleiermacher. Feeling, he says, is what man has in common with animals, 'est ist die tierische, sinnliche Form' (*Werke* 16 129).

45. Hegel's attitude to 'Minnesang' is ambivalent: 'Im deutschen Minnesang zeigt die Liebe sich empfindungsvoll, zart, ohne Reichhaltigkeit der Phantasie, spielend, melancholisch, einförmig' —'In German Minnesang, love is portrayed with delicate sentiment, without much imaginative variation, playful, melancholic, monotonous' (*Ä* II. 185).

46. In the first version the girl leaves the poet, in the second he leaves her, a detail Goethe thought significant enough to change.

CONCLUSION

1. Heinrich Theodor Rötscher, 'Das Verhältnis der Philosophie der Kunst und der Kritik zum einzelnen Kunstwerk', in *Abhandlungen zur Philosophie der Kunst*, Berlin, 1837, pp. 1–2.

2. Ibid. 10, 17.

3. Ibid. 18–24.

4. Ibid. 56–7.

5. It may be that sciences like physics and chemistry are themselves just rational hermeneutic exercises, but that is a controversy which cannot be entered into here. If they are, they still differ from art-criticism by being able to predict, because their object is nature, and not, like history, subject to the principle of non-repetition.

6. See also *Ä* I. 30, 32, 171.

7. *Ä* II. 164–5 and *Ä* III. 17, 434, 497–8, 507, 509.

8. Thus, surprisingly enough for an intellectual, Stuart Hampshire thinks it 'unnatural to ask "why is that picture or sonata good?"' (*Aesthetics and Language*, edited by Elton, p. 165). To ask it is unnatural in that it requires reflection, but it is not clear what follows from this. The question seems a perfectly 'natural' one in the art history and music faculties of most institutions of higher education.

9. 'Vorrede' to the *Rechtsphilosophie*, *Werke* 7. 26.

GLOSSARY

This glossary is intended to provide a quick reference source to the reader who is getting bogged down in Hegelianisms, and wants to extricate himself without starting again at page 1. A full explanation of the terms here would be a full exposition of the system, so what is provided is just a guide. Further details can usually be found somewhere in the main text. I have in general tried to use the convention of indicating a term with a particular Hegelian meaning by using a capital letter, as in 'Truth', 'Concept', and so on, the only exception being the names of the three art-forms. The reason for this is simply that a convention already exists whereby the artistic movement 'Romanticism' is written with a capital, and I wish to avoid confusion.

Absolute. As an adjective it means 'self-relating'. It implies difference (or there would be no relation), but it is internal to something. Hence 'the Absolute' is that instance whose identity is dependent only on its internal differences, not on anything outside itself—it encompasses 'otherness'.

Being. The *Logic of Being* (*Seinslogik*) is the first section of the *Logic*. It is distinguished by the fact that the categories which constitute it relate to each other purely contrastively. Their relationships are relatively little mediated, and therefore indeterminate. 'Being' in the text usually refers to the *Logic of Being* as a whole, but it can also mean the first category of Logic, pure Being ('das Sein').

Category. Used generally to refer to the 'determinations of Thought' reconstructed in Hegel's system. A category is a category because we have to use it at some point if we think systematically about how we have to think about anything, in other words it is encompassed by absolute Thought, thought which thinks about thinking. A category does not therefore make existential claims about reality, but claims to be something in terms of which reality can be understood.

Concept. 'Der Begriff'. The final section of Logic, and the one which provides the framework for reconstructing areas of reality such as art, politics, religion (that is 'Realphilosophie'). Its categories are highly mediated and determinate, and are such that they must be understood as universal, particular, and individual. The Concept of art must be shown to have those three 'moments': art must be something universal, something which appears in determinate relations to space and time, and something which appears in the context of history, making it irreducibly individual.

Determinacy. 'Bestimmtheit'. That in virtue of which anything is distinct from anything else. The *Logic* could be said to give a theory of determinacy.

Determination. 'Bestimmung'. The determinacy ascribable to something in virtue of which it is what it is and is not what it is not. Thus, the Concept of art gives its determination, and one could say that the purpose of Hegel's *Aesthetics* is to determine what art is. The purpose of the *Logic* is to determine what Thought is, which is why Hegel calls the categories 'determinations of Thought'.

Dialectics. The second of three steps in systematic reconstruction, which ought properly to be called the 'speculative method'. For example, the categories 'Something' and 'Other' are different determinations of the same determinacy (they are distinct by virtue of quality) which exclude each other. They could thus be said to stand in negative unity (each is what it is only by virtue of not being the other one) or to be dialectical.

Essence. The *Logic of Essence* (*Wesenslogik*) is the second section of the *Logic*, and is sometimes referred to as the *Logic of Reflection*. Its pairs of dialectical categories differ from those of Being in that they stand in a determinate relation to each other. One of the pair is essential and determines the other as its reflection, but this reflection is itself essential to Essence. Thus, 'Essence' refers to a moment which belongs with the other moment called 'Schein' (Reflection) through a relationship of reflection (which Hegel calls 'Scheinen in Anderes'), and it also refers to the whole structure. In the *Aesthetics* the content of art is to its form as Essence is to Reflection.

History. History has three meanings in Hegel. He constantly fails to distinguish them.

    1. A category of the *Philosophy if Spirit*, the third part of the system concerned with individuality. It forms the transition from *Objective Spirit* (the practical and political) to *Absolute Spirit* (art, religion, and philosophy). What is historical is governed by the principle of non-repetition, because an event is historical by virtue of altering the context of its own possibility and cannot therefore be repeated. Art is a historical object.

    2. The totality of past events.

    3. Chronological succession.

Idea. 'Idee'. The unity of Concept and reality. The Idea of something would be the actual realization of it.

Ideal. The Idea of art.

Individual. 'Das Einzelne' is the technical term; 'Individuum' and its cognates are sometimes used in the same context in their normal sense. Individuality is the third moment of Concept, the other two being universality and particularity. For the purposes of the *Aesthetics* one might understand individuality to be the realization of a universal (art) in a particular, spatio-temporally determinate context (the arts). Within the three-part system as a whole, Spirit is individual, Logic is universal, and Nature is particular.

Logic. The first part of Hegel's philosophical system, the *Encyclopedia of Philosophical Sciences*. It is universal, and thus stands in contrast with Nature and Spirit, which are the areas of regional philosophy ('Realphilosophie'). Logic is non-regional. It reconstructs all the categories used elsewhere, and all the relations between them in their purest form, and thus forms the basis for all the rest of Hegel's philosophy.

Method. What makes systematic reconstruction rational. As the system is a set of categories and their relations which are self-generating Logic is nothing more than an account of method.

Nature. The second part of the Hegelian system, accounting for the realm of the external (non-thought) as that of space and time (its first two categories). It is the context of the particular, the spatio-temporal.

Particular. 'Das Besondere'. The second moment of Concept. It is external, as opposed to the universal which is internal (thought), and identified with space and time. Within the system of the *Encyclopedia* it accordingly corresponds to Nature. Within the *Aesthetics* it should designate the arts themselves, though the text is equivocal on this point.

Realphilosophie. This is Hegel's term for Nature and Spirit taken together, in contrast with Logic. It might be called 'regional philosophy', and the aesthetics forms part of it. The terms it uses are determined in Logic, and in order to remain philosophy, the theories expounded in 'Realphilosophie' must restrict themselves to the framework Logic provides. They must likewise show that their various objects can be considered in those terms. Nature and Spirit can take the terms for granted, and operate solely on the level of Concept, which they then use to reconstruct the regions they are dealing with. Nature and Spirit are regional because they are placed (at the beginning of Nature) in the framework of space and time.

Reconstruction. 'Rekonstruktion' (*WL* I. 19) or 'Nachbildung' (*Enz.* § 12). All of Hegel's philosophy is reconstructive, that is, it translates the content of a representation, a vague, common-sense picture of something, into a Concept, determining it purely systematically and eliminating the picturing element. As categories are reconstructed, they imply, through their relations to each other, further steps. These steps, or systemic positions, are then named with an appropriate representation, and thereby the claim is made that a certain object has been determined. The medium of reconstruction is thought or language, there is no attempt to link a language on to the world. The language of philosophy is meta-theoretical, a language which makes claims about another language, that of representation. The representations, not 'the world', are the given.

Representation. 1. 'Vorstellung'. An epistemological term designating thought which is in principle separable from its object (and thus characteristically presupposes the opposition of consciousness). It provides systematic philosophy with its object-language, systematic philosophy beginning when the opposition of consciousness is eliminated at the end of the *Phenomenology of Spirit*. Only certain representations admit of systemic reconstruction, and the system must select those which are candidates for categorial status.

2. 'Darstellung'. This is not a technical term, but occurs frequently in the *Aesthetics*. It means more or less what 'representation' means in the context of aesthetics, and also 'presentation' or even 'performance' (as, alas, can 'Vorstellung').

Schein. See chapter 1, 'The Ideal'. I have translated 'Scheinen' as 'reflection' when used in its technical sense (see 'Essence'), otherwise rendering 'Schein' as 'appearance'. In the *Aesthetics* it is the form or appearance of art as posited or determined by its essence, and as such is itself essential. The German word had a wide range of meanings which Hegel exploits at various times, the main ones being those of 'illusion' or 'semblance' and of 'shine' or 'glow'. Thus, a full translation of 'Die Kunst ist Schein' would be something like: 'the illusion of art shines out at us, showing a reflection of essence'.

Speculative. The third step of systematic reconstruction, the determination of the category which resolves the contradiction of a pair of dialectical categories. Whereas dialectical categories could be said to stand in negative unity because they are related through their mutual exclusion, the speculative step is to place them in affirmative unity, understanding them as moments of a determination which includes them both. Hegel's method should properly be called 'speculative' rather than 'dialectical'.

Spirit. 'Der Geist'. This is the term for concrete subjectivity or individuality. The Concept of Spirit is consciousness which knows itself fully, that is, self-consciousness which is fully transparent to itself. The only way in which self-knowledge is reached is through the mediation of other objects, principally other instances of subjectivity. Self-consciousness is just a formal self-relation unless it has an object, and it cannot know what it is until it recognizes itself, and is likewise recognized by another self-consciousness. Hegel talks about Spirit only upon reaching this stage of mutual recognition, and the term is accordingly used mainly in a social context. The *Philosophy of Spirit*, which examines individuality, is the third part of the systemic triad, and indeed covers all aspects of social interaction (legal, moral, and political) in its second part. It is completed with the self-reflection of Spirit, *Absolute Spirit*, in which art is placed, to be succeeded by religion and philosophy.

Subjectivity. The logical structure of subjectivity is Concept, so in all cases in which Concept is used, one could legitimately talk about subjectivity. The salient feature of it is that a subject relates to itself, in Hegelian terms it is 'for-itself', it is capable of reflection. What is peculiar about Hegel's theory is that it understands human institutions as subjects, most notoriously the State. He can do this because subjectivity is defined in purely categorial terms, and he needs to do so in order to understand the nature of new unities formed by human social activity: a group loses the characteristics of its constituent individuals and takes on new ones of its own. Thus, a general election can be understood as the self-reflection of the State.

Sublate. 'Aufheben'. This is the term Hegel sometimes uses to describe the speculative step of systemic progression. In normal German the word has three meanings, all of which Hegel wishes to maintain:

1. to raise or hold up;
2. to annul, abolish, or suspend;
3. to keep or preserve.

The move to a higher (more determinate) category annuls that below it, whilst preserving it as a moment of the new one.

System. The result of 'bringing one's thoughts together' (see *WL* II. 496). The categories are brought together because of the relations they exhibit. Those relations constitute method, so the system is an account of it. It was generally accepted in Hegel's time that philosophy had to be systematic, but most philosophers started with some grounding principle or assumption. Hegel is unique in using systematicity alone. In the text I have used 'systematic' as a general term to designate a type of argument, as opposed to, say, 'historical' or 'empirical', and 'systemic' to refer to anything concerning a specific system. Thus, a 'systematic rationale' would be one relying on systematic rather than any other sort of argument, but a 'systemic rationale' would be one resulting from the position a category has in a system.

Thought. 'Das Denken'. When written with a capital letter it means specifically speculative categorial thinking as opposed to the first-order discourse of representation.

Truth. Hegel's theory of truth is peculiar in that it does not deal with judgemental truth: judgements are either correct ('richtig') or incorrect. Truth involves Concepts. Three things can be distinguished:

1. The theory of Truth, in the *Logic*, which determines Truth as Idea, the correspondence of Concept and reality. This combines the tradition of understanding truth as correspondence with the tradition of truth as coherence (for Concept is a result of systematic coherence). One might say that Hegel regards a claim about truth to be making the two claims 'This is a possible way for things to be' and 'This is the way things are'. Note that a Concept gives the determination of something, so that Truth, unlike judgemental correctness, means 'the whole truth'.

2. The Idea is used in 'Realphilosophie' to determine the adequacy of instances. They are 'true' to the extent to which they correspond to their Concept. Thus, in Hegel's usage, being a 'true work of art' is a matter of degree.

3. Truth is equated with the seriously held beliefs of a community. The way in which the human subject understands himself

at any time is what he considers to be the truth about himself, his identity. This will in general involve religion, and Hegel links this meaning of Truth, which really only has a place as a historical category in 'Realphilosophie', to the logical theory of Truth by claiming that the latter is an account of the Divine, a claim which can charitably be described as dubious.

Vorstellung. See 'Representation'.

SELECT BIBLIOGRAPHY

This bibliography lists works referred to in the text and certain others of importance. A bibliography of literature on the *Aesthetics* up to 1967, compiled by Wolfhart Henckmann, can be found in *Hegel Studien* 5 (1969).

1 Primary Texts

Hegel, G. W. F., *Aesthetics*, translated by T. M. Knox, Oxford, 1975.
— *Die Vernunft in der Geschichte*, edited by Johannes Hoffmeister, Hamburg, 1955.
— *Phänomenologie des Geistes* [*PhG*], edited by Johannes Hoffmeister, Hamburg, 1952.
— *Vorlesungen über Ästhetik*, edited by Rüdiger Bubner, Stuttgart, 1971.
— *Werke in Zwanzig Bänden* (*Theorie Werkausgabe*), edited by Eva Moldenhauer and Karl Markus Michel, Frankfurt, 1970.
— *Wissenschaft der Logik* [*WL*], edited by Georg Lasson, Hamburg, 1932.
Henckmann, Wolfhart (ed.), *G. W. F. Hegel–Einleitung in die Ästhetik*, Munich, 1967.
Lasson, Georg (ed.), *Die Idee und das Ideal*, Hamburg, 1931.

2 Secondary Literature on Hegel

Adorno, Th. W., *Drei Studien zu Hegel*, Frankfurt, 1974.
Apitzsch, Ursula, and Hinz, Berthold, 'Dialektik in Hegels Kunsturteil' in *Hegel Jahrbuch*, 1975.
Aschenberg, Reinhold, 'Der Wahrheitsbegriff in Hegels "Phänomenologie des Geistes"' in *Die Ontologische Option*, edited by Klaus Hartmann, Berlin, 1976.
Bradley, A. C., *Oxford Lectures on Poetry*, London, 1950.
Brinkmann, Klaus, 'Schellings Hegel-Kritik' in *Die Ontologische Option*, edited by Klaus Hartmann, Berlin, 1976.
Bröcker, Walter, 'Hegels Philosophie der Kunstgeschichte' in *Auseinandersetzungen mit Hegel*, Frankfurt, 1965.
Bubner, Rüdiger, 'Die "Sache selbst" in Hegels System' in *Dialektik in der Philosophie Hegels*, edited by Rolf-Peter Horstmann, Frankfurt, 1978.
Bukofzer, Manfred, 'Hegels Musikästhetik' in *Deuxième Congrès International d'Esthétique et de la Science de l'Art*, Paris, 1937.

Derrida, Jacques, 'Le Puits et la Pyramide' in *Marges de la Philosophie*, Paris, 1972.

Dove, Kenley Royce, 'Hegel's Phenomenological Method' in *Review of Metaphysics* 23, No. 4 (June 1970).

— 'Logik und Recht bei Hegel' in *Neue Hefte für Philosophie* 17 (1979).

Düsing, Klaus, *Das Problem der Subjektivität in Hegels Logik*, Bonn, 1976.

— 'Hegels Begriff der Subjektivität in der Logik und in der Philosophie des Subjektiven Geistes' in *Hegels Philosophische Psychologie* (*Hegel Studien, Beiheft* 19), Bonn, 1979.

Foster, Michael, 'The Opposition between Hegel and the Philosophy of Empiricism' in *Verhandlungen des III. Hegelkongresses*, edited by B. Wigersma, Tübingen, 1934.

Fulda, Hans Friedrich, 'Hegels Dialektik als Begriffsbewegung und Darstellungsweise' in *Dialektik in der Philosophie Hegels*, edited by Rolf-Peter Horstmann, Frankfurt, 1978.

Funke, Hermann, ΚΡΕΩΝ ΑΠΟΛΙΣ, in *Antike und Abendland* 12 (1966).

Gadamer, Hans-Georg, *Hegels Dialektik*, Tübingen, 1971.

Glockner, Hermann, 'Die Ästhetik in Hegels System' in *Hegel Studien, Beiheft* 2 (1965).

Gombrich, Ernst, 'Hegel und die Kunstgeschichte' in *Neue Rundschau* 88 (1977).

Harries, Karsten, 'Hegel on the future of art' in *Review of Metaphysics* 27 (1973–4).

Hartmann, Klaus, *Die Ontologische Option*, Berlin, 1976.

— 'Hegel—A Non-Metaphysical View' in *Hegel*, edited by Alasdair MacIntyre, London, 1972.

— 'Zur Neuesten Dialektik-Kritik' in *Archiv für Geschichte der Philosophie* 55 (1973).

Heidegger, Martin, *Identität und Differenz*, Pfullingen, 1957.

Helferich, Christoph, *Kunst und Subjektivität in Hegels Ästhetik*, Kronberg, 1976.

Heller, Erich, *The Artist's Journey into the Interior*, London, 1965.

Henrich, Dieter, 'Formen der Negation in Hegels Logik' in *Dialektik in der Philosophie Hegels*, edited by Rolf-Peter Horstmann, Frankfurt, 1978 (originally in *Hegel Jahrbuch* 1974).

— 'Hegels Grundoperation' in *Der Idealismus und seine Gegenwart. Festschrift für Werner Marx zum 65. Geburtstag*, edited by U. Guzzoni, B. Rang, and L. Siep, Hamburg, 1976.

— 'Hegels Logik der Reflexion' in *Hegel Studien, Beiheft* 18, Bonn, 1978.

— 'Kunst und Kunstphilosophie der Gegenwart' in *Immanente Ästhetik—Ästhetische Reflexion* (*Poetik und Hermeneutik* 2), edited by Wolfgang Iser, Munich, 1966.

— 'Kunst und Natur in der Idealistischen Ästhetik' in *Nachahmung und Illusion* (*Poetik und Hermeneutik* 1), edited by H. R. Jauß, Munich, 1964.

—— *Hegel im Kontext*, Frankfurt, 1971.

Herrmann, Hans, *Der Gegenwärtigkeitsgedanke in der theoretischen Behandlung des dramatischen Kunstwerks bei Lessing, A. W. Schlegel und Hegel*, Breslau, 1934.

Hofstadter, Albert, 'Die Kunst–Tod und Verklärung' in *Hegel Studien, Beiheft* 11, Bonn, 1974.

Horn, András, *Kunst und Freiheit*, The Hague, 1969.

Jähnig, Dieter, 'Hegel und die These vom "Verlust der Mitte"' in *Spengler Studien–Festgabe für Manfred Schröter zum 85. Geburtstag*, edited by A. M. Koktanek, Munich, 1965.

Kaminsky, Jack, *Hegel on Art*, New York, 1962.

Karelis, Charles, 'Hegel's Concept of Art: An Interpretative Essay' in *Hegels Introduction to Aesthetics*, translated by T. M. Knox, Oxford, 1979.

Kaufmann, Walter, 'The Hegel Myth and its Method' in *Hegel*, edited by Alasdair MacIntyre, London, 1972.

Koepsel, Werner, *Die Rezeption der Hegelschen Ästhetik im 20. Jahrhundert*, Bonn, 1975.

Krohn, Wolfgang, *Die Formale Logik in Hegels 'Wissenschaft der Logik'*, Munich, 1972.

Kroner, Richard, *Von Kant bis Hegel*, second edition, Tübingen, 1961.

Kuhn, Helmut, 'Die Gegenwärtigkeit der Kunst nach Hegels Vorlesungen über Ästhetik' in *Hegel Studien, Beiheft* 11, Bonn, 1974.

—— 'Die Vollendung der klassischen deutschen Ästhetik durch Hegel' in *Schriften zur Ästhetik*, edited by Wolfhart Henckmann, Munich, 1966 (originally in Kuhn, *Kulturfunktion der Kunst*, Berlin, 1931).

—— 'Hegels Ästhetik als System des Klassizismus' in *Archiv für Geschichte der Philosophie* 40 (1931).

Kuklinková, Theodora, 'Schöpferische Aktivität als Quelle des Schönen bei Hegel und in der marxistischen Ästhetik' in *Hegel Jahrbuch*, 1975.

Litt, Theodor, *Hegel–Versuch einer kritischen Erneuerung*, Heidelberg, 1953.

Lucas, Raymond, 'A Problem of Hegel's Aesthetics' in *Renaissance and Modern Studies* 4 (1960).

—— 'Hegel und die Abstraktion' in *Deutsche Vierteljahresschrift* 38 (1964).

Lukács, Georg, 'Über die Besonderheit als Kategorie der Ästhetik' in Lukács, *Werke* 10, Darmstadt and Neuwied, 1969.

Marcuse, Herbert, *Reason and Revolution*, second edition, London, 1955.

Marx, Karl, 'Kritik des Hegelschen Staatsrechts' in *Marx/Engels Werke* 1, Berlin, 1956.

Metscher, Thomas W., 'Hegel und die philosophische Grundlegung der Kunstsoziologie' in *Literaturwissenschaft und Sozialwissenschaften*, Stuttgart, 1971.

Mure, G. R. G., *A Study of Hegel's Logic*, Oxford, 1950.

Nowak, Adolf, *Hegels Musikästhetik*, Regensburg, 1971.

O'Brien, George Dennis, *Hegel on Reason and History*, Chicago and London, 1975.

Oelmüller, Willi, 'Hegels Satz vom Ende der Kunst' in *Die Unbefriedigte Aufklärung*, second edition, Frankfurt, 1979 (originally in *Philosophisches Jahrbuch* 73 (1965-6)).

Patočka, Jan, 'Die Lehre von der Vergangenheit der Kunst' in *Beispiele. Festschrift für Eugen Fink zum 60. Geburstag*, edited by L. Landgrebe, The Hague, 1965.

Popper, Karl, *The Open Society and its Enemies*, London, 1945.

Pöggeler, Otto, *Hegels Kritik der Romantik*, Bonn, 1956.

Puntel, L. Bruno, *Darstellung, Methode und Struktur*, Bonn, 1973.

Reed, T. J., 'Critical Consciousness and Creation: The Concept "Kritik" from Lessing to Hegel' in *Oxford German Studies* 3 (1968).

Rosenkranz, Karl, 'Hegels Ästhetik' in *Jahrbücher für Wissenschaftliche Kritik*, 1836 (Halbband 1) and 1839 (Halbband 1), reprinted in *Kritische Erläuterungen des Hegelschen Systems*, Königsberg, 1840.

— *G. W. F. Hegels Leben*, Berlin, 1844.

Rüsen, Jörn, 'Die Vernunft der Kunst' in *Philosophisches Jahrbuch* 80 (1973), reprinted in Rüsen, *Ästhetik und Geschichte*, Stuttgart, 1973.

Schelling, F. W. J., 'Zur Geschichte der Neueren Philosophie' in *Werke*, edited by Manfred Schröter, Hauptband V, Munich, 1928.

Schulz-Seitz, Ruth-Eva, '"Sein" in Hegels Logik: Einfache Beziehung auf sich' in *Wirklichkeit und Reflexion—Walter Schulz zum 60. Geburtstag*, edited by H. Fahrenbach, Pfullingen, 1973.

Smith, John E., 'Hegel's Critique of Kant' in *Review of Metaphysics*, 26, No. 3 (Mar. 1973).

Stoikov, Athanas, 'Hegel et le destin de l'art' in *Hegel Jahrbuch*, 1971.

Szondi, Peter, *Poetik und Geschichtsphilosophie I*, Frankfurt, 1974.

— *Poetik und Geschichtsphilosophie II*, Frankfurt, 1974.

Taylor, Charles, *Hegel*, Cambridge, 1975.

Theunissen, Michael, *Hegels Lehre vom absoluten Geist als theologisch-politischer Traktat*, Berlin, 1970.

— *Sein und Schein*, Frankfurt, 1978.

Wagner, Frank Dietrich, *Hegels Philosophie der Dichtung*, Bonn, 1974.

Weisse, Christian Hermann, Review of Hegel's *Aesthetics* in *Hallische Jahrbücher für Wissenschaft und Kritik*, 1–7 Sept. 1838.

Wiehl, Reiner, 'Über den Handlungsbegriff als Kategorie der Hegelschen Ästhetik' in *Hegel Studien*, Beiheft 11, Bonn, 1974.

Wolandt, Gerd, 'Standpunkte der Kunstphilosophie' in *Die Aktualität der Transzendentalphilosophie—Hans Wagner zum 60. Geburtstag*, edited by Schmidt and Wolandt, Bonn, 1977.

Zander, Hartwig, *Hegels Kunstphilosophie*, Ratingen, 1970.

3 Other Theoretical Works

Adorno, Th. W., *Ästhetische Theorie*, Frankfurt, 1970.

Batteux, Charles, *Les Beaux Arts réduits à un même principe*, second edition, 1773 (reprinted Geneva, 1969).

Benjamin, Walter, *Ursprung des deutschen Trauerspiels*, edited by Rolf Tiedemann, Frankfurt, 1978.

Bense, Max, *Aesthetica I*, Stuttgart, 1954.

Bubner, Rüdiger, 'Über einige Bedingungen gegenwärtiger Ästhetik' in *Neue Hefte für Philosophie* 5 (1973).

Casey, John, *The Language of Criticism*, London, 1966.

Collingwood, R. G., *The Principles of Art*, Oxford, 1938.

Croce, Benedetto, *Estetica–come scienza dell'espressione e linguistica generale*, sixth edition, Bari, 1928.

Culler, Jonathan, *Structuralist Poetics*, London, 1975.

Ellis, John M., *The Theory of Literary Criticism: A Logical Analysis*, California, 1974.

Gadamer, Hans-Georg, *Die Aktualität des Schönen*, Stuttgart, 1977.

— *Wahrheit und Methode*, fourth edition, Tübingen, 1975.

Gallie, W. B., 'The Function of Philosophical Aesthetics' in *Aesthetics and Language*, edited by William Elton, Oxford, 1967.

Goodman, Nelson, *The Languages of Art*, London, 1969.

Hamburger, Käte, *Wahrheit und ästhetische Wahrheit*, Stuttgart, 1979.

— *Die Logik der Dichtung*, second edition, Stuttgart, 1965.

Hampshire, Stuart, 'Logic and Appreciation' in *Aesthetics and Language*, edited by Elton, Oxford, 1967.

Hanslick, Eduard, *Vom Musikalisch-Schönen*, Leipzig, 1854.

Hartmann, Klaus, *Die Marxsche Theorie*, Berlin, 1970.

Hirt, Alois, 'Versuch über das Kunstschöne' in *Die Horen*, 7. Stück, 1797.

Hook, Sidney (ed.), *Art and Philosophy*, New York, 1966.

Kant, Emmanuel, *Werke–Akademie Textausgabe* (reprint of *Kants gesammelte Schriften. Herausgegeben von der Königlichen Preußischen Akademie der Wissenschaften*), Berlin, 1968.

Katchadourian, Haig, 'Common Names and "Family Resemblances"' in *Wittgenstein*, edited by George Pitcher, London, 1968.

Kennick, W. E., 'Does traditional aesthetics rest on a mistake?' in *Philosophical Review* 66 (1957), reprinted in *Collected Papers on Aesthetics*, edited by C. Barrett, Oxford, 1965.

Lake, Beryl, 'A Study of the Irrefutability of two Aesthetic Theories' in *Aesthetics and Language*, edited by Elton, Oxford, 1967.

Lukács, Georg, *Die Theorie des Romans*, Darmstadt, 1971.

— *Heidelberger Ästhetik*, Darmstadt and Neuwied, 1974 (*Werke* 17).

Lyotard, Jean-Francois, *Discours, Figure*, Paris, 1978.

Macdonald, Margaret, 'Some Distinctive Features of Arguments used in Criticism of the Arts' in *Aesthetics and Language*, edited by Elton, Oxford, 1967.

Marx, Karl, *Grundrisse der Kritik der Politischen Ökonomie*, Berlin, 1974.

Nietzsche, Friedrich, *Zur Genealogie der Moral*, Munich, 1964.

Puntel, L. Bruno, *Wahrheitstheorien in der Neueren Philosophie*, Darmstadt, 1978.

Quine, Willard van Orman, *From a Logical Point of View*, second edition, New York, 1961.

Rötscher, Heinrich Theodor, *Abhandlungen zur Philosophie der Kunst*, Berlin, 1837.

Rosenkranz, Karl, *Ästhetik des Häßlichen*, Königsberg, 1853.

Schelling, F. W. J., *Schriften von 1806–13*, Darmstadt, 1976.

— *Philosophie der Kunst* (1859), reprinted Darmstadt, 1976.

Schiller, Friedrich, *Über die ästhetische Erziehung des Menschen*, edited by Wolfhart Henckmann, Munich, 1967.

Schopenhauer, Arthur, *Sämtliche Werke*, edited by Arthur Hübscher, Wiesbaden, 1960.

Scruton, Roger, *Art and Imagination*, London, 1974.

— *The Aesthetics of Architecture*, London, 1979.

Solger, C. W. F., *Vorlesungen über Ästhetik*, edited by K. W. L. Heyse, Leipzig, 1829.

Staiger, Emil, *Grundbegriffe der Poetik*, Zurich, 1946.

Strawson, P. F., 'Aesthetic Appraisal and Works of Art' in *Oxford Review* 3 (Michaelmas, 1966).

Vischer, Friedrich Theodor, *Kritische Gänge* 1, Tübingen, 1844.

Wagner, Hans, *Philosophie und Reflexion*, third edition, Munich and Basle, 1980.

Weisse, Christian Hermann, *System der Ästhetik als Wissenschaft von der Idee der Schönheit*, Leipzig, 1830.

Wollheim, Richard, *Art and its Objects*, Harmondsworth, 1970.

4 Historical and Critical Works and Other Texts

Aeschylus, *Oresteia*, translated by Richard Lattimore, *Aeschylus I* in *The Complete Greek Tragedies*, edited by David Grene and Richard Lattimore, Chicago and London, 1953.

Auerbach, Erich, *Dante als Dichter der Irdischen Welt*, Berlin and Leipzig, 1929.

— *Mimesis*, Berlin, 1946.

Battcock, Gregory (ed.), *Idea Art*, New York, 1973.

Boardman, John, *Greek Art*, revised edition, London, 1973.

Capell, Richard, *Schubert's Songs*, revised edition, London, 1957.

Clark, Sir Kenneth, *The Nude*, Harmondsworth, 1960.

Creuzer, Friedrich, *Symbolik und Mythologie der Alten Völker, besonders der Griechen*, second edition, Leipzig and Darmstadt, 1819.

Dante Alighieri, *The Divine Comedy*, translated by John D. Sinclair, Oxford, 1971.

de Boor, Helmut (ed.), *Das Nibelungenlied*, Wiesbaden, 1967.

— *Die Düsseldorfer Malerschule* (exhibition catalogue), Mainz, 1979.

Dorfles, Gillo, *Der Kitsch*, translated by Birgid Mayr, Tübingen, 1969.

Eckermann, Johann Peter, *Gespräche mit Goethe in den letzten Jahren seines Lebens* (1836), edited by Paul Stapf, Wiesbaden.

Finnegan, Ruth, *Oral Poetry*, Cambridge, 1977.

Friedrich, Hugo, *Die Struktur der modernen Lyrik*, Hamburg, 1956.

Fülleborn, Ulrich, *Das Deutsche Prosagedicht*, Munich, 1977.

Georgiades, Thrasybulos, *Musik und Sprache*, Berlin, Heidelberg, New York, 1954.

Gladstone-Bratton, F., *A History of Egyptian Archaeology*, London, 1967.

Goethe, Johann Wolfgang, *Sämtliche Werke* [*SW*], edited by Ernst Beutler, Zurich, 1950.

Goldschmidt, Hugo, *Die Musikästhetik des 18. Jahrhunderts*, Zurich and Leipzig, 1915.

Gombrich, Ernst, *The Story of Art*, twelfth edition, London, 1972.

Gosebruch, Martin, *Unmittelbarkeit und Reflexion*, Munich, 1979.

Gould, Cecil, *The Paintings of Correggio*, London, 1976.

Grimm, Herman, *Das Leben Raphaels*, Berlin, 1886.

Hawkes, Jacquetta, *The First Great Civilizations*, London, 1973.

Heine, Heinrich, *Sämtliche Schriften*, edited by Klaus Briegleb, Munich, 1968–76.

Heinse, Wilhelm, *Ardinghello und die glückseligen Inseln*, edited by Max L. Baeumer, Stuttgart, 1975.

Herder, Johann Gottfried, *Sämmtliche Werke*, edited by Bernhard Suphan, Berlin, 1877–1913.

Herodotus, *The Histories*, translated by Aubrey de Sélincourt, revised edition, Harmondsworth, 1972.

Hibbard, Howard, *Masterpieces of Western Sculpture*, London, 1977.

Hirt, Alois, *Die Baukunst nach den Grundsätzen der Alten*, Berlin, 1809.

— *Geschichte der Baukunst bei den Alten*, Berlin, 1821–7.

Homer, *The Iliad*, translated by E. V. Rieu, Harmondsworth, 1950.

— *The Odyssey*, translated by E. V. Rieu, Harmondsworth, 1946.

Jump, John (ed.), *Shakespeare: Hamlet*, in the *Casebook* series, London, 1969.

Klopstock, Friedrich Gottlieb, *Werke*, edited by A. L. Back, Berlin, 1876.

Klessmann, Rüdiger, *The Berlin Gallery*, translated by D. J. S. Thomson, London, 1971.

Kristeller, Paul O., 'The Modern System of the Arts' in *Journal of the History of Ideas* 12 (1951) and 13 (1952).

Lavater, Johann Caspar, *Physiognomische Fragmente, zur Beförderung der Menschenkenntniß und Menschenliebe*, Leipzig and Winterthur, 1775.

Markowitz, Irene, *Die Düsseldorfer Malerschule*, Düsseldorf, 1969.

Meyer, Johann Heinrich, *Geschichte der bildenden Künste bei den Griechen*, Dresden, 1824–36.

Milton, John, *Paradise Lost*, edited by Alastair Fowler, London, 1971.

Morris, James, *Pax Britannica*, Harmondsworth, 1979.

Müller-Seidel, Walter, *Probleme der literarischen Wertung*, second edition, Stuttgart, 1969.

Nisbet, H. B., 'Laocoon in Germany: the Reception of the Group since Winckelmann' in *Oxford German Studies* 10 (1979).

Oppé, Paul, *Raphael*, revised and edited by Charles Mitchell, New York, 1970.

Panofsky, Erwin, *Early Netherlandish Painting*, Harvard, 1966.

Philips, Duncan, *The Leadership of Giorgione*, Washington, 1937.

Prawer, S. S., *The Penguin Book of Lieder*, Harmondsworth, 1964.

Richter, G. M. A., *The Sculpture and Sculptors of the Greeks*, New Haven and London, 1970.

Rimbaud, Arthur, *Œuvres*, edited by Suzanne Bernard, Paris, 1960.

Rosen, Charles, *The Classical Style*, revised edition, London, 1976.

Rumpf, A., *Archäologie*, Berlin, 1953.

Schiller, Friedrich, *Sämtliche Werke*, edited by Gerhard Fricke and Herbert Göpfert, Munich, 1965–75.

Sedlmayr, Hans, *Die Entstehung der Kathedrale*, Zurich, 1950.

—— *Verlust der Mitte*, ninth edition, Salzburg, 1976.

Shakespeare, William, *King Henry IV (Part 2)*, *King Lear*, *Macbeth*, *Othello*, *Richard II*, in *The Arden Shakespeare*, edited by Harold F. Brooks, Harold Jenkins, and Brian Morris.

—— *Hamlet*, edited by John Dover Wilson, second edition, Cambridge, 1936, in *The New Shakespeare* series.

Söring, Jürgen, *Die Dialektik der Rechtfertigung*, Frankfurt, 1973.

Sophocles, *Oedipus the King*, translated by David Grene; *Oedipus at Colonus*, translated by Robert Fitzgerald; *Antigone*, translated by Elizabeth Wyckoff; *Sophocles I* in *The Complete Greek Tragedies*, edited by David Grene and Richard Lattimore, Chicago and London, 1954.

Tieck, Ludwig, *Frühe Erzählungen und Romane*, edited by Marianne Thalmann, Munich, 1964.

Vasari, Giorgio, *Lives of the Artists*, translated by George Bull, Harmondsworth, 1965.

Vickers, Brian, *Towards Greek Tragedy*, London, 1973.

Vitruvius, *Ten Books of Architecture*, translated by Morris Hicky Morgan, New York, 1960.

von Boehm, Max, *Giorgione und Palma Vecchio*, Bielefeld and Leipzig, 1908.

von Simson, Otto, *The Gothic Cathedral*, New York, 1956.

Voß, Johann Heinrich, *Luise*, Tübingen, 1807.

Wackenroder, Wilhelm Heinrich, and Tieck, Ludwig, *Herzensergießungen eines kunstliebenden Klosterbruders*, edited by A. Gillies, Oxford, 1948.

Watkin, David, *The Rise of Architectural History*, London, 1980.

Winckelmann, Johann Joachim, *Sämtliche Werke*, edited by Joseph Eiselein, Donaueschingen, 1825–29, reprinted Osnabrück, 1965.

Wittkower, Rudolf, *Architectural Principles in the Age of Humanism*, fourth edition, London, 1973.

—— *Sculpture*, Harmondsworth, 1979.

INDEX

absolute
    defined, 28
    absolute Idea, 4
    absolute Spirit, 26–9, 31–4,
        43–4, 49–50, 52, 64, 75–6
Adorno, Theodor Wiesengrund, 74
    defends aesthetics, 13 and n. 2
    on natural beauty, 15 n. 13
    and value judgements, 44 n. 67
    on dissonance, 48 n. 81
    on form and content, 65 n. 16
    on music, 137 n. 73
Aeschylus, 168–71
    Oresteia, 168–71, 173
aesthetic judgement, 16–18, 49–50
aesthetics
    in ill repute, 13
    need of the time, 23
    term criticized by Hegel, 13–14
    sceptic implicitly indulges in it, 22
Alberti, Leon Battista, 106
Anthropology, Hegel's, 40
Apollo Belvedere, 118
architecture, 99–108
    is symbolic, 90, 101–4
    relation to space and time, 91–3
    first of the arts, 99–101
    classical, 104–7
    Gothic, 107–8
Aristophanes, 173
Arnim, Achim von, 140
art-forms, 39, 51–61, 64–7
artist
    and aesthetics, 16, 20
    common views of, 35
    affected by reflection, 80–2
    object of modern art, 84, 86–7
    lack of material a problem for, 88
Auerbach, Erich, 160–1

Bach, J. S., 133–4
Batteux, Charles, 33 n. 54, 90 n. 65
Baudelaire, Charles, 87–8, 148
Beethoven, Ludwig van, 137

Begriff (see Concept)
Bense, Max, 47 n. 78
Bernini, Gian Lorenzo, 112
Brentano, Clemens, 140
Broch, Hermann, 95
Bröcker, Walter, 74
Bubner, Rüdiger, 31 n. 48, 72, 84 n.
        51, 88 n. 56

Celan, Paul, 87
Cervantes, 163
Cézanne, Paul, 83
Champollion, Jean François, 102
Christ
    representation in painting, 122,
        131
El Cid, 61, 153–4
classical art-form, 57–8
    form and content in, 58–60, 65–7
    representation in, 71
    sculpture and, 90, 93
    architecture and, 90, 104–7
    and lyric, 182–3
classicism
    role of in aesthetics, 21–2
    Hegel's theory privileges, 22, 71
    Hegel rejects, 34, 125
clothing
    in sculpture, 117–18
    used by Sohn, 125
Collingwood, R. G., 43–4, 46–7
colour
    in sculpture, 109–11
    Titian's use of, 130
    transition to music, 134
columns
    Greek, 105
    engaged, 106
    Gothic, 107
comedy, 173
    limit of art, 75, 81–2, 145–6
    contrasted with tragedy, 151
common sense (see Vorstellung)
    in philosophy, 26, 35–6

Concept (*see Logic of Concept*)
  eliminates picturing element from
      representation, 3
  in Realphilosophie, 27–8
  as content, 40, 45
concept art, 47–8
content
  of art, 30–3, 40, 45
  and form, see form and content
  Hegel's definition changes, 37–9
  rationale for division of subject,
      51–2
  and religion, 30–1, 58–61
  of painting, 121–2
  of music, 134–7
Correggio, Antonio Allegri da, 123,
      130
  Mary Magdalen, 126–7
criticism
  sceptic's view of, 20
  grounded by aesthetics, 18, 23,
      49–50, 189
  mixed in with, 54–5
Croce, Benedetto, 21 n. 34, 46–7,
      72

dance, 90, 92
Dante, 154, 159–62, 167
definitions, 25, 42
Denner, Balthasar, 130
Derrida, Jacques, 104 n. 7
Des Knaben Wunderhorn, 140, 186
dialectics
  negative implication of Concepts,
      4
didacticism, 30
Diderot, Jacques, 126
divine (*see* God)
  art expresses, 29–30, 76
  and Truth, 6, 43, 60–1
  in art, 34, 43
  and art, 66–7, 43–4
drama, 165–78
  action in, 147, 150–1
  conflict in, 150–2, 165–72
  guilt in, 152, 166–8
  ancient, 166–73
  Shakespearian, 173–5
  contemporary, 175–8
Dürer, Albrecht, 130
Durante, Francesco, 133

Eckermann, Johann Peter, 166, 167

Egypt, Ancient
  identified with symbolic art, 57
  architecture of, 101–4
  eschatology of, 102 n. 6
Eliot, T. S., 43–4, 87–8
empiricism, 17–18, 20
Encyclopedia of Philosophical Sciences,
      7, 26, 28–9, 31, 32–3, 35, 36
epic, 147, 149–50, 153–65
  action in, 146–7, 149–50
  content of, 147
  conflict in, 149–50
  heroes in, 150, 153–4, 157–9
  style in, 153, 159
  social background to, 154–6
  gods in, 155–6
  in modern world, 155, 163–5
eurhythmy, 107
Euripides, 172
  Iphigenia contrasted with Goethe's,
      177
excellence
  in art, 44, 63 and n. 15, 67–70
eye
  surface of work of art, 39, 50
  in sculpture, 110–12

feeling, 45–6, 180 n. 44
  and music, 134–5
Flaubert, Gustave, 68, 88
  Madame Bovary, 168
form and content, 33, 34–5, 36–42,
      50, 51–2, 54–8, 62–71
freedom
  art is free, 29–30
  content of art, 39

Gadamer, Hans-Georg, 15 n. 10, 40 n.
      63, 58 n. 13, 70 n. 18, 74
galleries
  known to Hegel, 124
genius
  in Kant, 14
  views of, 35
genre painting, Dutch, 72, 131–3
genres
  origins of, 146–53
George, Stefan, 87, 143
Giorgione, 123
Glockner, Hermann, 72
Gluck, Christoph Willibald, 133
God
  in philosophy, 1

of Christianity, 6, 60–1, 76–7,
    121–3
of Greeks, *see* Greeks
as Truth, 6
in painting, 122
Goethe, Johann Wolfgang, 26,
    37–8 and n. 59, 84 n. 49, 87,
    118, 127, 140, 143, 151
    attitude to engaged columns, 106
    ballads of, 183–5
    criticizes Hegel's view of tragedy,
        166, 167
    instinctiveness of, 68, 113–14,
        182–3
    lyric poetry of, 177–8
    theory of colour, 109
    Die Leiden des Jungen Werthers,
        182–3
    Faust, 177–8
    Götz von Berlichingen, 176
    Hermann und Dorothea, 164–5
    Iphigenia, 143, 176–7
    Reinecke Fuchs, 164–5
    Torquato Tasso, 87, 176
    Von Deutscher Baukunst, 106
    West-Östlicher Divan, 87, 186–7
    Wilhelm Meisters Lehrjahre, 175
    Willkommen und Abschied, 185–6
Gombrich, Ernst, 115
Goodman, Nelson, 46, 47 n. 80
Gothic architecture, 101, 107–8
graffiti, 146
Greek art
    fulfils highest function, 34
    real norm for Winckelmann, 34,
        125, 132 n. 62, 190
    and religion, 67, 72
    architecture, 101, 102, 104–7
    sculpture, 110–20, 190
    painting, 121–2
    Greek profile in, 116–17, 125
Greeks (*see* Greek art)
    instinctive, 107
    Hegel biased towards, 21
    expressed Divine as embodied, 60
    gods of, 20–1, 76–7, 79, 93–4,
        155–6
    lack interiority, 111–12

Handel, George Frederick, 133
harmony, 106–7
Harries, Karsten, 73
Haydn, Joseph, 133

Heidegger, Martin, 71 n. 21, 73, 74
Heinse, Wilhelm, 188 and n. 34, 137
    n. 71
    Ardinghello on Raphael, 128–30
Helferich, Christoph, 58 n. 11, 72–3
Heller, Erich, 74
Henrich, Dieter, 15 n. 8, 74
Herder, Johann Gottfried, 137 n. 71,
    153
Herodotus, 102, 146, 155
Hesiod, 156
Hirt, Alois, 26, 37 and n. 57, 38, 106,
    115 n. 31, 124
history
    as chronology, 6
    as principle of non-repetition, 6,
        78–9
    products individual, 6
    contrasted with philosophy, 55
    contrasted with literature, 145
Hölderlin, Friedrich, 151
Hofstadter, Albert, 74
Homer, 64–5, 70, 79, 132, 153–9
    Iliad, 64–6, 156–9
    Achilles, 64–5, 154, 156–8, 163,
        164, 178
    model of epic, 152
    objectivity of, 147, 153, 159
    Odyssey, 157
Hotho, Gustav Heinrich, 6–7, 14 n. 7,
    35, 53 and n. 2, 71
humour, 145–6
Huysmans, J. K., 88

Idea
    art and philosophy a form of, 2
    theory of Truth, 5–6
    of Beauty, 39, 41
    art forms examples of, 60
individuality
    moment of Concept, 5, 51–61
    theme of Spirit, 26
intentions, 45
irony, 87–8

Jähnig, Dieter, 71 n. 21, 74, 94 n. 69
jokes, 145–6
Judd, Don, 19–20
judgement
    element in public's attitude, 23,
        79–80
    role of in Hegel and Kant, 16
    role in aesthetics, 16–19, 23–4, 75

judgement (*cont.*)
  grounded by aesthetics, 21, 49, 88
  needed to discuss works of art, 54
  Hegel's, 99, 123, 124–7, 133,
    189–90

Kafka, Franz, 85, 87
Kaiser, G. Ph. Chr., 14 n. 5
Kallistik, 14 n. 5
Kant, Emmanuel, 38–9, 134, 137 n.
    71
  Critique of Judgement, 14, 16,
    18, 39
  understanding of philosophy, 1
  primacy of natural beauty in, 14
  two aesthetic theories, 16
  judgement of taste in, 18, 88, 190
  system of the arts, 89
kitsch, 95
Klopstock, Friedrich Gottlieb, 86, 179
  poetry of, 179–81
  Messias, 162–3, 181
  Selmar und Selma, 180
Koepsel, Werner, 74
Kristeller, Paul, 89 n. 60, 90
Kuhn, Helmut, 58 n. 13, 71 n. 21, 74

language
  Hegel's conception of, 137, 142–3
  used by philosophy, 3, 15, 21
  of art criticism, 54–5, 68, 191
  of songs, 138–9
  in literature, 143–4
  in Homer, 153
Laocoon, 118–19, 172
Lasson, Georg, 6–7, 14 n. 7, 53 n. 2
Lavater, Johann Caspar, 116 n. 32
Leonardo da Vinci, 127
literature, 142–87
  Hegel most interested in, 22
  as representation, 32, 142
  relation to space and time, 91–3
  gives subjects for painting, 125–6
  determined, 142–6
  and history, 145
Litt, Theodor, 72
Logic,
  first part of system, 3–5
  quoted, 8, 41
  advantage of having one, 45–6
  grounds epic/drama, 149
  relevance to aesthetics, 188
Logic of Being, 4

model for epic, 149
Logic of Concept, 4–5, 31–2, 40, 179,
    188
Logic of Essence, 4–5, 40
  form and content derived from, 36,
    62–3
  used in literature, 143, 149
Lotti, Antonio, 133
lyric, 178–87
  origins of, 147–9
  systematic ordering of, 178–7
  national role of, 179, 181, 182

Madonna, portrayals of, 122–3, 127,
    137
Mallarmé, Stéphane, 87–8
Mann, Thomas, 87
Marmontel, Jean François, 140
Marx, Karl
  criticism of Hegel, 2
  regards socio-economic as primary,
    29
  view of epics, 155, 156, 164
Medici Venus, 118–19
Mendelssohn, Felix, 133
Mendelssohn, Moses, 36, 137 n. 71
Mengs, Anton Raphael, 125
Metastasio, Pietro, 140
Meyer, Johann Heinrich, 26, 37–8
Michelangelo, 112, 115, 127
middle
  art as middle between mind and
    esence, 36, 38–9, 42
  loss of, 88–9
  sculpture is middle of art, 93–5
  of sculpture, 109
Milton, John, 154 and n. 16, 160
mimesis
  Hegel bans from aesthetics, 15, 188
Minnesang, 180 and n. 45
Mörike, Eduard, 140
morality
  art's relation to, 43, 48–50, 88, 95
  art confused with, 47
Mozart, Wolfgang Amadeus, 54, 87,
    133
  Magic Flute, 140
Murillo, Bartolomé Estéban, 124
music, 89, 133–41
  themes in, 65 n. 16, 135–6
  is romantic, 90, 121, 134–5
  relations to space and time, 91–3,
    134–5

content in, 134-8
words and, 137-41
mythology, 64-6, 82, 84-6, 88, 168,
181

natural Beauty, 14-15
nature
Philosophy of Nature, 4, 134
and art, 15 and n. 12, 41
realm of particular, 54
vs. self-consciousness in *Oresteia*,
169-71
necessity, 29, 69
Nietzsche, Friedrich, 94-5, 118
Novalis, 140, 178 n. 42

Oedipus, *see* Sophocles
Oelmüller, Willi, 73, 85
ordinary language (*see* Vorstellung)
raw material of philosophy, 3, 15,
26, 35

painting, 121-33, 137
is romantic, 90, 121
relations to space and time, 91-3,
121
vs. sculpture, 119, 120
of Greeks, 121-2
and Christianity, 120, 121-3, 127
contemporary, 124-6
colour in, 127, 130
Italian, 124, 127-30
Dutch, 72, 124, 127, 131-3, 190
portrait, 130-1
Palestrina, Giovanni Pierluigi de, 133-4
Palladio, Andrea, 106
Palma Vecchio, 123
Parthenon frieze, 115-16, 119
particularity, 5, 51-61
Pater, Walter, 94
Patočka, Jan, 74
Pericles, 113
Phenomenology of Spirit, 26-7, 31,
76, 153 n. 14, 168
Phidias, 76, 79, 110, 113, 114, 132,
156
philosophy, 1-3
relation to art, 2, 5, 29, 34-5, 42,
69
Philostratus, 8 n. 59
Pindar, 86
Plato, 25, 80, 113, 191
Pliny, 100, 110

Pöggeler, Otto, 74
poetry, 143-4, 149, 178-87
used for songs, 139-41
sound of words in, 143
politics, 28
Polyklitos, 112
portrait painting, 130-1
Praxiteles, 110
prose poem, 148-9
Proust, Marcel, 83
Psychology, 32
public
in Scruton, 17
in Hegel, 23
reflectiveness of, 79-80, 82, 120
pyramid, 88, 102-4, 108

Raphael, 123, 125, 130
central figure of Italian painting,
127-30
Transfiguration, 128-30
Rauch, Christian Daniel, 113
Realphilosophie, 42
Nature and Spirit, 4
reconstructs with Concept, 5
method in, 24-5, 31-3
reconstruction
translation of Vorstellung into
Concepts, 3-4
in Realphilosophie, 24-5
Introduction as example of, 35-40
Reed, T. J., 74
reflection
relationship between categories in
Essence, 4-5
regional philosophy, *see* Realphilosophie
religion (*see* God)
Egyptian, 58, 60
Greek, 60, 70-1, 76-7, 79, 119
Christian, 6, 60-1, 76-7
related to art, 5, 28, 29-34, 42,
60-1, 64, 84-6
Religion, Philosophy of, 53, 58, 167
religions
in art-forms, 58-61, 66, 76-7
Renaissance, 114
ignored, 106
Reni, Guido,
sentimentality of, 126
representation (*see also* form and
content)
religion and literature as, 32

representation (*cont.*)
  in art, 70-1, 75-7
  of God, 77-8, 122-3
  in sculpture, 94, 119
  in genres, 146-7
rhetoric, 144
Rilke, Rainer Maria, 143
Rimbaud, Arthur, 148-9
Rötscher, Heinrich Theodor, 3, 188-9, 191
Romans
  architecture criticized, 104-5
romantic
  Hegel's use of, 57 and n. 7
romantic art-form, 57-8
  form and content in, 59-61, 67
  representation in, 71
  end of, 79-82, 88
  painting and, 90, 93, 121-3
  music and, 90, 93, 134-5
  architecture and, 107-8
  sculpture and, 115
  and lyric, 182-3
Romanticism
  end of Romantic art-form, 81
Rossini, Gioacchino, 133
Rosenkranz, Karl, 3, 31, 48, 90
Rubens, Peter Paul, 123
Rückert, Friedrich, 87, 140
Rüsen, Jörn, 73
Rumohr, Carl Friedrich von, 123

scepticism, 19-22
Schadow, Johann Gottfried, 109
Schadow, Wilhelm von, 124, 125-6
Schein, 8, 40-1 and n. 61, 45, 153
Schelling, F. W. J., 15 n. 9, 23
Schiller, Friedrich, 38-9, 151
  poetry unsuitable for music, 140-1
  early plays, 175-6
  poetry, 181-2, 184
Schleiermacher, Friedrich, 180 n. 44
Schönberg, Arnold, 83
Schopenhauer, Arthur, 94-5, 135
Schubert, Franz, 140-1
Schütz, Heinrich, 133
Scruton, Roger, 13 n. 3, 15 n. 10, 17-18, 48-50, 101 n. 3
sculpture, 108-20, 156
  privileged by Hegel, 22
  is classical, 90, 113-14
  relations to space and time, 91-3
  as middle, 93-5

confused with architecture, 100-1
  colour in, 109-10
  eyes in, 111-12
  movement in, 109, 112
  clothing of, 117-18
  heads in, 116-17
  vs painting, 119, 120, 132-3
  coldness of, 120
self-consciousness, 26-8
self-reflection, 28, 93
  art as form of, 32-4
  characteristic of 'us', 23
Shakespeare, William, 65, 67-9, 72, 143, 173-5
  Hamlet, 173-5, 178
sign, 57, 102-4
Socrates, 113, 116
Sohn, Carl Ferdinand, 124-5
Solger, C. W. F., 15, 45
song, 137-41, 179
Sophocles, 113, 132
  Antigone, 152-3, 166-8, 172
  Oedipus plays, 44, 171-2
speculative method, 4, 35, 36-7
Sphinx, 88
Spirit
  third part of system, 4, 26
  meaning in Hegel, 26-8
  art is need of Spirit, 29
  deduction of art in, 31-4
Stoikov, Athanas, 72
Stravinsky, Igor, 88
subjectivity, 5
Superman
  as modern Achilles, 163
symbol, 57, 59, 70 n. 18, 102-4
symbolic art-form, 56-9
  form and content in, 58-60
  representation in, 71
  as end of romantic art-form, 88
  architecture and, 90, 93, 101-4

Tasso, Torquato, 124
taste, 190-1
  Hegel's, 75
  modern, 120
thought
  the object of philosophy, 3
  art contains, 40-2
Thucydides, 113
Tieck, C F., 109
Tieck, Ludwig
  comments on Raphael in, 128-30

Titian, 127, 130
tragedy (*see* drama), 152-3, 165-78
    contrast with comedy, 151
    classical, 166-73
    modern, 173-8
truth
    as Idea, 2
    Hegel's concept of, 5-6
    as unity of coherence and cor-
        respondence, 5
    as social beliefs, 6, 66
    art and, 36, 42-4, 48-50, 66,
        75-7, 79, 83

ugliness, 47-8, 66
    in Greek art, 119
universality
    moment of Concept, 5, 51-61
    in art is abstract, 29

van Eyck, Jan and Hubert, 127, 131-3
van Gogh, 83
Vasari, Giorgio, 115
Venetian painting, 132-3
Vickers, Brian, 166-7
Virgil, 154
Vitruvius, 106-7
Vorstellung
    imaging thought, 3

input to theory, 15, 26, 35-6, 51
religion and literature as, 32, 75
Hegel's use of, 89-90, 100
Voss, Johann Heinrich
    Luise, 164

Wackenroder, Wilhelm Heinrich, 127,
    131 n. 71
Wagner, Frank Dietrich, 58 n. 12, 74,
    90
Wagner, Richard, 83, 88, 181
Weisse, Christian Hermann, 3, 15 n. 12,
    31, 55-6, 71, 73, 84-6, 89
Wiehl, Reiner, 74
Wilde, Oscar, 88
Winckelmann, J. J., 94, 114-18, 127
    regarded Greek art as real norm, 34,
        125, 132, n. 62, 190
Wittgenstein, Ludwig, 20-1
Wölfflin, Heinrich, 127
Wolandt, Gerd, 29 n. 46, 72
Wollheim, Richard, 19 n. 27, 45

Xenophon, 113

Zelter, Karl Friedrich, 133
Zweckmässigkeit
    in Kant, 14
    in architecture, 104-6